# AMERICAN
# MUCKRAKER

## RETHINKING JOURNALISM
## FOR THE 21ST CENTURY

# JAMES O'KEEFE

Post Hill
PRESS

A POST HILL PRESS BOOK
ISBN: 978-1-63758-090-5
ISBN (eBook): 978-1-63758-091-2

American Muckraker:
Rethinking Journalism for the 21st Century
© 2022 by James O'Keefe
All Rights Reserved

Post Hill Press
New York • Nashville
posthillpress.com

Published in the United States of America
1  2  3  4  5  6  7  8  9  10

For Mom; who instilled in me humility, authenticity, forgiveness, and balance.

For Dad; who taught me drive, resilience, indefatigability, and common sense.

For my Sister; who was with me during the nadir.

# TABLE OF CONTENTS

# PREFACE
# SUFFERING

*The quality of a revolutionary is inversely proportional to the system he fights against – The more oppressive and cruel the system, the more heroic and self-sacrificing is the rebel; in other words, the better and more indulgent the system, the more flippant the revolutionary.[1]*

-Leopold Tyrmand, Polish Anti-Communist,
*Tyrmand's Law*[2]

T here are two questions the American muckraker is asked repeatedly. Number one: Do *you* fear for your life? Number two: What can *I* do? The first question calls upon a library of material written by past muckrakers, broadcasters, lawyers, judges, and academics who risked their lives and careers to expose corruption and maleficence in society's institutions. Professional truth-seekers do not fear for their life when they are called to this higher purpose, for their life is the vehicle in which defenders of press freedom conduct their crusade in our brave new world of video journalism. When people ask, "What can I do?" what they're really asking—what they're truly seeking—is what Viktor Frankl describes as "the striving and struggling of some goal worthy" of themselves.[3] During times of universal deceit, a good place to start is telling the truth. Doing this, as George Orwell reportedly said, is, in itself, a "revolutionary act."[4] The muckraker's revolution is not one of reform or radicalism, but a return to truth, for there is only one true reality.

---

1    Leopold Tyrmand, *Notebooks of a Dilettante* (New York: The Macmillan Company, 1970), 147.
2    Matthew Tyrmand, Leopold Tyrmand's son, serves on the board of directors for Project Veritas.
3    Viktor Frankl, *Man's Search for Meaning* (New York: Pocket Books, 1985), 184.
4    Although usually attributed to Orwell, no firm source for this quote has been identified.

## THE PURSUIT OF HAPPINESS VS. THE PURSUIT OF MEANING

Rebellion against the system will inevitably cause the muckraker a fair share of pain, political persecution, even prosecution, so piercing, so excruciating, that his continuation down this path risks crossing the line into masochism. He will enter into what Empedocles described as a "region of adversity" fraught with "suffering and toil," enduring "failures of insight and character" along the way.[5]

Outside observers feel a combination of wonder and fascination with the muckraker's art. This creates a curiosity that the muckraker has a hard time understanding. We all know the tale of Pentagon Papers whistleblower Daniel Ellsberg, who said that his former friends and colleagues "regarded him with neither admiration nor censure, but with wonder, as though he were a space-walking astronaut who had cut his lifeline to the mother ship."[6]

The muckraker finds himself identifying with Sisyphus, the sufferer of Greek lore consigned to push a rock up a hill for eternity only to see it roll back down every time. Despite his manifest successes, even legendary muckraker Upton Sinclair felt his task more than a little Sisyphean. "You are listening," he wrote in *The Brass Check*, "to a man who for fourteen years has been in a battle, and has seen his cause suffering daily wounds from a cruel and treacherous foe."[7]

Over time, the muckraker finds himself increasingly alienated from those who marvel at his mission. He wonders how these good people cannot themselves be doing what he is doing. When thanked, the muckraker wonders what he is being thanked for. His job is not over. It is never over. He has barely scratched the surface.

Training and experience have coached him, wrote Rudyard Kipling, to "meet with triumph and disaster...just the same."[8] It culminates with wisdom described by Aleksandr Solzhenitsyn as, "Do not rejoice when you have found, do not weep when you have lost," in his book, *The Gulag*

---

5    Sissela Bok, *Secrets: On the Ethics of Concealment and Revelation* (New York: Random House, 1989), 103. Bok brings up Empedocles. There is a universality to the truth-teller's struggle. What Empedocles faced twenty-five hundred years ago in Greece, muckraker Andy Ngo has faced these past several years in the streets of Portland.
6    C. Fred Alford: *Whistleblowers: Broken Lives and Organizational Power* (Ithaca and London: Cornell University Press, 2001), 5.
7    Upton Sinclair, *The Brass Check: A Study of American Journalism; Evidence and Reasons Behind the Media's Corruption* (Adansonia Press, First Published in 1919), 31.
8    Rudyard Kipling, *'If-' and other poems* (London: Michael O'Mara Books Limited, 2016).

*Archipelago*.[9] The muckraker knows the fragility of his success because of what he has endured, what he imagines he will endure, and the price he will have to pay for his endurance.

David Daleiden, whose exposé of the baby parts trafficking racket that almost brought down Planned Parenthood, glimpsed into that future. Daleiden vividly recalls taking out the trash "on an idyllic southern California spring day" when the unthinkable happened:

> As I rounded the corner, the door of a large, white, windowless van swung open, and a tall, uniformed officer stepped out and blocked my path. "Are you David Daleiden?" he asked. "Yes," I said nervously as I started to freeze from confusion and surprise. "We have a search warrant for your apartment from the California Department of Justice," he said as he shoved papers at me. No less than 11 armed CA DOJ agents, accompanied by K-9 dogs, filed out of the van and sprung out of surrounding police cars. Only half of them fit in my apartment to search it, the rest waited outside with their dogs and assault rifles. The leader of the agents tried to prevent me from calling my lawyer and threatened to seize my phone while I was talking to legal counsel. They overturned my entire apartment, looking behind statues and icons of the Virgin Mary for "evidence." They thumbed through invoice printouts for fetal body parts from StemExpress, Advanced Bioscience Resources, and the admitted criminal DaVinci companies but left those behind, instead seizing all my hard drives and equipment with the original undercover footage and my laptops going back to high school. I felt powerless, like I was drowning, and it felt like the search lasted forever.[10]

Daleiden was targeted because of the institution he investigated and the truth he uncovered. His success was his undoing. So was Andy Ngo's. Working with just a phone and a GoPro camera, the young citizen journalist was doing America's best reporting on the mounting Antifa terror in Portland, Oregon. In June 2019, Antifa decided they had had enough:

---

9   Aleksandr Solzhenitsyn, *The Gulag Archipelago 1918-1956 An Experiment in Literary Investigation*, trans. Thomas P. Whitney and Harry Willets, abr. Edward E. Ericson, Jr. (New York: HarperCollins Publishers, 2007). All future references to Solzhenitsyn in this chapter will be italicized without attribution. The muckraker who wavers in his faith, and all do at some point, does well to absorb the life lessons of Solzhenitsyn. Dispatched to a gulag for daring to criticize Josef Stalin in a private letter, Solzhenitsyn emerged to continue challenging the Soviet State in a series of books.
10  David Daleiden, email to James O'Keefe, March 12, 2021.

Suddenly, clenched fists repeatedly struck my face and head from all directions. My right knee buckled from the impact. The masked attackers wore tactical gloves - gloves hardened with fiberglass on the knuckles. It's likely some of them used brass knuckles as well. I put my arms up to surrender, but this only signaled to them to beat me more ferociously. Someone then snatched my camera - my evidence…The mob roared in laughter as I stumbled away.[11]

As was true with Daleiden, the mainstream media either ignored Ngo's plight or quietly cheered on his attackers. As to the authorities, writes Ngo, "At no point did police intervene to help."[12]

Having observed the fate of truth-tellers like Ngo and Daleiden, the American muckraker has nightmare visions of text exchanges laid bare, freedom of association rights stripped away, donor names illegally leaked and published, police turning a blind eye, and federal agents pounding at his door. The muckraker watches with disgust as the governor of New York defends himself during a 2021 press conference, proclaiming, "I'm not going to argue this issue in the press" when it comes to allegations of his own professional misconduct.[13] The muckraker knows full well that the "press" was where that governor of New York went when motivated to defame an ideological opponent, evidenced when a letter written by his own attorney general to this muckraker, somehow arrived at the *Daily News*, before this muckraker received it. The front-page headline screamed, GOTCHA.[14] Yet they said they did not try cases in the press.

This muckraker had broken no laws in New Orleans, yet was stripped of his freedoms, incarcerated, broken, and made an example. His SD chip with the footage that would have set him free was destroyed by a federal magistrate judge, and the powers that be escaped all liability precisely *because* this fact of evidence destruction was not mentioned in the press. In shackles, this muckraker gave up his Miranda rights and spoke to the FBI, and even the muckraker's allies would ask, "Why would you do such a thing?"[15] In shackles, you'd be surprised at what you'd do.

11  Andy Ngo, *Unmasked: Inside Antifa's Radical Plan to Destroy Democracy* (New York: Hachette Book Group, 2021), 9.
12  Ngo, *Unmasked*, 9.
13  Yahoo Finance, "Governor Cuomo holds press briefing (Audio only)," March 12, 2021, YouTube video, 34:00.
14  See Chapter Secrecy, Secrecy of Donors, describing the New York attorney general coordinating with the press. The attorney general was Eric Schneiderman, who resigned in disgrace after a *New Yorker* article by Jane Mayer and Ronan Farrow detailed evidence of sexual misconduct.
15  James O'Keefe, *Breakthrough: Our Guerilla War to Expose Fraud and Save Democracy* (New York: Threshold Editions, 2014), 151–152.

*You are under arrest... the verist simpleton amongst us, drawing on all life's experience, can gasp out only: "Me? What for?" ... in your desperation the fake circus moon will blink at you: "It's a mistake! They'll set things right!"*

Meanwhile, Rob Sawicki, the press secretary for the senator you were investigating, was telling the press that the one imprisoned muckraker "should save his feeble explanation for the FBI and judge."[16] But the federal prosecutors were not saving their explanations. These prosecutors were simultaneously and anonymously blogging about them in the mainstream media. "Sure they should be punished. Throw the book at them,"[17] wrote one prosecutor under a pseudonym in the comments section of *The New Orleans Times-Picayune*. The prosecutors' violations of federal ethics laws were so egregious, they would one day be used as a "what not to do" example in the curricula prepared for US attorneys. Yet somehow, they also had the gall to say *we don't try cases in the press.*

This muckraker knew what was happening at the time but was never sure that the rest of the world knew themselves. It would take five years and surface as a veritable footnote.[18] In truth, the prosecutors had total influence over the press, from the op-ed columns of the *New York Times* to this muckraker's Wikipedia page—one so repugnant it evokes audible gasps from anyone who has witnessed his muckraking up close.[19]

Yes, the world is round, but the lies about me swirl endlessly in a vortex of propaganda and circularly sourced citations on crowdsourced aggregated encyclopedias, with algorithms regurgitating what Chomsky refers to as the "authorized knowers" in society.[20] At the core of this vortex are the tech platforms that freely circulate falsehoods while banning the truthful videos of the muckraker. So disorienting is the result that the unknowing citizen sees the American muckraker as an agent of disinformation. Whereas in the Soviet Union, people knew *Pravda* was a lie, these days there is still a substantial portion of the American people who truly believe what they read in the chyrons on CNN while waiting for their flight's departure.

---

16   Jonathan Tilove, "Activist says Landrieu plot was to uncover dodged phone calls," *The Times-Picayune*, January 30, 2010.

17   Project Veritas Action, "O'Keefe Exposes DOJ Corruption in Louisiana US Attorney Office and DOJ Civil Rights Division," December 4, 2014, YouTube video, 7:54.

18   The prosecutors punished for their role were former Assistant U.S. Attorney Sal Perricone, former Assistant U.S. Attorney Jan Mann, and former U.S. Attorney Jim Letten.

19   Tim Pool's personal comment on the Project Veritas Wikipedia page. It has also been said that it reads like a political party press release.

20   Edward S. Herman and Noam Chomsky, *Manufacturing Consent: The Political Economy of the Mass Media* (New York: Knopf Doubleday Publishing Group, 2011).

For the muckraker, scorn and defamation follow, and these are, ironically, directly proportional to the veracity of the reporter's work. This unending drumbeat of defamation often leads to the surrender of supposed allies who once fought alongside the muckraker in the battle for truth. Neil Gorsuch noted in a recent criticism of *New York Times v. Sullivan* that the published falsehoods are on a scale so great, "it has come to leave far more [Americans defamed] without redress than anyone could have predicted."[21]

## THE NADIR

Just like any survivor of psychological abuse, the American muckraker over time starts to realize a new kind of superpower. Reborn through baptism by fire, he is invigorated by the knowledge that he is no longer a slave to fear.[22] Fear may grow inside of him, but he does not let it affect his decision making.

No one can deprive him of his reputation; he has already been deprived of that too many times through declarations from "credible journalists."[23] Credible, not by virtue of the evidence they present, but by virtue of their own decree that they are indeed credible, because they say so. Their "credible sources," anonymously sourced, are permitted to contradict incontrovertible evidence. So, the deprivation of your reputation is based upon the vanity of a self-anointed racket. Although pernicious, this still brings a new type of freedom.

*And there is one more freedom. No one can deprive you…you have already been deprived of them. What does not exist - not even God can take away. And this is a basic freedom.*

This is an age where the loss of one's Twitter account is treated like the loss of one's life. It is an age where people assign more value to their perceived image on Instagram than they do their own reality. They will hesitate to speak the truth because, in this age, there is a perverse incentive that actually rewards people who *don't* speak the truth.

21  Shkelzen Berisha v. Guy Lawson. 594 U.S. (2021). Justice Gorsuch, dissenting. It seems "to leave even ordinary Americans without recourse for grievous defamation."

22  Ngo, *Unmasked,* 40. "I thought about it and decided I couldn't live in perpetual terror," writes Andy Ngo about his decision to resume reporting after being beaten senseless in the streets of Portland.

23  The *Washington Post*'s Jacob Bogage dripped with hubris when referring to himself and his colleagues as "credible journalists" to Anderson Cooper while lying about postal worker Richard Hopkins. See Meredith Digital Staff, "Report: Postal worker recants claim of ballot tampering," Fox10 News, November 11, 2020.

The reward for chronic dishonesty could come in the form of a guest spot on CNN, a book review in the *New York Times*, or a coveted blue check mark. These are treated as the *ultimate* rewards in a successful life. Therefore, the lie becomes a form of existence. People survive "*unharmed only in a superficial bodily sense. And inside…they become corrupt.*"

And it is the result which counts in this life.

Or is it?

*It is not the result that counts. It is not the result - but the spirit!*

Incarcerated, shackled, terminated from his job, and ostracized from polite society, the American muckraker lands without a safety net, not knowing what the future might hold. Ralph Nader observed that the cruelty of the State and the media was invasive not just of his privacy, but also "of the self."[24] It can make an otherwise confident man question his own perceptions of reality. This is more terrifying than the concerns others have for the muckraker's life. Misery endures. Yet, meaning also endures because he is somehow still standing. He exists in a state of being in which there is nothing to hold on to, "Except the Will which says…'Hold on!'"[25]

A mailman sits in a hotel room in Erie, Pennsylvania—alone, unemployed, with a *Washington Post* headline syndicating that he "Recanted allegations of ballot tampering, officials say." The justification for the headline cites "three officials briefed on the investigation."[26] There were only two men in the room with the mailman when the interaction was recorded. However, in a Kafkaesque game of telephone, "officials briefed" somehow supercedes the audio record of what occurred, including the part when the government official threatened the mailman in a coercive way.[27] The now unemployed mailman sits in a chair, staring at the paintings on the hotel room wall, his mind instinctively responding to the trauma of being gaslit. The paint melts in a surreal way akin to Dali's *Persistence of Memory*. He sees his four-year-old daughter.

24 Thomas Whiteside, *The Investigation of Ralph Nader* (New York: Arbor House, 1972), 85
25 Rudyard Kipling, "If-"
 *If you can force your heart and nerve and sinew*
 *To serve your turn long after they are gone,*
 *And so hold on when there is nothing in you*
 *Except the Will which says to them: 'Hold on!'*
26 Shawn Boburg and Jacob Bogage, "Postal worker recanted allegations of ballot tampering, officials say," *Washington Post*, November 10, 2020.
27 "I'm not scaring you but I am scaring you. Hoping your mind will twist…" Russell Strasser, Office of the Inspector General.

*She doesn't know anything about this…I'm hoping one day she's proud of what I'm doing here.*[28]

The mailman, the Marine Corp's insignia Eagle, Globe, and Anchor displayed on his ballcap, says aloud to this muckraker, "I'll tell y'all, I'd rather be out, back in Afghanistan, getting shot at by Afghans, honest to God, than having to be in this kind of position."[29] It's reminiscent of whistleblower Jeffrey Wigand in his hotel room directly across from the legal department of tobacco giant Brown & Williamson's headquarters, shouting at the *60 Minutes* producer, "That's where they fuck with my life." The producer responds, "I'm running out of heroes, man. Guys like you are in short supply."[30]

Throughout the twentieth century, most whistleblowers lost their homes, their families, and the strain became unbearable.[31] Families were targeted. Marriages destroyed. Reputations besmirched. As the attorney hired by the State of Mississippi to assist with suing Big Tobacco explained so eloquently to Wigand:

> In combat, events have a duration of seconds, sometimes minutes. But what you're going through goes on day in and day out…week in, week out. Month after month…you're assaulted psychologically. You're assaulted financially, which is its own special kind of violence because it's directed at your kids…You feel your whole family's future's compromised, held hostage.[32]

When and where the system cannot persuade or propagandize, it punishes through coercion. Short of gulags, authorities content themselves with getting the muckraker fired, rendered unemployable, bankrupted, shunned—even by friends and family. "This is not 'death' exactly," writes Michael Anton, "but how much less cruel is it, really, to cut people off from human contact and the means of making a living? And how much real misery - and desperation - does it produce?"[33]

Fifteen years after the events featured in *The Insider*, another piece of true-crime fiction is happening: four young men live under the shadow of federal pre-trial release for a crime they did not commit, targeted not

28  Project Veritas, "USPS Whistleblower Richard Hopkins Gives New Interview Detailing Coercion Tactics Used by Federal Agents," November 11, 2020, YouTube video, 7:02.
29  Project Veritas, "USPS Whistleblower Richard Hopkins."
30  *The Insider*, directed by Michael Mann, Touchstone Pictures, 1999.
31  Alford, *Whistleblowers: Broken Lives and Organizational Power*, 19.
32  *The Insider*, 1999.
33  Michael Anton, "The Continuing Crisis," *Claremont Review of Books*, Winter 2020/2021.

for what they did, but for what they were trying to expose and for what they stood for. Sitting in jail, the idea "descended on them like a tongue of fire…they were not screwing them over in spite of the fact they were journalists, but *because* they were."[34]

*Yes, you have been imprisoned for nothing. You have nothing to repent before the State and its laws.*

Facing nine felony counts in California, a young muckraker who exposed Planned Parenthood finds little comfort in the truth that, as one muckraker said about the other, if he had exposed the unethical and commercial destruction of puppies (as opposed to the sale of aborted baby body parts), the country would have rallied to his defense.[35]

So, this moment becomes the nadir.[36]

*Your soul, once dry, ripens with suffering.*

A cloud of claustrophobia forms, hovers, swallows. You curse your circumstances. You simultaneously regret the actions that led you to where you are, yet at the same time you have no regrets at all, because you told the truth and followed your conscience. You are being *punished* for doing the right thing! But with this self-torture reveals the dichotomy of man. You start to embrace the punishment; a break away from evolutionary instinct of responding to positive stimuli as the good and true, and that is where your ascent begins.

The undercover muckraker Jaime Phillips burned and branded as "humiliated" by media pariahs for attempting to expose the *Washington Post* (how dare she go after a venerable institution like that!) sits in exile in a Vermont cabin to shield her friends and roommates from the fallout. She says to herself, *I'm a warrior and we're at war*. It was in this moment she made the decision and resolved to accept the consequences of what she was about to do.

---

34 O'Keefe, *Breakthrough*, prologue, xi.
35 "The verdict in the David Daleiden case is a complete travesty of justice and a significant wound to the First Amendment." @jamesokeefeiii is permanently suspended from Twitter.
36 *Nadir* – lowest point.

## THE ASCENT

You are pushed further and deeper into a higher level of consciousness. As you sit atop a heap of defamatory articles, you are pushed further and deeper. You are broke, unemployed, and abandoned. Your allies whisper and murmur about how toxic you are and whether you can survive this latest "misstep." Amidst this, you tend to go over your life with a fine-tooth comb and ponder that unrelated *"transgression of yours for which you have now received this blow."*

*. . . There is no punishment that comes to us in this life on earth which is undeserved.*

You repent in a more private place than the confessional; not before the State or before the yellow journalists. Yes, you do begin to repent, but before yourself.

*You will know that life is pain, that each of us hangs always upon the cross of himself. And when you know that this is true of every man, woman, and child on earth, you will be wise.*[37]

You may find that being confined to a room for three years nourished your soul.

*Your clean conscience, like a clear mountain lake, shines in your eyes.*

Political persecution, no matter the degree, inflicts a unique type of torture. Maybe it was the New Orleans crooked cop-cum-FBI officer accusing you of "willfully and maliciously interfering with a telephone system operated and controlled by the United States of America" in an affidavit, when the only true crime committed was to enter a federal building wearing hard hats and orange vests as telephone repairmen for the purpose of capturing video of Senator Landrieu ignoring her constituents' concerns.[38]

Maybe it was federal magistrate judge Daniel Knowles, with impunity, ordering the destruction of the SD chip containing video recording that,

---

37  Whittaker Chambers, *Witness* (Washington DC: Regnery Publishing, 1969).
38  "Affidavit of Stephen Rayes PDF," cbsnews.com. Accessed August 30 2021.

arguably, would have freed you, or at least prevented the ocean of words casting you as a felon the day after your arrest.[39]

Maybe it was federal prosecutor Sal Perricone orchestrating the anonymous commenting on his case through various media websites.[40] Although US Attorney Jim Letten resigned in disgrace years later for his media mischief, maybe it was the muckraker who watched mutely in real time as all this unfolded, helpless, akin to the Ludovico technique administered to Alex DeLarge in Anthony Burgess's *A Clockwork Orange.*

Maybe it was the coercion by federal agent Russell Strasser who manipulated you with the admission that he was trying to "twist you a little bit so your mind can kick in," with the mission of leaking the fruits of his labor to the *Washington Post*, a newspaper with the audacity to proclaim the tagline, "Democracy Dies in Darkness." Or maybe it's watching in horror as your Torquemada, California attorney general, who sent a team of lackeys to descend upon your apartment, confiscates your hard drives containing your reporter notebooks, and then watching as she becomes the vice president of the United States.

You witness oppressors repeatedly manipulate their power. You witness those under the banner of justice declare, like the tyrant O'Brien did in Orwell's *1984*, that "the object of persecution, is persecution."[41] As Chris Hedges said in his diatribe of the political order, *Wages of Rebellion*: "For the object of persecution is to break the will," and to deter others by sending a message that moral courage is "defined by the state as treason."[42] You watch over the course of a decade all the powerful institutions project onto you what they are. They are what they seem to hate. They become what they hate. You learn in this life:

> Laws are written for the lofty aim of "the common good" and then acted out in life on the basis of the common greed. In this world irrationality clings to man like his shadow so that the right things are done for the wrong reasons - afterwards, we dredge up the right reasons for justifications. It is a world not of angels but of angles, where men speak of moral principle but act on power principles...[43]

39  No major media outlet covered the evidence being destroyed. It was only posted on a little-known blog. Patterico, "Exclusive: Judge Orders Potentially Exculpatory Evidence in O'Keefe Case to Be Destroyed," The Patterico Pontifications Blog, entry posted May 5, 2010.
40  WDSU News, "Mann, Perricone gave up licenses 'in lieu of disciplinary action'," May 1, 2014, YouTube video, 2:24.
41  George Orwell, *1984* (New York: Signet Classics, 1950).
42  Chris Hedges, *Wages of Rebellion: The Moral Imperative of Revolt* (New York: Perseus Books Group, 2016), 59.
43  Saul D. Alinsky, *Rules for Radicals* (New York: Random House, 1971), 13.

These forces seek to stop you in your tracks. But to walk toward the fire and keep going, as your mentor once said, "is sending a message to the people who are rooting for you, who are agreeing with you. The message is that they can do it, too."[44] Even this statement, said in the abstract, does not entirely make sense in the beginning of your journey.

It is precisely in the moments of grief and uncertainty, as Maria Callas sang, that love and truth come to you.[45] Michael O'Brien echoes this sentiment in his book *Eclipse of the Sun*: "He understood suddenly…what the sailors and the poets knew, what the sparrows in the holly knew. He understood, despite his blindness, blinder than the eyeless snail: Time is an illusion of the mind. Only love remains."[46] To love what you do without the will to see it through, although well-intended, is an empty gesture. Whittaker Chambers, twentieth-century whistleblower, wrote: "Without courage, kindness and compassion remain merely fatuous postures."[47]

You are simultaneously broken and unbroken.

*Once upon a time you were sharply intolerant…You have come to realize your own weakness—and you can therefore understand the weakness of others. And be astonished at another's strength. And wish to possess it yourself.*

And so, you begin to live like you are dying. Or put another way, you conduct your muckraking journalism as if you have no fear of death.

*He could beat anything, he thought, because no thing could hurt him if he did not care.*[48]

Others ask if you fear for your life. Your answer, whether in the negative or affirmative, will make you sound prideful, or worse, self-aggrandizing.

*…a beneficial calming fluid pours through your blood vessels - patience.*

Upon ascendance, you begin to realize there are some things more important than praise and validation by a digital—yet invisible—sea of armchair critics and journalists. The realization then: yes, you've been tortured in a sense, and they've taken away so much, but in a more existential sense,

44  Andrew Breitbart, *Righteous Indignation* (New York: Grand Central Publishing, 2011).
45  *The Very Best of Maria Callas*, 06 "La Mamma Morta" from Andrea Chenier, comp. Umberto Giordano, EMI Classics CD57230, 2002.
46  Michael O'Brien, *Eclipse of the Sun* (San Francisco: Ignatius Press, 1999).
47  Chambers, *Witness,* 113.
48  Ernest Hemingway, *The Snows of Kilimanjaro and Other Stories* (New York: Scribner, 1961).

*some higher need was now being satisfied.* The experience ceases to be about rewards but instead now becomes about the salvation of *your own soul.*

*It is not the result that counts, but the spirit!*
As the muckraker from *To Kill a Messenger* said:

> I was winning awards, getting raises, lecturing college classes, appearing on TV shows, and judging journalism contests. And then I wrote some stories that made me realize how sadly misplaced my bliss had been. The reason I'd enjoyed such smooth sailing for so long hadn't been, as I'd assumed, because I was careful and diligent and good at my job…The truth was that, in all those years, I hadn't written anything important enough to suppress.[49]

So, the muckraker has to be prepared to suffer. British writer Freya India sagely describes suffering as "a requisite for growth." She continues, "It compels self-reflection, transformation, and transcendence: it precedes our resurrection, dragging us down before reviving us as wiser, more lucid versions of ourselves."[50]

You endured reputationally what Ernest Shackleton, quoting poet Robert Service, endured being stuck three years in the arctic ice: "We had 'suffered, starved, and triumphed, groveled down yet grasped at glory, grown bigger in the bigness of the whole.'"[51]

From this point of view, the crooked federal agents who interrogated Richard Hopkins, their allies in the establishment press who buy ink by the barrel, the oppressors who continuously live by lies, the prosecutors who blogged anonymously on newspaper columns while they tried your case, and the governor of New York, who claims to not *try cases in the press*, while his whole modus operandi is *to try cases in the press*—they are the ones devolving and being tortured.

*From that point of view our torturers have been punished most horribly of all. They are turning into swine, they are departing downward from humanity…*

*They* are the ones who are truly suffering.

---

49   Gary Webb, *Into the Buzzsaw: Leading Journalists Expose the Myth of a Free Press*, ed. Kristina Borjesson (New York: Prometheus Books, 2004).

50   Freya India, "My Generation Isn't Suffering Enough," The Quillette Blog, entry posted February 28, 2021, accessed August 30, 2021.

51   "We had pierced the veneer of outside things." Ernest Shackleton, *South: The Story of Shackleton's Last Expedition* (New York: The Macmillan Company, 1920).

## THE HUNTER BECOMES THE HUNTED

At the commencement of this ascent, you had become too well-known, and would now need to do something nobody has ever done before: something the German muckrakers described as a vision in the analog days of the 1970s, where there were only pencil-written accounts of submersion journalism. This was a strategic vision articulated but never pulled off: "I can see only one way out - to create five, six, a dozen [Günter Wallraffs]."[52]

So, one becomes two, two becomes four, and four becomes eight. The same experiences that tortured you engender trust with those who come to you. And suddenly, there are one hundred and more muckrakers and whistleblowers manifest. They look to you; they depend upon you. The Silicon Valley engineer jumps on a grenade and then makes the statement to you: "I'll fall to ashes one day. I want this to mean something after I'm gone."[53] The arc of the moral universe is long, but it bends toward justice. The first frame has now bent. Those one hundred American muckrakers turn into thousands hoping you can answer their question, "What can I do?" They, too, are willing to give up their lives to answer that question, so long as you are willing.

You've crossed the event horizon. No defamation or incarceration can now stop the momentum. This is your juncture, and it is yours alone. Yes, they do have tremendous power. But in part, it is because we give it to them. We are nothing, but we are not alone. To be awesome, one cannot be afraid, for we cannot live in fear. So, "a new truth, on top of the truth revealed in his reports, emerges in the reactions of those concerned."[54]

> The reaction from the opposition starts to become essential for the success of the muckraker's campaign...not only that the action is in the reaction, but that action is itself the consequence of reaction and of reaction to the reaction, ad infinitum. The pressure produces the reaction, and constant pressure sustains actions.[55]

> Thanks to the reactions of society, the facts disclosed appear as the elements of a system, brought into the consciousness of ordinary people.[56]

52  Günter Wallraff, *The Undesirable Journalist* (Woodstock: The Overlook Press, 1979).
53  Project Veritas, "Project Veritas Features – Pinterest Insider Speaks Out: 'The tech companies can't fight us all,'" June 13, 2019, YouTube video, 19:33.
54  Wallraff, *The Undesirable Journalist*, 3.
55  Alinsky, *Rules for Radicals*, 129.
56  Wallraff, *The Undesirable Journalist*, 4.

The balance of political forces has now changed. The role of the oppressor is now reversed. "David assumes new strength, while Goliath is attacked on all sides. The hunter has become the quarry."[57]

The hunter becomes the hunted…

*Hope!*

*Veritas lux mea!*

---

57   Wallraff, *The Undesirable Journalist*, 4.

# PREFACE
# SUFFERING

## WORKS CITED

Alford, C. Fred. *Whistleblowers: Broken Lives and Organizational Power*. Ithaca and London: Cornell University Press, 2001.

Alinsky, Saul D. *Rules for Radicals*. New York: Random House, 1971.

Bok, Sissela. *Secrets: On the Ethics of Concealment and Revelation*. New York: Random House, 1989.

Breitbart, Andrew. *Righteous Indignation*. New York: Grand Central Publishing, 2011.

Chambers, Whittaker. *Witness*. Washington DC: Regnery Publishing, 1969.

Frankl, Viktor. *Man's Search for Meaning*. New York: Pocket Books, 1985.

Hedges, Chris. *Wages of Rebellion*. New York: Perseus Books Group, 2016.

Hemingway, Ernest. *The Snows of Kilimanjaro and Other Stories*. New York: Scribner, 1961.

Herman, Edward S. and Noam Chomsky. *Manufacturing Consent: The Political*

*Economy of the Mass Media*. New York: Knopf Doubleday Publishing Group, 2011.

Kipling, Rudyard. *'If-' and other Poems*. London: Michael O'Mara Books Limited, 2016.

Ngo, Andy. *Unmasked: Inside Antifa's Radical Plan to Destroy Democracy*. New York: Hachette Book Group, 2021.

O'Keefe, James. *Breakthrough: Our Guerilla War to Expose Fraud and Save Democracy*. New York: Threshold Editions, 2014.

Orwell, George. *1984*. New York: Signet Classics, 1950.

Shackleton, Ernest. *South: The Story of Shackleton's Last Expedition*. New York: The Macmillan Company, 1920.

Sinclair, Upton. *The Brass Check: A Study of American Journalism; Evidence and Reasons Behind the Media's Corruption*. Adansonia Press, 1919.

Solzhenitsyn, Aleksandr. *The Gulag Archipelago 1918-1956 An Experiment in Literary Investigation*. Translated by Thomas P. Whitney and Harry Willets. Abridged by Edward E. Ericson, Jr. New York: HarperCollins Publishers, 2007.

Wallraff, Gunter. *The Undesirable Journalist*. Woodstock: The Overlook Press, 1979.

Webb, Gary. *Into the Buzzsaw: Leading Journalists Expose the Myth of a Free Press*. Edited by Kristina Borjesson. New York: Prometheus Books, 2004.

Tyrmand, Leopold. *Notebooks of a Dilettante*. New York: The Macmillan Company, 1970.

## LEGAL CASES

Shkelzen Berisha v. Guy Lawson. 594 U.S. (2021).

## DIGITAL DOCUMENTS

"Affidavit of Stephen Rayes PDF." cbsnews.com. Accessed August 30, 2021. https://www.cbsnews.com/htdocs/pdf/Landrieu_tampering_affadavit.pdf.

## MORE INFORMATION

On Aleksandr Solzhenitsyn: https://www.solzhenitsyncenter.org/

# CHAPTER 1
# MEDIUM

---

*It seemed to me that the walls of the mighty fortress of greed were on the point of cracking. It needed only one rush, and then another, and another.*[58]

-Upton Sinclair; *Early Twentieth-Century American Muckraker*

---

## A JOURNEY THROUGH TIME

Three quarters of a century ago, Canadian futurist Marshall McLuhan helped reshape our understanding of reality with this deceptively simple concept: "The medium is the message." In other words, the means we use to express our thoughts changes our perception of the world around us. The choice of medium, McLuhan observes, "shapes and controls the scale and form of human association and action."[59] Throughout history, a great deal has changed in the way news is disseminated, but, until recently, little has changed in way the act of journalism is performed.[60]

## THE PRINT ERA

When the printing press arrived in Venice five centuries ago, some powerful nobles and aristocrats promptly called for it to be outlawed. They saw printing as a dangerous and destabilizing new medium that spread the flow of ideas beyond the control of a learned few.

---

58  Upton Sinclair, *The Autobiography of Upton Sinclair* (London: Harcourt, Brace, and World, 1962), 121.
59  Marshall McLuhan, *Understanding Media: The Extensions of Man* (New York: McGraw Hill, 1964), 9.
60  Stephan Lesher, *Media Unbound* (Boston: Houghton Mifflin Company, 1982), 56.

If anything, they underestimated the power of the printed word. English philosopher Francis Bacon credited printing, along with gunpowder and the compass, as having "changed the whole face and state of things throughout the world."[61] Indeed, the printing press led directly to the Protestant Reformation and, indirectly, to the rise of the nation-state.

When the telegraph was invented three centuries later, social critic Henry David Thoreau said mockingly, "We are in great haste to construct a magnetic telegraph from Maine to Texas; but Maine and Texas, it may be, have nothing important to communicate."[62] Author Jack London saw it differently: "The telegraph annihilates space and time. Each morning, every part knows what every other part is thinking, contemplating, or doing."[63] If proof were needed, Abraham Lincoln knew the results of the 1860 presidential election before he went to bed on election night.

## THEY SAW PRINTING AS A DANGEROUS AND DE-STABILIZING NEW MEDIUM THAT SPREAD THE FLOW OF IDEAS BEYOND THE CONTROL OF A LEARNED FEW.

The *New York Times* later famously criticized the telephone's invention as an invasion of privacy. An 1887 op-ed writer worried that it forced people to be "transparent heaps of jelly to each other."[64] Another critic of the era complained that the telephone deprived the individual of the ability to cut another off with a simple look or gesture.[65] In 1890, when future Supreme Court Justice Louis Brandeis and his colleague Samuel Warren wrote their famous *Harvard Law Review* article, "The Right to Privacy," they envisioned the telephone as one of many new "mechanical devices" that threatened this heretofore unstated right. Instantaneous photography and the rapid dissemination of newspapers heightened their fears. And while Brandeis expressed concern over future technologies, he had no way of knowing that moving pictures with synchronized sound recording were just around the new century's corner. The telegraph and the telephone, however, did not replace the dominant print medium. They made it more efficient.

---

61 Francis Bacon, *The New Organon,* ed. Lisa Jardine and Michael Silverthorne (New York: Cambridge University Press, 2000), 129.
62 Henry David Thoreau, *Walden* (Boston: Beacon Press, 2004), 48.
63 Jack London, *War of the Classes, The Question of the Maximum* (Scotts Valley, CA: CreateSpace Independent Publishing, 2016).
64 Mitchell Stephens, *The Rise of the Image, the Fall of the Word* (New York: Oxford University Press, 1998), 31.
65 Stephens, 31.

Before the twentieth century, the press was supported in part by political parties. In the 1800s, even small towns had journals reflecting the will of the political parties of that day—Federalist, Democrat, Republican, and Whig. On one level, this open partisanship started to fade with the emergence of papers like the *New York Times* that still promise, however insincerely, to report "without fear or favor." On a deeper level, a new breed of reporter arrived on the scene. Independent investigative writers, willing to take chances with unproven tactics, began chasing stories that deeply resonated with the public. A constant struggle emerged in American journalism between the forces that want to control and the forces that want to expose.

For a time at least, journalists seemed to be motivated by "low tolerance for fraud, misuse of power, faith in the power of exposure to achieve correction."[66] Journalists couldn't save society, they understood, but they could provoke others to take action. As historian of journalism James Dygert notes, the press would serve as a vehicle to "promote reform, expose injustice, enlighten the public, and discourage knavery."[67] The Founding Fathers, Dygert argues, thought an informed populace, "a necessary condition for the intelligent exercise of democratic rights and duties."[68] Adolph Ochs agreed. "For much of the twentieth century," writes Ashley Rindsberg in his book *The Gray Lady Winked*, "the *Times* was seen as a standard bearer of the truth. It is because of this unique standing that the seven words that constitute the *Times'* famous slogan. 'All the News That's Fit to Print,' have been printed atop each day's edition since 1897 without irony or embarrassment."[69]

Even when operating under a benign corporate flag, however, journalists were only as valuable and efficient as their ability to be self-directed, self-managed, and even self- rewarded. In the best of days, reporters were kept on a short leash by management. Creative, gutsy work was the exception, not the rule. Sensing a void in the early twentieth-century marketplace, *McClure's*, a bellwether illustrated monthly, was determined not only to report on the world around it, but also to change that world.[70] The journal's editors aimed to "describe, to recognize, to denounce, and to cause change."[71] *McClure's* star reporter, Ida Tarbell, openly expressed her desire to attach herself to a cause greater than herself. Reporting, wrote Tarbell,

---

66  James H. Dygert, *The Investigative Journalist: Folk Heroes of a New Era* (Hoboken: Prentice-Hall, 1976).

67  Dygert, *The Investigative Journalist.*

68  Dygert, *The Investigative Journalist.*

69  Ashley Rindsberg, *The Gray Lady Winked: How the New York Times' Misreporting, Distortions and Fabrications Radically Altered History* (Monee, IL: Midnight Oil Publishers, 2021), 16.

70  Stephanie Gorton, *Citizen Reporters: S.S. McClure, Ida Tarbell, and the Magazine That Rewrote America* (New York: HarperCollins Publishers, 2020), 128.

71  Wallraff, *The Undesirable Journalist*, 9.

"aroused my flagging sense that I had a country, that its problems were my problems."[72] Tarbell's relentless reporting on Standard Oil led eventually to the dissolution of that powerful monopoly. Tarbell was perhaps the most prominent "muckraker," but she was in good company. The undercover work, for instance, of Julius Chambers and Nellie Bly, writing for the *New York Tribune* and *World* respectively, led to new laws, new facilities, and the closure of some of the more inhumane mental health facilities.[73]

## *"INVESTIGATIVE DISCLOSURES, IRONICALLY, OFTEN HAVE LITTLE IMPACT UNLESS THEY ARE PICKED UP AND EXPANDED BY OTHER NEWS MEDIA."*

Tarbell, Bly, and others in this school came from humble backgrounds. Through sheer tenacity, they forced their way into an arena previously dominated by the privileged few and, in so doing, tipped the social scales of power within newsrooms whose work product was no longer seen as mere "commodity."[74] Serious investigative reporters everywhere soon adopted this style of reporting. Throughout the first decades of the twentieth century, these reporters pounded their readers with a barrage of exposés, more than a few of which would evolve through tenacious reporting into perpetual crusades. Writes Pulitzer Prize-winning journalist Clark Mollenhoff, "If you want to be effective in this business…you've got to follow through."[75] Without follow-through, he adds, "The exposure alone may be counterproductive in that it results in a public display of the success of an arrogant and corrupt machine."[76] Ideally, that follow-through is collective. Dygert elaborates: "Investigative disclosures, ironically, often have little impact unless they are picked up and expanded by other news media."[77]

Then, as now, the media establishment resisted change. Despite his successes—most notably his game-changing 1906 exposé of the meatpacking industry, *The Jungle*—muckraker Sinclair felt himself, "An animal in a cage," one whose "bars were newspapers."[78] He told the story of his struggles in his 1919 exposé, *The Brass Check*, not of the packing plants, but of his era's corrupt journalistic establishment.

72   Ida M. Tarbell, *All in the Day's Work: An Autobiography* (New York: Macmillan, 1939), 179.
73   Gorton, *Citizen Reporters*, 125.
74   Gorton, *Citizen Reporters*, 125.
75   Clark Mollenhoff, *Investigative Reporting: From Courthouse to White House* (New York: Macmillan, 1981), 78.
76   Mollenhoff, *Investigative Reporting*, 78.
77   Dygert, *The Investigative Journalist*, 48.
78   Sinclair, *The Brass Check*, 42.

While Sinclair was out scrambling in the stockyards, many of his more gentlemanly peers were still wearing their fedoras and carrying walking sticks, eschewing the telephone for the personal visit and the calling card.[79] For most reporters, journalism was an "easier, tidier" enterprise than it was for the Sinclairs and the Tarbells.[80] Especially in Washington, there emerged a chumminess between press and politicians that led to an institutionalized blind eye. "The Rooseveltian rule" kept the private life of public figures private and undisclosed. During FDR's four-term presidency, for instance, most of the public did not even know he was confined to a wheelchair, let alone that he had a string of mistresses.

## THE BROADCAST ERA

While the muckrakers fought to expose injustices, the dominant media helped protect secrets. Up until about 1950, the public received its news almost exclusively through print, radio, and cinema newsreels. Both print and radio are examples of what McLuhan describes as "hot" media. Both require only one sense and "do not leave," writes McLuhan, "so much to be filled in or completed by the audience."[81] Television, by contrast, is "cool." It engages several senses, but less intensely than either print or radio, and demands more interaction on the part of the audience. Edited video leaves informational gaps that force the viewer to deduce a conclusion themselves. This is unavoidable, as is the nature of the medium.

The transition of the dominant media from hot to cool was part of a great, but little-noticed, informational revolution. Newspapers and magazines were yielding their customers and their independence to television. By the 1960s, virtually every household in America had a television, and television was making a difference. A contributing factor to the conclusion of our civil rights turmoil was the ubiquity of this medium. For the first time in history, people could actually see recent and relevant footage on the evening news of peaceful protests, ugly riots, and police brutality. This new visual code "enlarged notions of what is worth looking at and what we have a right to observe," writes Susan Sontag. The television "gave us the sense that we can hold the whole world in our heads," and offered finally "incontrovertible proof that the thing has happened." [82]

Negating the potential truth-telling power of television, however, was its tight control by the executives of three New York-based net-

79  David Halberstam, *The Powers That Be* (Champaign, IL: University of Illinois Press, 2000), 7.
80  Larry Sabato, *Feeding Frenzy: Attack Journalism and American Politics* (Baltimore: Lanahan Publishers, 2000), 26.
81  McLuhan, *Understanding Media*, 39.
82  Susan Sontag, *On Photography* (New York: Picador, 1977), 3.

works, two of them dominant, CBS and NBC. Heading these networks, in theory at least, was what Walter Lippmann, the dean of American journalists, calls a "specialized class" of "responsible men" who, he believed, were smart enough to figure things out. Wrote Lippmann, "The common interests elude public opinion entirely."[83] Not everyone thought this control was a good thing. Noam Chomsky and Edward Herman argue in *Manufacturing Consent* that the media became a system-supported propaganda function that engineered the public's responses.[84] Newspaper editor and social critic John Lofton observes, "Newspapers have tended to go along with the efforts to suppress deviations from the prevailing political and social orthodoxies of their time and place rather than to support the right to dissent."[85]

### THE TELEVISION "GAVE US THE SENSE THAT WE CAN HOLD THE WHOLE WORLD IN OUR HEADS," AND OFFERED FINALLY "INCONTROVERTIBLE PROOF THAT THE THING HAS HAPPENED."

For years, the journalist who best represented that "specialized class" was CBS's uber-anchor Walter Cronkite. "It is increasingly clear to this reporter," said Cronkite on air in February 1968, "that the only rational way out [of Vietnam] then will be to negotiate, not as victors, but as an honorable people who lived up to their pledge to defend democracy and did the best they could."[86] Cronkite had just returned from a visit to Vietnam, still reeling in the wake of the Tet Offensive in early 1968. Upon hearing this, President Lyndon Johnson was widely believed to have said, "If I've lost Cronkite, I've lost middle America."[87] This event marked the pinnacle of power for media empires like CBS. They had become nearly as powerful as the military and the government. Writes David Halberstam in *The Powers that Be*, "It was the first time in American history a war had been declared over by an anchorman."[88]

83  Quoted in Noam Chomsky, *Media Control: The Spectacular Achievements of Propaganda* (New York: Seven Stories Press, 2002), 15.

84  Herman and Chomsky, *Manufacturing Consent,* 15.

85  John Lofton, *The Press as Guardian of the First Amendment* (Columbia, SC: University of South Carolina Press, 1980), 279.

86  NPR, "Final Words: Cronkite's Vietnam Commentary," All Things Considered hosted by Guy Raz, broadcast on July 18, 2009.

87  Joseph W. Campbell, *Getting It Wrong: Ten of the Greatest Misreported Stories in American Journalism* (Berkeley: University of California Press, 2010).

88  Halberstam, *The Powers That Be,* 514.

This specialized class of responsible men maintained their power throughout the 1970s. In his famed 1978 Harvard address, Soviet dissident Aleksandr Solzhenitsyn observed, "The press has become the greatest power within the Western countries, more powerful than the legislative power, the executive, and the judiciary."[89] Thanks largely to the dominance of television news, the "fourth estate" was able to chase one president out of the White House and the American military out of Vietnam. But, as Solzhenitsyn asked of the press, "By what law has it been elected and to whom is it responsible?"[90]

In the 1970s, that question was rarely raised. The assumption was that journalists were choosing their targets by the Ochs family standard: "…impartially, without fear or favor, regardless of party, sect, or interests involved."[91] Few in the public suspected that Cronkite had his own pronounced biases, and his constant worry was that he would be found out. "I thought that some day the roof was going to fall in," he would later confess. "Somebody was going to write a big piece in the newspaper or something. I don't know why to this day I got away with it."[92] In a similar vein, the *Washington Post*'s Watergate reporting was being managed by an editor, Ben Bradlee, whose best buddy had been JFK and who remained too tight with the Washington establishment.

## "ANONYMOUS" SOURCES

During the Watergate era, journalists speculated that Robert Woodward and Carl Bernstein's anonymous source, "Deep Throat," was a composite, not a real person. They were right to speculate. The *Washington Post* based much of its reporting on a single, anonymous source who was unknown even to the *Post*'s editor, Ben Bradlee.[93] Years later, it was revealed that there was a core figure who was romanticized into the Deep Throat character, an FBI higher-up named Mark Felt. In retrospect, though, it is clear Felt steered the reporting in a direction that served both his agenda and the *Post*'s. Although the *Post* would never admit it, the truth was secondary to the urge to "get Nixon."

---

89  Solzhenitsyn Center, "Harvard Address," April 12, 2013, YouTube video, 1:02:29. Accessed August 31, 2021.
90  Solzhenitsyn Center, "Harvard Address."
91  David W. Dunlap, "Looking Back: 1896 'Without Fear or Favor,'" *New York Times*, August 14, 2015.
92  Douglas Brinkley, *Cronkite* (New York: HarperCollins Publishers, 2012).
93  Gillian Brockell, "Deep Throat's identity was a mystery for decades because no one believed this woman," *Washington Post*, September 27, 2019.

The course of journalism was forever changed with the Watergate scandal that cost Republican Richard Nixon the presidency upon his resignation in 1974. Journalism became more adversarial, more puritan, more cynical, and less tolerant. Reporters hungered after fame and sought to become stars like the *Post*'s Woodward and Bernstein.

In the process, the press was being poisoned by the reporters' desire to "change the world" on the cheap, not by fixing what was broken but by taking down targets such as Richard Nixon. The end goal became the cathartic "we got 'em" moment. Having largely abandoned traditional ways of gathering information, journalists had a harder time obtaining meaningful information about public officials' character and personalities.

### *REPORTERS HUNGERED AFTER FAME AND SOUGHT TO BECOME STARS LIKE THE POST'S WOODWARD AND BERNSTEIN.*

What was "supposed to be straight news" no longer was.[94] Journalists jumped from scandal to scandal. Private lives became public, and nothing sold better than sex as presidential contender Gary Hart learned the hard way in the bellwether "Monkey Business" scandal of 1987. After Watergate, writes Stephan Lesher, journalism became "bellicose, bullying, smug, sullen and self-righteous."[95] In economic terms, the commercial imperative of the news led papers to try to maximize circulation and avoid alienating readers by choosing sides. Intense competition and corporate control led to a dwindling audience share. Star journalism led to timidity in reporting, pseudo-celebrities, e-girls, and infotainment. A power reversal was in order.

### THE DEMOCRATIZATION OF THE MEDIA

Newspapers started losing their audience to television. By the 1980s, television was the people's choice by a two-to-one margin.[96] Yet, nearly forty years into the television revolution, the content of that news was being controlled by a handful of like-minded and increasingly dishonest people. The advent of broadcast satellite technology was best seen utilized at Ted Turner's CNN in Atlanta, Georgia, the first twenty-four-

---

94  Sabato, *Feeding Frenzy*, 164.
95  Lesher, *Media Unbound*, 6.
96  Sabato, *Feeding Frenzy*, 31.

hour cable news channel, and among the first to disrupt the monolithic television networks who had become ubiquitous in the worlds of news and entertainment. The hegemony of those powerful networks would soon be challenged, not as much by cable news, the obvious competitor on the horizon, as by the handheld video camcorder. Live video recording became affordable on an industrial scale. Handheld cameras could circle the globe like never seen before. For the first time, the individual could choose what was worth recording and, thanks to the VCR, could share that information freely. The medium changed the way we view the world around us and the way we viewed ourselves.[97] The millions of camcorders leveled the boundaries of privacy. A media revolution had just begun, but few took notice.

For years, hidden camera visuals and their near kin, ambush-style interviews, were the preserve of Big Media. Mike Wallace, the late veteran of CBS News, once proudly employed both. He claimed to have abandoned these practices after failing to achieve the reporter's ultimate goal. "The problem became this: We became a caricature of ourselves," he said. "We were after light, and it began to look as though we were after heat, not to reveal some information or not to find out the story."[98]

Upon abandoning these tactics, Wallace would argue that such video had the potential to "convey any picture you want."[99] Although the same could be said of all journalistic media, hidden camera video, done responsibly, became the most honest medium of all. It is the one medium that can honestly address *motive*.

## THE MEDIUM CHANGED THE WAY WE VIEW THE WORLD AROUND US AND THE WAY WE VIEWED OURSELVES.

This was a cop-out on Wallace's part, an excuse. It also wouldn't be the first time he caved under pressure. In 1997, when CBS News took on one of the biggest culprits of all, Big Tobacco, Wallace kowtowed to corporate interests. At CBS, the separation of editorial and business sides of the news had begun to blur. As ownership of the major media companies consolidated, the drive to be profitable oozed deep into the newsroom.[100]

---

97  Andrew J. McClurg, "Bringing Privacy Law Out of the Closet: A Tort Theory of Liability for Intrusions in Public Places," *North Carolina Law Review* 73, no. 3 (March 1995).

98  NPR, "Fresh Air Remembers Mike Wallace Of '60 Minutes,'" Fresh Air, broadcast on April 9, 2012.

99  Harry Stein, "How '60 Minutes' Makes News," *New York Times*, May 6, 1979.

100  Clarence Jones, *Winning with the News Media: A Self-Defense Manual When You're the Story* (Holmes Beach: Winning News Media, 1983), 18.

The money men certainly gave the impression of calling the shots when it came to major news decisions.

The sale of CBS to Westinghouse almost caused CBS to shelve a lengthy exposé critical of Big Tobacco. The chief lawyer for CBS told the executive producer for *60 Minutes* that no story should put the network at risk. "[The lawyer] was proposing something unprecedented in the history of CBS News - stopping an important history in midstream for fear of a lawsuit that hadn't been threatened," reported Marie Brenner in *Vanity Fair*. The complication was that Andrew Tisch, the chairman of Lorillard Tobacco Company, was the son of CBS chairman Laurence Tisch. Andrew was among the tobacco executives to have testified under oath that nicotine was not addictive.[101] According to Brenner, the CBS lawyer asked, "How do you expect us to go on the air with a piece that might put the chairman's son in jail?"[102] Finally, CBS made the extraordinary decision to run the story but to leave out "critical information." Wallace even admitted on the air that CBS "had seen fit to give in to perceived threats of legal action against us by an industry giant."[103]

In the late 1980s, deregulation paved the way for talk radio. Largely shut out of other broadcast media, conservatives found their voice on the AM side of the dial. Thirty-three years after Rush Limbaugh hit the airwaves, journalists at the *New York Times* still had not reconciled themselves to the possibility of alternative viewpoints. They characterized talk radio as the "id of American conservative thought," and worried openly about the "unguarded nature of talk radio, where hosts indulge in edgier fare than on TV networks like Fox News and listeners call in to say what they really think."[104] It clearly bothered the *Times* and others in the "mainstream" that someone like Limbaugh was articulating the things people were thinking but were too afraid to say, didn't know how to say, or just needed to hear said.

However, radio had its limitations. Although admittedly in pitched battle with the mainstream media, the late Andrew Breitbart did not embrace talk radio as his weapon of choice. "In a world in which media is everything, AM radio is the lowest form of communication," Breitbart said during a 2011 interview with Web TV host Peter Robinson. "It's tinny. It's not robust. It's not *Avatar*. I want *Avatar*."[105]

101 Michael Janofsky, "On Cigarettes, Health and Lawyers," *New York Times*, December 6, 1993.
102 Marie Brenner, "The Man Who Knew Too Much," *Vanity Fair*, April 1, 2004.
103 WGBH/Frontline, "Anatomy of a Decision: Facts and context in the '60 Minutes' decision not to air a tobacco industry expose," PBS, 1999.
104 Michael M. Grynbaum, Tiffany Hsu, Katie Robertson, and Keith Collins, "How Right-Wing Radio Stoked Anger Before the Capitol Siege," *New York Times*, February 12, 2021.
105 Conor Friedersdorf, "Andrew Breitbart Talks Down Talk Radio," *The Atlantic*, June 17, 2011.

No one understood the media better than Breitbart, the foremost of this muckraker's mentors. *Avatar* was an epic Hollywood film of the era that soft-pedaled messages of social equity, little known at that time, amidst a dazzling color spectacle of light and sound in participatory three-dimensions (3D). The hidden camera visual, which Breitbart championed, was not *Avatar*, but like the film, it invited the audience in. Unlike talk radio, it allowed viewers to participate and draw conclusions on their own. Although a cool medium by McLuhan standards, it generated heat. Viewers weren't told what to think or how to feel. If the content was powerful, they arrived at the state of what Ida Tarbell called "righteous indignation" on their own.[106] For McLuhan, the medium may have been the message, but at the inception of a new guerilla journalism organization, Project Veritas, content has always been king. At its best, hidden camera visual weds a powerful participatory medium with equally powerful content, and the result is low-budget *Avatar*.

## THE INTERNET ERA

Amplifying the power of the hidden camera visual, of course, was the internet. If product for the VCR had to be produced in a studio and distributed through snail mail, the product spread through the internet was instant and could be produced on a desktop or even in one's own cell phone. "Because the new media provides the tools and there are millions out there who are outraged," said Breitbart in 2010. "Now they realize, 'Wow anybody can do that. We can hold these people accountable. We have the means. We have the technology.'"[107]

Those who study journalism history must have anticipated the pushback from those with the power to control information flow. Fifteen years into the internet era, there would be an information sea change that would shatter illusions and shift the balance of informational power. Almost as soon as the internet established its liberating influence, centralizing forces moved in to counter that liberation. One of those forces was the US government. The surveillance age had begun before 9/11 but accelerated thereafter. Whistleblower Edward Snowden called the resulting intrusiveness "the end of the internet as I knew it."[108] Snowden described the remaking of the world thus: "Everything about us that we revealed, knowingly or not, was being surveilled and sold in secret." Even the FBI admitted that

---

106 Cecelia Tichi, *Exposés and Excess: Muckraking in America, 1900/2000* (Philadelphia: University of Pennsylvania Press, 2011).

107 Noah Shachtman, "How Andrew Breitbart Hacked the Media," *Wired*, March 11, 2010.

108 Edward Snowden, *Permanent Record* (New York: Metropolitan Books, 2019), 5.

the individual's television was capable of spying on that person.[109]

Madison Avenue moved in as well. As 2010 approached, the *Financial Times* reported, "With the advent of the internet, online platforms such as Craigslist and eventually Google and Facebook snatched up most of the advertising revenue that supported the local press."[110] Even as the internet was demolishing traditional business models, Amazon founder Jeff Bezos purchased the *Washington Post* in 2013. Bezos shifted the coverage from local to national and global distribution via the internet. No longer "relying on relatively few subscribers paying lots of money," the *Post*'s management was intent on "persuading many more subscribers to buy cheaper digital-only subscriptions."[111] Bezos, in an extraordinary admission of the power of narrative amplified through Big Tech, called his stewardship of the *Post*, "something I will be most proud of when I'm 90 and reviewing my life."[112] The digital subscriptions of both the *New York Times* and the *Washington Post* began to increase, and the two media giants strengthened their shares of the print journalism oligopoly.

## "WE CAN HOLD THESE PEOPLE ACCOUNTABLE. WE HAVE THE MEANS. WE HAVE THE TECHNOLOGY."

Holman Jenkins argued in the *Wall Street Journal* that these two newspapers consciously abandoned the advertisers' historic model of reaching as "many customers as possible." Wrote Jenkins, "If you think the *New York Times* and *Washington Post* mind in the least that their coverage is off-putting to a large number of Americans, you misunderstand the business they're in."[113] The business they are now in is one that caters to the needs of an increasingly narrow audience of affluent ideologues.

The *Times*' audience, in particular, seemed largely unaware that the Gray Lady had changed styles. It had slowly slipped off its "without fear

109 Karl Bode, "The FBI Says Your TV Is Probably Spying On You," Techdirt, December 6, 2019.

110 Anna Nicolau and James Fontanella-Khan, "The Fight for the Future of America's Local Newspapers," *Financial Times*, January 20, 2021.

111 Marc Tracy, "How Marty Baron and Jeff Bezos Remade the Washington Post," *New York Times*, February 27, 2021.

112 Mr. Bezos's pride in transforming the *Post* to a partisan digital publication gauges his success in terms of acquired power, and not in journalistic integrity, considering the *Post* does little to investigate the malfeasance and corruption Silicon Valley monopolies hold over DC politicians and in swaying national elections to tech-friendly candidates.Jeff Bezos, "No thank you, Mr. Pecker," Jeff Bezos blog on *Medium*, entry posted February 7, 2019.

113 Holman W. Jenkins, Jr., "How to Have More Police Shootings," *Wall Street Journal*, April 23, 2021.

or favor" look in favor of "critical theory," a Marxist fashion first imported from Europe in the 1930s. Writes Rindsberg in his dissection of the *Times*:

> The job of critical theory was to look at the power structures that lie beneath any theory and how those theories work to oppress others. A critical theory thus became one that did not aim first and foremost at finding "truth" - something critical theory holds is produced according to the needs of a power structure - but, instead, at effecting social change.[114]

While the *Times* was increasing its dominance and growing more and more indifferent to "truth," local and state newspapers shuttered or became distressed assets purchased by hedge funds like Alden Global Capital.[115] Budgets were slashed, and investigative reporters were laid off, deemed inessential. Just about all that was left were "ghost" papers, "unable to produce much in the way of original local journalism."[116] Digital reporters at outlets all across the political spectrum no longer produced meaningful content. Now their papers became chop shops with some reporters required to spit out as many as a dozen articles a day.

### THE MUCKRAKER ONCE WORKED WITHIN THE FRAMEWORK OF ESTABLISHMENT JOURNALISM. TODAY, THE MUCKRAKER IS ON HIS OWN.

Editors became all too familiar with the tactic of "stealth editing" to make up for the rise in errors and aggregated untruths. Stealth editing consisted of the editor or reporter going back into an already published story, making just enough edits to avoid plagiarism charges, and then passing off the article as original. In some cases, outlets do not even track who is making the changes. This leaves little room for accountability when massive mistakes enter print and blow up in the editor's face. Many a stealth editor has found their way to an honored place on the Project Veritas Wall of Shame, where retracted claims live in infamy at Project Veritas headquarters.

---

114 Rindsberg, *The Gray Lady Winked*, 226.
115 Margaret Sullivan, "The 'audacious lie' behind a hedge fund's promise to sustain local journalism," *Washington Post*, February 17, 2021.
116 Jenkins, "How to Have More Police Shootings."

The larger papers still standing became colonial outposts of the Big Media oligopoly. Rather than seeking the truth, they rehashed tired social change messaging and shed their more conservative customers as they hewed steadily leftward. Over time, they sacrificed their journalistic integrity by yielding to the temptation to pander to their paying subscribers' political fantasies. Collectively, they made a mockery of Ochs's "without fear or favor" pledge. The muckraker once worked within the framework of establishment journalism. Today, the muckraker is on his own.

## THE RISE OF THE OLIGARCHY

American life in the late twentieth century had been trending toward an increase in anonymity. The popularity of private autos, automatic garage doors, and suburban homes without front porches left many Americans "drowning in privacy."[117] The twenty-first century reversed that momentum. In exchange for instant information and communication, Americans all but welcomed the Big Tech companies into their living rooms and into their lives. These companies engaged in mass surveillance in ways that not even science fiction writers had anticipated. Big Tech freely gathered the individual's most intimate data and sold it on the open market. Writes Edward Snowden, arguably America's foremost whistleblower, "Our attention, our activities, our locations, and our desires - everything about us that we revealed, knowingly or not, was being surveilled and sold in secret, so as to delay the inevitable feeling of violation."[118] Like the benighted citizens of Orwell's Oceania, today every American worth watching can be kept under perpetual watch by the digital police and within the sound of official propaganda twenty-four hours a day.

Mass surveillance, at least when done by the government, notes Snowden, "afflicts the innocent far more than the guilty."[119] Objections to the use of the hidden camera reporting by the elites have tended to be about *mitigating* or blunting the truth. They have also professed dissatisfaction with the content in cases where the content wasn't at issue.

The Big Tech oligarchs did not discourage individuals from launching their own platforms on individual niche channels such as Instagram, or even becoming their own platforms. An iPhone 10 or 11, equipped

---

117 Jonathan Franzen, "Imperial Bedroom," *New Yorker*, October 5, 1998.
118 Snowden, *Permanent Record*, 5.
119 Snowden, *Permanent Record*, 5.

with cameras more powerful than the DSLR cameras a decade previously, had become addictive "fantasy machines" for many an aspiring "influencer."[120] In the nineteenth century, the French poet Mallarmé said that things existed in order to end up as a book.[121] To paraphrase Susan Sontag, by the end of the second decade of the twenty-first century, things existed in order to end up on Instagram.[122]

Writer for the *New York Times* Jon Caramanica agreed, "Whereas Twitter fomented arguments, Instagram became, 'polished beyond feeling.'"[123] If these "things" did not threaten the oligarchs' control of the message, they were permitted for permanent residency in the mansions of Instagram, Twitter, or Facebook.

Open the Books, a non-profit organization lobbying for government accountability, sports the motto: "Transparency is transformative."[124] Heinrich Böll's introduction to Wallraff's book highlights the transformative effects fact-finding can have on society's progression: "To describe reality precisely is an essential step toward transforming it."[125] The world saw how devastatingly effective video could be. Citizen video journalism, arguably launched with the video recording of Rodney King being beaten by Los Angeles cops in 1991, created a media domino effect on a scale that was never seen before.

Despite their best efforts, the oligarchs could not control information as well as they hoped. In the 2016 election year, for instance, hundreds of people worked without compensation to expose wrongdoing in their city halls, state houses, and federal centers. In that one year alone, journalists without credentials, armed with video, did everything from shaking the foundations of policing on city streets to exposing shady political maneuverings among the consultant class during the presidential election.

## *BY THE END OF THE SECOND DECADE OF THE TWENTY-FIRST CENTURY, THINGS EXISTED IN ORDER TO END UP ON INSTAGRAM.*

---

120 Sontag, *On Photography*, 14.
121 Alex Ross, "Encrypted: Translators confront the supreme enigma of Stephane Mallarme's poetry," *New Yorker*, April 4, 2016. Accessed September 29, 2021.
122 Sontag, *On Photography*, 24.
123 Jon Caramanica, "The Young Men's Style Council of TikTok," *New York Times*, July 8, 2021.
124 Open the Books, "Every Dime. Online. In Real Time.," Openthebooks.com, 2021.
125 Wallraff, introduction by Böll, *The Undesirable Journalist*, 9.

## JOURNALISTS AS SLAVES TO ACCESS

Generally speaking, beat reporters became wholly dependent upon their access to those in power. What results, writes media scholar Stephan Lesher, is that reporters "tend to play stenographer precisely when they should exercise independence, and they tend to expound their own ideas when they should be quoting someone much more knowledgeable to help us better comprehend the event."[126] The muckraker who employs hidden camera technology is not so conflicted.

Throughout the twentieth century, there was a "tension between access and autonomy" in the media.[127] On one end of the spectrum, there were adversarial journalists who, given their lack of access, did not have a realistic understanding of what was happening on the inside of a given institution. In his book on Watergate, Mark Feldstein traces the beginning of "scandal culture" to that bellwether event, one that he believes led to a trivialization of political discourse and eventually to sensationalism.[128] Following the Watergate scandal, the mood of journalists, observes Paul Weaver, was one of "truculent independence from government and officialdom."[129] In extreme cases, where there is no truce whatsoever between politicians and the press, writes Sissela Bok, "Adversary relations engender biases of their own."[130] Aggressiveness is admired, notes Lesher, but "moderations in reaching judgments...often is mistaken for weakness or wrong-headedness."[131]

Press that becomes too adversarial, Weaver adds, "allies itself with a political faction and so becomes partisan - an ideologically divisive factor rather than a politically unifying force."[132] One example, cited in *Trump v. Media*, states, "The premise was that most journalists would inevitably agree that Trump was a dangerous demagogue, and that they should continue to stay on the Trump beat even though they were unable or unwilling to change their opinion."[133] Another example, in 2016, a column on

---

126 Lesher, *Media Unbound,* 58.
127 Gregory Magarian, "The Jurisprudence of Colliding First Amendment Interests: From the Dead End of Neutrality to the Open Road of Participation Enhancing Review," 83 *Notre Dame Law Review* 185, 2007.
128 Mark Feldstein, *Poisoning the Press: Richard Nixon, Jack Anderson, and the Rise of Washington's Scandal Culture* (New York: Farrar, Strauss, and Giroux, 2010), 4.
129 Paul H. Weaver, "The new journalism and the old - thoughts after Watergate," *National Affairs,* Spring 1974.
130 Bok, *Secrets,* 258.
131 Lesher, *Media Unbound,* 42.
132 Weaver, "The new journalism and the old," 87.
133 Mollie Ziegler Hemingway, *Trump vs. The Media* (New York: Encounter Books, 2017), 29-30.

the front page of the *New York Times* titled, "Trump is Testing the Norms of Objectivity in Journalism," Jim Rutenberg boldly advocated for the abandonment of the concept of "fairness." Wrote Rutenberg, "You have to throw out the textbook American journalism has been using for the better part of the past half-century."[134] Rutenberg wrote this extraordinary confession *before* Trump was elected president. Rather than condemning it, the executive editor of the *Times* Dean Baquet responded, "I thought Jim Rutenberg's column nailed it."[135]

In beat reporting, there exists in this paradigm a "structured independence" in which "each side knows its role." Given the "reciprocity of interest," a symbiotic relationship exists between media officials and sources.[136] This kind of relationship tends to corrupt journalism, and, to paraphrase Lord Acton, the closer the relationship between journalist and source, the more corrupt. This was never more the case than during the Kennedy presidency when reporters reveled in their acceptance by, and association with, the glamorous, dashing, wealthy, jet-setting president.[137]

Kennedy was not the first president to enjoy such widespread media support. Franklin D. Roosevelt manipulated his cozy relationship with the press as well. FDR would try to shape the stories, using peer pressure, to keep any wandering journalist in line. "If I were writing that story," he would say, "I would write it along the lines…"[138]

The interview between a government source and a journalist is inevitably a "contrived occurrence" and is often "phony and extremely cooperative."[139] An interview of this nature between journalist and source is yet another prime example of what Daniel Boorstin would call a "pseudo-event."[140] Boorstin references a 1869 article from *The Nation* publication, "The interview as at present managed, is generally the joint product of some humbug of a hack politician, and another humbug of a reporter."[141]

J. Anthony Lukas, two-time winner of the Pulitzer Prize, thought along similar lines as Boorstin. A relationship between reporter and source, Lukas argues, is "mutually manipulative, particularly one of long term, is

134 Jim Rutenberg, "Trump is Testing the Norms of Objectivity in Journalism," *New York Times*, August 7, 2016.
135 James Taranto, "Finale," *Wall Street Journal*, January 3, 2017.
136 Herman and Chomsky, *Manufacturing Consent*.
137 Sabato, *Feeding Frenzy*, 26.
138 Halberstam, *The Powers That Be*, 9.
139 Charles Stewart and William B. Cash, *Interviewing: Principles and Practices* (Englewood, NJ: McGraw Hill Education, 2021).
140 Daniel J. Boorstin, *The Image: A Guide to Pseudo-Events in America* (New York: Vintage Books, 1961).
141 "The Interview," *The Nation*, January 28, 1869, cited in Boorstin, *The Image*.

filled with collaboration and manipulation," but, Lukas adds, "it is very much more likely to be the man in power who is manipulating the reporter."[142] According to muckraker Jack Anderson, "Reporters consider it their function to court the high and mighty rather than condemn them; to extol public officials rather than expose them." [143]

*Guardian* editor in chief Alan Rusbridger laid out the three categories into which accredited media usually slot themselves:

> Some do a very good job of attempting to determine whether they are being misled, and always run the risk of being cut adrift for doing so. Others, while not gullible, appear at times to suspend their disbelief in the hope of picking up a good story. The people in this group are guilty in my opinion of a rather British journalistic vice: deference…The journalists in the third category are those who are so impressed by the supposed mystique of the agencies that they appear to go weak at the knees at the thought of an off-the-record briefing.[144]

## "REPORTERS CONSIDER IT THEIR FUNCTION TO COURT THE HIGH AND MIGHTY RATHER THAN CONDEMN THEM; TO EXTOL PUBLIC OFFICIALS RATHER THAN EXPOSE THEM."

The *Washington Post*'s Jacob Bogage fell clearly into that third category. As was discussed earlier, Bogage reported in a headline that Project Veritas whistleblower USPS carrier Richard Hopkins "recanted his allegations of ballot tampering." Bogage relied on information from "three officials briefed on the investigation." To the *Post*'s misfortune, Project Veritas had a live recording of what transpired between the federal agents and Hopkins. The *Post* based its reporting not on the recording, but on the anonymous "three officials" that were merely "briefed." In this regard, the federal agents were using the *Washington Post* to advance what Boorstin characterizes as a form of "domestic counterintelligence inappropriate in a Republic." The *Post*'s characterization that Hopkins "fabricated the allegations"[145] corresponds to Boorstin's description of the media pseudo-event being "fuller

142 Martin Gottlieb, "Dangerous Liaisons? Journalists and their sources," *Columbia Journalism Review* 28, no. 2 (July/August 1989).
143 Jack Anderson and George Clifford, *The Anderson Papers* (New York: Random House, 1974), 5.
144 Alan Rusbridger, *News and How to Use It: What to Believe in a Fake News World* (Edinburgh: Canongate Books, 2020).
145 Boburg and Bogage, "Postal worker recanted allegations."

of ambiguity, with a welcome atmosphere of confidence and intrigue… more appealing to all concerned."[146] Much media distortion, argues Lesher, derives "from the nature of journalism, not from the nature of journalists."[147] Whatever its cause, during the Trump era, there was a whole lot of abysmal journalism. Relying on anonymous sources, *The Atlantic* claimed Trump insulted dead American servicemen, although the claim was actually disputed by some of those who were there. Likewise, the *Times* ran a major pre-election story on Trump's tax returns that did not produce any evidence, any on-the-record sources, or even a single document.[148]

Traditionally, journalists have been driven by two imperatives: to be first on the story and to keep costs down. Taking information from sources that were "presumed credible" reduced investigative expenses.[149] Reluctant to get into what veteran journalist James Dygert has called "an exposed position where it might be accused of affecting events rather than just reporting them," the average TV news program has a tendency to report the obvious. Television producers, writes Dygert, historically preferred to investigate a story that's already been broken elsewhere. They are cautious "about breaking new ground."[150] The need to influence events, rather than merely chronicle them, came slow to TV newsrooms.

On the other end of the spectrum are journalists who depend for facts completely on their access to sources. Ken Silverstein is not one of them. In 2007, Silverstein posed as a representative of a London-based energy firm looking to find a DC lobbying firm that would help his business partners in Turkmenistan "whitewash the image of that country's Stalinist regime."[151] He had no trouble finding two such firms. Although accused of deception, Silverstein strongly defended the "rich benefits" that undercover journalism can deliver. Wrote Silverstein in *Harpers*, "Unfortunately, few news outlets are willing to use undercover journalism to get a story, or to practice investigative journalism in general. It's just too expensive and risky; media organizations would rather spend their money on tables at the White House Correspondents Dinner and watch Karl Rove rap."[152]

---

146 Boorstin, *The Image*, 31.
147 Lesher, *Media Unbound*, 15.
148 David Barstow, "Donald Trump Tax Records Show He Could Have Avoided Taxes for Nearly Two Decades, the Times Found," *New York Times,* October 2, 2016.
149 Anderson and Clifford, *The Anderson Papers*, 5.
150 Dygert, *The Investigative Journalist*.
151 Ken Silverstein, "Lobby Shops for Turkmenistan: Will lie for money," *Harper's Magazine*, June 24, 2007.
152 Silverstein, "Lobby Shops for Turkmenistan."

Silverstein caught considerable heat from the journalism establishment for his deceptive tactics. Among those who came to his defense was media watchdog Mark Lisheron. Wrote Lisheron in the *American Journalism Review*, "Beltway reporters walked a rutted beat all the way around the inner sanctum of the Washington lobby."[153] All of them knew what was happening with these high-priced lobbying firms, but none got the story. Silverstein explained why:

> There is a certain smugness on the high end of the Washington press corps, indecently close personal and professional relationships between reporters and the people they are supposed to cover. What is lost here in the interest of phony balance is any sense of right and wrong.[154]

The beat reporter is often mired in a conundrum. By relying upon the same sources for information, she feels compelled, observes Edward Wasserman, the dean of UC Berkeley's school of journalism, to "sit on a perfectly newsworthy story that would embarrass the source she relies on." Her alternative is "to write it and sacrifice her future effectiveness as a police reporter."[155]

### *"WHAT IS LOST HERE IN THE INTEREST OF PHONY BALANCE IS ANY SENSE OF RIGHT AND WRONG."*

## THE TRUMP DISRUPTION

In 2016, not coincidentally, Donald Trump was elected president. Trump's ascendancy, argued Barton Swaim in the *Wall Street Journal*, represented the "spectacular failure of America's expert class," one "that would have been impossible without the willing support of a credulous news media."[156] A colleague of senior ABC correspondent David Wright, Andy Fies, explained the nature of that failure to an undercover Project Veritas reporter:

> It's about the fucking horse race…people in New York are constantly, I think, fascinated by how can people like Donald Trump, how can people understand. You know, well fuck,

153 Mark Lisheron, "Lying to Get the Truth," *American Journalism Review*, October/November 2007.
154 Silverstein, "Lobby Shops for Turkmenistan."
155 Edward Wasserman, "The Insidious Corruption of Beats," Edward Wasserman blog archive of columns written while employed at the *Miami Herald*, January 8, 2007.
156 Barton Swaim, "Trump and the Failure of the Expert Class," *Wall Street Journal*, January 22, 2021.

cross the Hudson now and then, and come out and spend some time, and you'll hear why.[157]

The disconnect between public sentiment and corporate media culture was echoed in 2017. CNN employees reluctant to speak publicly, did so privately to Project Veritas. A twenty-five-year veteran of CNN said of his employer:

> I hate what we've become…we could be so much better than we are…All they gotta do is take an anchor, and put him at the desk, and tell the news…We're so busy trying to get appointment viewership…Even though we're totally left-leaning, we're not, we don't wanna admit it. [158]

Although most journalists have been unwilling to acknowledge this bias out loud, people as different as Glenn Greenwald, Noam Chomsky, and President Trump have not shied from pointing it out, especially Trump when he talks about "fake news." Despite the public silence, in private, even a CNN supervising producer admitted his network's shabby motives. That producer, John Bonifield, told a Project Veritas undercover reporter that the reason CNN constantly focused on Russia was "ratings." Bonifield added, "It's mostly bullshit right now. Like, we don't have any big giant proof [of Russian interference]."[159] Not one to mince words, the *Wall Street Journal*'s Barton Swaim called Russia collusion "an idiotic conspiracy theory."[160] Another hidden camera recording at a bar in New Hampshire caught Andy Fies, an ABC News producer, admitting, "We fucked up four years ago [2016], and we're fucking up in the same ways today."[161]

## *"EVEN THOUGH WE'RE TOTALLY LEFT-LEANING, WE'RE NOT, WE DON'T WANNA ADMIT IT."*

The effects are astonishing. Big Media had become a Goliath itself decades before, but as 2020 approached, the press, prominent CEOs, and the

157 Project Veritas, "'Socialist' ABC Reporter Admits Bosses Spike News Important to Voters, 'Don't Give Trump Credit,'" February 26, 2021, YouTube video, 7:31.
158 Project Veritas, "Part 3: CNN Field Manager: Zucker's 9am Calls 'BS;'…Totally Left-Leaning…Don't Want to Admit It," October 17, 2019, YouTube video, 15:48.
159 Project Veritas, "American Pravda: CNN Producer Says Russia Narrative 'bullsh*t,'" June 27, 2017, YouTube video, 8:48.
160 Swaim, "Trump and the Failure of the Expert Class."
161 Russia Today, "The truth suffers: ABC employee in leaked tape by Project Veritas," February 27, 2020, YouTube video, 1:07.

administrative state "[found] themselves in closer political alignment than at any time in decades."[162] Now, however, the citizen journalist advanced thanks to new technologies while the oligarchy could only play defense. As undercover German muckraker Günter Wallraff said, "David assumes new strength while Goliath is attacked on all sides. The Hunter becomes the quarry."[163] David suddenly had the power to upend Big Tech and Big Media as well as the political machine. "Once Gunther [*sic*] gets on stage," writes radical activist Abbie Hoffman, "We begin to see things in a different focus." For Hoffman, Wallraff's technique is, "[j]ournalism as guerrilla theater. The reporter as life-actor."[164]

Throughout that year and in the years that followed, those specialized classes of responsible men, bewildered by their failure to anticipate Trump's populist appeal, attacked citizen journalists when they weren't belittling their work product. After months spent mocking these uncredentialled journalists and the people who relied on their information, the more honest of these responsible men and women admitted to their own unbearable smugness, what CBS Digital's managing director Will Rahn called, "a profound failure of empathy in the service of endless posturing."[165]

Social media had rapidly become the main source of information for many Americans. By 2020, four billion people worldwide were on the various platforms.[166] Critics put increasing pressure on social media executives to, in the words of one tech insider, "demonstrate their legitimacy."[167]

Tech companies were forced to make high stakes gut decisions "under extreme duress."[168] Facebook's head of global affairs, Nick Clegg, revealed on a leaked internal staff call published by Project Veritas:

> Ideally, we [Facebook] wouldn't be taking these decisions on our own. We would be taking these decisions in line with and in conformity with democratically agreed rules and principles. At the moment, those democratically agreed rules don't exist. We still have to make decisions in real-time.[169]

162 The Editorial Board, "Speech and Sedition in 2021: The progressive press decides that dissenters should be suppressed," *Wall Street Journal*, January 29, 2021.

163 James S. Ettema and Theodore L. Glasser, *Custodians of Conscience: Investigative Journalism and Public Virtue* (New York: Columbia University Press, 1998), 4.

164 Abbie Hoffman, *Square Dancing in the Ice Age* (Boston: South End Press, 1982), 144.

165 James O'Keefe, *American Pravda: My Fight for Truth in the Era of Fake News* (New York: St. Martin's Press, 2017), 9.

166 Brian Dean, "Social Network Usage & Growth Statistics: How Many People Use Social Media in 2021?," BackLink, August 10, 2021.

167 Richard Waters and Hannah Murphy, "Donald Trump, Twitter and the messy fight over free speech," *Financial Times*, January 15, 2021.

168 Kevin Roose, "In Pulling Trump's Megaphone, Twitter Shows Where Power Now Lies," *New York Times*, January 11, 2021.

169 Project Veritas, "Facebook Insider Leaks: Zuckerberg & Execs Admit Excessive Power," January 31, 2021, YouTube video, 2:15.

Clegg, in the recording leaked to Project Veritas, discussed a veritable "Supreme Court" of outside experts of journalists, politicians, and judges leaning on his company to yield to the powers that be.

The unprecedented amplification of certain voices frightened Goliath. Big Tech honchos responded by setting the algorithms on the major social media platforms to monitor content that "moves, inspires, and/or terrifies us," and by reacting accordingly.[170] This led to the outright exclusion of those citizens who terrified those gatekeepers of information, including the president of the United States. It also meant excluding certain targeted media, including Project Veritas. Such exclusion has always and everywhere been a detriment to the truth, but the scale and speed of this exercise in social control was unprecedented. An individual or a media entity could lose a million followers in a heartbeat with no viable recourse.

At present day, the tech companies have reached a concentrated form of political power not unlike leaving a "loaded gun on the table."[171] During the 2020 election, they regularly engaged in "phony fact check" exercises, removed articles and videos that troubled them, and employed the kind of circular sourcing that would have impressed Orwell's Ministry of Truth.[172] By 2020, they had the power to sway an election and ultimately shape policy, and that is exactly what they did. Said Benny Thomas, Facebook's Global Planning Lead: "Facebook and Google are no longer companies, they're countries.... They're more powerful than any country.... They must be stopped."[173]

Section 230 of the Communications Decency Act gave the social media giants immunity from the libel and defamation laws under which other media labor. Republicans have put pressure on the tech companies to be neutral. Some have even sought to end the Section 230 exemption altogether, but no congressional effort would have resolved the core dilemma. While the Republicans wanted policy reform in order to minimize censorship, Democrats were proposing bills to increase censorship by holding tech companies "accountable for enabling cyberstalking, targeted harassment, and discrimination."[174]

As Charles Murray argued in his book, *By the People*, "American gov-

---

170 Christopher Mims, "GameStop, Bitcoin and QAnon: How the Wisdom of Crowds Became the Anarchy of the Mob," *Wall Street Journal*, January 29, 2021.

171 Barak Richman and Francis Fukuyama, "How to Quiet the Megaphones of Facebook, Google and Twitter," *Wall Street Journal*, February 12, 2021.

172 The Editorial Board, "Fact-Checking Facebook's Fact-Checkers," *Wall Street Journal*, March 6, 2021.

173 Project Veritas, "FB exec says Zuckerberg is too powerful," March 16, 2021, YouTube video, 2:01.

174 Christopher Mims, "How Congress Might Upend Section 230, the Law Big Tech is Built On," *Wall Street Journal*, February 13, 2021.

ernment was now in an advanced stage of institutional sclerosis where solutions were beyond the reach of the electoral and legislative process." [175]

During and after the 2020 election, *both* major American political parties yielded to the Silicon Valley cartel with regard to voter fraud. In imposing unprecedented censorship policies in the midst of a contested election, Big Tech shook the pillars of the American Experiment to its very core, and the political classes scarcely protested.

Perhaps the only way out of this impasse, in a world in which media is very nearly everything, would be full transparency over the content decisions of tech and media companies. This would involve some combination of *cinéma vérité* and libel suits to force transparency through discovery. In this case, it would be *Project Veritas v. The New York Times Company*. Jonathan Turley found the court's decision to reject the *Times'* motion to dismiss and grant Project Veritas discovery noteworthy, "because it calls out the *New York Times* for blurring the line between opinion and fact." Turley described it as "a shot across the bow," one that might well restrain the oligarchy's power.[176] Though slim, David had forced a crack in Goliath's shield.

**"AMERICAN GOVERNMENT WAS NOW IN AN ADVANCED STAGE OF INSTITUTIONAL SCLEROSIS WHERE SOLUTIONS WERE BEYOND THE REACH OF THE ELECTORAL AND LEGISLATIVE PROCESS."**

---

175 Charles Murray, *By The People* (New York: Crown Forum, 2016), 10.
176 Jonathan Turley, "Project Veritas Wins Victory Against *New York Times* in Defamation Action," March 21, 2021,

# CHAPTER 1
# MEDIUM

## WORKS CITED

Anderson, Jack and George Clifford. *The Anderson Papers*. New York: Random House, 1974.

Bacon, Francis. *The New Organon*. Edited by Lisa Jardine and Michael Silverthorne. New York: Cambridge University Press, 2000.

Bok, Sissela. *Secrets: On the Ethics of Concealment and Revelation*. New York: Random House, 1989.

Boorstin, Daniel J. *The Image: A Guide to Pseudo-Events in America*. New York: Vintage, 2012.

Brinkley, Douglas. *Cronkite*. New York: HarperCollins Publishers, 2012.

Campbell, Joseph W. *Getting It Wrong: Ten of the Greatest Misreported Stories in American Journalism*. Berkeley: University of California Press, 2010.

Chomsky, Noam. *Media Control: The Spectacular Achievements of Propaganda*. New York: Seven Stories Press, 2002.

Dygert, James H. *The Investigative Journalist: Folk Heroes of a New Era*. Hoboken, NJ: Prentice-Hall, 1976.

Ettema, James S. and Theodore L. Glasser. *Custodians of Conscience: Investigative Journalism and Public Virtue*. New York: Columbia University Press, 1998.

Feldstein, Mark. *Poisoning the Press: Richard Nixon, Jack Anderson, and the Rise of Washington's Scandal Culture*. New York: Farrar, Strauss, and Giroux, 2010.

Gorton, Stephanie. *Citizen Reporters: S.S. McClure, Ida Tarbell, and the Magazine That Rewrote America*. New York: HarperCollins Publishers, 2020.

Halberstam, David. *The Powers That Be*. Champaign, IL: University of Illinois Press, 2000.

Hemingway, Mollie Ziegler. *Trump vs. The Media*. New York: Encounter Books, 2017.

Herman, Edward S. and Noam Chomsky. *Manufacturing Consent: The Political Economy of the Mass Media*. New York: Knopf Doubleday Publishing Group, 2011.

Hoffman, Abbie. *Square Dancing in the Ice Age*. Boston: South End Press, 1982.

Jones, Clarence. *Winning with the News Media: A Self-Defense Manual When You're the Story*. Holmes Beach, FL: Winning News Media, 1983.

Lesher, Stephen. *Media Unbound*. Boston: Houghton Mifflin Company, 1982.

Lofton, John. *The Press as Guardian of the First Amendment*. Columbia, SC: University of South Carolina Press, 1980.

London, Jack. *War of the Classes, The Question of the Maximum*. Scotts Valley, CA: CreateSpace Independent Publishing, 2016.

McLuhan, Marshall. *Understanding Media: The Extensions of Man*. New York: McGraw Hill, 1964.

Mollenhoff, Clark. *Investigative Reporting: From Courthouse to White House*. New York: Macmillan, 1981.

Murray, Charles. *By The People*. New York: Crown Forum, 2016.

O'Keefe, James. *American Pravda: My Fight for Truth in the Era of Fake News*. New York: St. Martin's Press, 2017.

Rindsberg, Ashley. *The Gray Lady Winked: How the New York Times' Misreporting, Distortions and Fabrications Radically Altered History*. Monee, IL: Midnight Oil Publishers, 2021.

Rudbridger, Alan. *News and How to Use It: What to Believe in a Fake News World*. Edinburgh: Cannongate Books, 2020.

Sabato, Larry. *Feeding Frenzy: Attack Journalism and American Politics*. Baltimore: Lanahan Publishers, 2000.

Sinclair, Upton. *The Autobiography of Upton Sinclair*. London: Harcourt, Brace, and the World, 1962.

Sinclair, Upton. *The Brass Check: A Study of American Journalism; Evidence and Reasons Behind the Media's Corruption*. Adansonia Press, First Published in 1919.

Snowden, Edward. *Permanent Record*. New York: Metropolitan Books, 2019.

Sontag, Susan. *On Photography*. New York: Picador, 1977.

Stephens, Mitchell. *The Rise of the Image, the Fall of the World*. New York: Oxford University Press, 1998.

Stewart, Charles and William B. Cash. *Interviewing: Principles and Practice*. Englewood, NJ: McGraw Hill Education, 2021.

Tarbell, Ida M. *All in the Day's Work: An Autobiography*. New York: Macmillan, 1939.

Tichi, Cecelia. *Exposés and Excess: Muckraking in America, 1900/2000*. Philadelphia: University of Pennsylvania Press, 2011.

Thoreau, Henry David. *Walden*. Boston: Beacon Press, 2004.

Wallraff, Gunter. *The Undesirable Journalist*. Woodstock: The Overlook Press, 1979.

## JOURNAL ARTICLES

Gottlieb, Martin. "Dangerous Liaisons? Journalists and their sources," *Columbia Journalism Review*, July 1989.

Magarian, Gregory. "The Jurisprudence of Colliding First Amendment Interests: From the Dead End of Neutrality to the Open Road of Participation Enhancing Review." 83 *Notre Dame Law Review* 185, 2007.

McClurg, Andrew J. "Bringing Privacy Law Out of the Closet: A Tort Theory of Liability for Intrusions in Public Places." 73 *North Carolina Law Review* 989, 1995.

# CHAPTER 2
# IMAGE

---

*Photography is truth. The cinema is truth twenty-four times per second.*[177]

-Jean-Luc Godard; French-Swiss New Wave Filmmaker

---

The introduction of the still camera nearly two centuries ago changed not only the way we see the world, but also the course of human history. Nineteenth-century poet and polymath Oliver Wendell Holmes Sr. called the photograph a "mirror with a memory" and a "pencil of fire," one capable of burning away unnatural things like "pomp and vanity."[178] Famed twentieth-century photographer Edward Weston saw the camera as an "honest medium," adding, "Only with effort can the camera be forced to lie."[179] Like Holmes, he thought it capable of doing away with dishonesty, pomposity, and vanity. "Images transfix. Images anesthetize," said writer and filmmaker Susan Sontag. "An event becomes more real than it would have been if one had never seen the photographs."[180] Those in power have long understood this, which is why Stalin kept photographers out of his gulags and the Biden White House tried to keep Project Veritas cameras away from the border.

---

177 *The Cinema Alone: Essays on the Work of Jean-Luc Godard 1985-2000*, ed. Michael Temple and James S. Williams (Amsterdam: Amsterdam University Press, 2000), 84.
178 Oliver Wendell Holmes, "The Stereoscope and the Stereograph," *The Atlantic*, June 1859.
179 Edward Weston, *The Daybooks of Edward Weston* (New York: Aperture, 1990), xx.
180 Susan Sontag, "War and Photography," in *Human Rights, Human Wrongs: The Oxford Amnesty Lectures*, ed. Nicholas Owen (Oxford: Oxford University Press, 2002), 263.

## FIRST-PERSON PERSPECTIVE

As with the still camera, the power of video is visual, not verbal. "Video is a language made up of much more than words,"[181] argues Kevin O'Neill in a noteworthy legal brief on the ethics of the ambush interview. "Seeing is believing," said NBC field producer Bob Windrem, a veteran of both TV and print. "That's why television has higher credibility than print."[182] Surreptitiously recorded audio/video opens up the world to another dimension, still. A medium this honest becomes potentially *too true*, and its accuracy and potency becomes a liability.

### *WITH CINÉMA VERITÉ, THE FINISHED REPORT IS NOT MORAL DISCOURSE, BUT SIMPLY INFORMATION ITSELF.*

The French introduced the term *cinéma vérité* to refer to a film style devoid of artificiality. In those days, they characterized the 1920s Soviet documentary trend innovated by visual theorists like Dziga Vertov and Sergei Eisenstein, displayed in cinema mainstays *Man with a Movie Camera* and *Battleship Potemkin*. The twenty-first-century muckraker takes cinéma vérité another step closer to the true. This technique harkens to a form of direct cinema characterized by 1960s American filmmakers like D. A. Pennebaker, where the camera was hidden from view and unnoticed by documentary subjects, like John F. Kennedy in Pennebaker's *Primary*, the candidate's responses unclouded by the setup production and scripted banter. In the Project Veritas adaptation of cinéma vérité, the footage is *self-evident* and in its purest form. The captured conversations do not require verification because the statements are inherently newsworthy. They are such because of the nature of the *moving image with synchronized sound*.[183] With cinéma verité, the finished report is not moral discourse, but simply

181 Kevin O'Neill, "The Ambush Interview: A False Light Invasion of Privacy?" *Case Western Reserve Law Review* 34, no. 1 (1983).
182 Quoted in Diane Leenheer Zimmerman, "I Spy: The Newsgatherer Under Cover," *University of Richmond Law Review* 33, no. 4 (2000).
183 As an example, Jered Ede was asked by *Columbia Journalism Review* professor Bill Grueskin why we didn't call Liban Mohamed for comment, the Minneapolis Somali man who recorded himself saying he had ballots all over his car. "Numbers don't lie. Numbers don't lie. You Can See My Car is Full. All These Here Are Absentee Ballots. Can't You See? Look at All These, My Car is Full." Bill Grueskin: "At any point did anybody who identified themselves as Veritas journalists reach out to Liban Mohammed?… There are some pretty serious accusations about what he may have done." Jered Ede: The Allegations against Liban Mohammed were made by himself in his own snapchat videos. *That effectively was his comment.*"

information itself. [184] It makes no sense for anybody, especially a journalist, to reject the "unmediated and unfettered access to the world"[185] that cinéma vérité journalism brings.

Given the media hysteria about the muckraker's use of pretense and undercover reporting, one would think that Project Veritas had invented these practices. Not so. The Project Veritas method has a long and storied journalistic history. Among others, veteran investigative reporter Edward Jay Epstein has written that journalists are rarely, if ever, in a position to establish the truth about an issue themselves. To establish truth requires one to be in a position to capture truth, and as such, requires firsthand observation of the problems. "We needed to *see* the problem at Walter Reed with our own eyes," agreed Anne Hull, a reporter who won the Pulitzer Prize for documenting the deplorable conditions at Walter Reed Army Medical Center in 2008.[186]

Acclaimed *Los Angeles Times* reporter David Shaw affirmed this position more than forty years ago. "I'm a great believer in the reporter as an observer. Firsthand observation is the ultimate documentation," observed Shaw. "Almost every big story I've done, I've had to impersonate someone." [187] The first-person perspective matters. As former *Harper's* editor Richard Hodge has observed, "In times such as these, healthy citizenship requires the insertion of a human proxy into the stream of historical happenstance."[188] Writes Andy Ngo, "There's a lot of reporting one can do from a distance away, but at some point it requires being on the ground."[189] In reporting on Seattle's notorious CHAZ, Capitol Hill Autonomous Zone, Ngo dressed in black bloc-style clothing both to improve his reporting and to protect himself from retaliation.

### *"ALMOST EVERY BIG STORY I'VE DONE, I'VE HAD TO IMPERSONATE SOMEONE."*

184 Ettema and Glasser, *Custodians of Conscience*, 9.
185 Bill Nichols, *Representing Reality* (Indianapolis: Indiana University Press, 1991), 43.
186 Al Tompkins, "Anatomy of a Pulitzer: Q&A with Hull and Priest," PoynterOnline, uploaded by New York University, April 8, 2008.
187 Bok, *Secrets*, 263.
188 Roger Hodge, Intro, *Submersion Journalism*, ed. Bill Wasik (New York: New Press, 2008), x.
189 Ngo, *Unmasked*, 40.

In his authoritative guide to ethical journalism, Philip Meyer makes the case for undercover journalism. "Participant observation is straightforward, enabling a reporter to see and hear things with his own eyes and ears, and that is a virtue," writes Meyer. "In fact, given that accuracy is journalism's fundamental objective, it is an extremely important virtue, one that should not be readily sacrificed to a rigid rule against deception."[190], [191] Don Hewitt, the producer of *60 Minutes*, introduced what legal scholar Kevin O'Neill considered an "enormously successful concept," namely, "casting the correspondent as a stalwart, facing down foes."[192]

What holds true in the United States holds true in India as well. "As going undercover allows the reporter to witness events from the inside, as a participant-observer, undercover newsgathering has proven effective in exposing fraud, corruption, and illegal activity in government and industry," writes Indian author Parikshit Khari. "Thus, has become intrinsic to the high standard of new age journalism."[193]

In its controversial investigation of the Food Lion grocery store chain, ABC News directed two of its reporters to gain employment at the grocery stores and put hidden cameras in their wigs. The producers could have simply purchased samples of repackaged fish and rotting meat and brought them to laboratories for analysis, but such findings, reported the *New York Times*, "would have been no substitute for the on-the-spot evidence of malpractice."[194] Firsthand observation is the purest form of journalism. It allows the muckraker to see and hear with his own eyes and ears. When evidence is offered through video and audio, viewers have more confidence in the legitimacy of the reporting than if they were merely told about the same. This sentiment rings true in the Barbara Kopple documentary *Harlan County, USA*, where a poor Kentucky coal-mining community unifies on strike for fair wages and acceptably safe working conditions in the face of monolithic Duke Power, all captured via first

---

190 Philip Meyer, *Ethical Journalism: A Guide for Students, Practitioners, and Consumers* (Harlow: Longman, 1987), 81.
191 *Columbia Journalism Review* professor Bill Grueskin inquired, "You don't see [the ballot harvester's] face, you don't really know who they are," even though Project Veritas reporter was a participant observer and played a recording of the voice on the other end. Grueskin was arguing whether authority (of the *New York Times* relying on their credibility) versus material (from Project Veritas) determines truth. "Aren't you asking the consumer of that story, the viewer to take it on faith that this is the person the reporter is saying who it is?" This author responded, "No, because in one case you're showing videotaped evidence of the person. I'm not showing you the interpretation of the events. I'm showing you the actual events."
192 Lesher, *Media Unbound,* 151.
193 Lyrissa C. Barnett, "Intrusion and the Investigative Reporter," 71 *Texas Law Review* 433, 1993.
194 Walter Goodman, "Beyond ABC v. Food Lion," *New York Times*, March 9, 1997.

person video; a fly on the wall of life as reality unfolds before the cinéma vérité filmmaker-journalist.

The camera eliminates the need for the first-person newspaper account. Pulitzer Prize-winning *Chicago Tribune* reporter William Gaines observed, "In television, a camera eliminates the need for the first-person account because when the camera goes undercover the viewer experiences the story."[195] Eyewitness evidence makes the motives and characterizations of the reporter irrelevant. In fact, video is nothing more than an evolution of the reporter's notebook. It brings a story to life in a far more impactful way than a reader could have ever before internalized. The leaders of *1984*'s Oceania certainly understood the power of visual evidence: "The party told you to reject the evidence of their own eyes and ears. It was their final, most essential command."[196]

While the Supreme Court has upheld that there is no *legal* issue for reporters to rely on a single, unverifiable source (and a failure to investigate is not necessarily done in bad faith),[197] undercover videos, when properly executed, do not require *verification* because the statements recorded and identities portrayed are unfiltered. The content is manifestly damning on its own. Consider Tucker Carlson's response to the Project Veritas sting showing Ron Schiller, CFO of NPR, meeting with people he thought were members of the Muslim Brotherhood: "I may have aesthetic qualms about it, but the point of journalism is the story." Carlson inquired, "The main question you ask is, is it true?"[198]

### THE PRODUCERS COULD HAVE SIMPLY PURCHASED SAMPLES OF REPACKAGED FISH AND ROTTING MEAT AND BROUGHT THEM TO LABORATORIES FOR ANALYSIS.

The aesthetic properties of the finished product—the graininess of the images, the audio quality of the recording, even the motives of the muckraker—do not undermine the reality of the events that occurred. As an application of the empirical method, the medium does indeed provoke "aesthetic qualms." These are what Eric Weinstein referred to when he tweeted:

---

195 William Gaines, "Lost art of infiltration," *SAGE Publications* 8, no. 5: 2007.

196 Orwell, *1984*, 103.

197 "Holding that to show actual malice, plaintiff must show 'high degree of awareness of probably falsity.'" St. Amant v. Thompson, 390 U.S. 727 (1968).

198 Howard Kurtz, "NPR's Polarizing Shake-Up: Vivian Schiller Resigns Over O'Keefe Video," *Daily Beast*, July 13, 2017.

"I also have to admit: I hate this shitty hidden camera 'gotcha' crap."[199] Weinstein was referencing a Project Veritas video that recorded ABC News correspondent David Wright.

Said the muckraker in disbelief: "You hate 'this shitty hidden camera gotcha crap?' Wright was in a public space speaking freely among his peers. In newspapers, that's called 'reporting.' Your prejudice against the method doesn't make any sense. You prefer I report this *without* the audio 'anonymously sourced?'"[200]

## INTENTIONS OF VIDEO JOURNALISM

Journalism scholar Theodore L. Glasser writes: "The use of a concealed tape recorder, at least when one party is present, is not nearly the moral quandary its opponents would have us believe: it is not an invasion of privacy, it is not act of deception, it is not a form of eavesdropping, and it does not constitute entrapment."[201]

The cinéma vérité muckraker simply presents natural information. His reporting meets classic journalistic standards. It involves no exercise of conscience, but only an application of the empirical method itself.[202] It is meant to be "so utterly disinterested as to be transparent. The report was to be virtually the thing itself, unrefracted by the mind of the reporter."[203] ABC reporter David Wright was *recorded* saying, "The commercial imperative is incompatible with the news."[204] The muckraker didn't quote the veteran correspondent. He merely let him talk. He offered no additional comment, forced no narrative, refrained from propaganda.

> **"WRIGHT WAS IN A PUBLIC SPACE SPEAKING FREELY AMONG HIS PEERS. IN NEWSPAPERS, THAT'S CALLED 'REPORTING.'"**

Unquestionably, the expansion of media, video especially, has affected traditional privacy safeguards and the social norms that comprise community standards. Unquestionably, too, a printed account does not threaten privacy or reputation the way a televised image does. It is

199 @EricRWeinstein, Twitter, February 26, 2020.
200 @jamesokeefeiii, Twitter, February 26, 2020. Accessed before permanent suspension.
201 Ettema and Glasser, *Custodians of Conscience*, 82.
202 Ettema and Glasser, *Custodians of Conscience*, 9.
203 Jack Fuller, *News Values: Ideas for an Information Age* (Chicago: University of Chicago Press, 1997), 14.
204 Jamie Ross, "ABC News Suspends Correspondent David Wright Over Secret Video Footage: Report," *Daily Beast*, February 26, 2020.

much easier to deny words on a page than images on a screen. Furthermore, printed words require a reader's comprehensive investment. A single image or video clip only takes a viewer's moment for its power to be realized, and like a brook trout, cast back out again down the cyber stream to continue its journey.

Sanford Socolow, a former executive producer for CBS Evening News, suggested that accurate video journalism—even when presented responsibly—can still be misleading. He observed, for instance, that the effect of weeks of studious journalism covering topics of public importance could all be erased with just one two-minute broadcast of, say, a battle in the Vietnam War.

If video in the twentieth century was three-dimensional, accommodating the intonation, cadence, and gestures of those on camera, videotape in the twenty-first century adds a potential fourth dimension, spontaneity. Consider the case of Patrick Davis, the manager of field operations at CNN, who was secretly recorded by colleague Cary Poarch, a CNN satellite technician. Disturbed by CNN's open betrayal of its cited mission, namely, to present objective news, Poarch turned whistleblower and contacted Project Veritas. He recorded Davis expressing a sentiment that many at CNN say in private, but none would say in public: "I'm not super thrilled with what we do on our air anymore. '95; I've been here for a little while. So, I hate seeing what we were and what we could be and what we've become. It's just awful."[205] Poarch's objective was not to embarrass Davis. Davis said nothing to be embarrassed about. Ted Turner would likely agree, quoted in a 1982 interview airing on BBC:

> Our editorial policy is to present the news as it is, and when there's contrasting viewpoints on controversial issues we seek out the leading proponent of each side and get them to air their views, and then let the American people that are watching make up their own minds as to what they want to believe. That's my philosophy, at least, of how a free society should operate. Of course, in a controlled country like Cuba or Russia, everything is controlled by the government, and they don't run much news in those places that's not favorable to the government. Here we have freedom of the press.[206]

---

205 Project Veritas, "Project Veritas Action - Patrick Davis Manager of Field Ops at CNN," January 16, 2020, YouTube video, 0:39.
206 Brit Junior, "The Man from Atlanta," August 24, 2014, originally broadcast by BBC, August 23, 1982, YouTube video, 39:35.

## IN THEIR OWN WORDS: THE CASE OF SHIRLEY TETER

There is no legal problem with capturing the actual words of a given subject. This became clear during the case in which Shirley Teter, sixty-nine-year-old sufferer of chronic obstructive pulmonary disease, sued Project Veritas. Teter first made the news when she was allegedly "assaulted" at a September 2016 Trump rally in North Carolina by a Trump supporter. For days, the media delighted in running headlines such as this one from local station WLOS, "69-year-old woman allegedly punched in face by Trump supporter outside NC rally."[207]

After Project Veritas recorded Democratic operative Scott Foval bragging that Teter was a "bird-dogger" who deliberately provoked the incident, Ms. Teter unwisely chose to sue. During the muckraker's deposition in the Teter case, he had the following exchange with four high-priced attorneys for Ms. Teter:

> **Lawyer:** Was Shirley Teter a bird-dogger?
>
> **Muckraker:** I can only speak to what Scott Foval said about Ms. Teter.
>
> **Lawyer:** Well, was she?
>
> **Muckraker:** I can only report what Scott Foval said about her, about these incidents.[208]

With Project Veritas as the defendant, the case went all the way to the verdict stage in a federal jury trial. It was at this point that Federal Judge Martin K. Reidinger called for a Rule 50 motion hearing to decide whether a directed verdict was in order.[209] Referencing the deposition excerpt above, the attorney for Teter, Ms. Dixie Wells, implored Reidinger to force the muckraker to opine on what Foval was saying.

Wells complained that when asked what his opinion was, the muckraker would merely say, "My duty as a journalist is to report accurately

---

207 Aaron Adelson, "69-year-old woman allegedly punched in face by Trump supporter outside NC rally," WLOS ABC-13, updated May 9, 2017.

208 Shirley Teter v. Project Veritas Action Fund, et al., United States District Court, Civil No: 1:17-cv-256 (2019).

209 "Rule 50. Judgement as a Matter of Law in a Jury Trial; Related Motion for a New Trial; Conditional Ruling," Legal Information Institute, Cornell Law School.

what people tell me." This frustrated Wells. "He doesn't stand behind what he said in the video," she told Reidinger. Clearly irritated, the judge disagreed with the ethical direction in which Wells was prodding the court. Reidinger's response is worth reading at length:

> Well, again - and I don't need you to read through all those. I can go back and look at it. But this is exactly the conversation that you and I just had a few minutes ago. The first two rounds of questions are, essentially, Mr. O'Keefe will you in fact vouch for the 100 percent veracity of your source? No journalist would do that. No lawyer would do that. I mean we lawyers pay lip service to it when we argue to the jury, but that's our job. Or should I say that's your job. It's not my job anymore. But, then, when it goes to, well, what's your opinion? Well, a journalist's opinion about his source is utterly irrelevant. I would question the ethics of a journalist who opines about the opinions - about the veracity of the people he reports on. That's not what journalists do. *I mean that's what pundits do.*[210]

Judge Reidinger was not through with Wells. In his extraordinary defense of the First Amendment, he added: "There are some parts of your argument that, if you made that argument about Mike Wallace, people in the room would laugh." There was more to come: "I'm very concerned about making any ruling that is not only detrimental to the First Amendment but eviscerates the First Amendment." As a judge, he was free to opine, and this he did generously: "If I've gotten this wrong, and the Fourth Circuit says that this is not what the law is, I hesitate to think where the First Amendment is going in this country."[211]

### "A JOURNALIST'S OPINION ABOUT HIS SOURCE IS UTTERLY IRRELEVANT. I WOULD QUESTION THE ETHICS OF A JOURNALIST WHO OPINES ABOUT THE OPINIONS."

The judge brought up a unique point. Traditionally, according to the Society of Professional Journalists (SPJ) Code of Ethics, a journalist seeks out multiple witnesses, finds and discloses multiple sources, and asks for comment. The Committee of Concerned Journalists defines this practice as the "discipline of verification." According to the Committee, "This discipline of verification is what separates journalism from other forms of com-

---

210 Shirley Teter v. Project Veritas Action Fund, excerpt of proceedings, May 21, 2019.
211 Shirley Teter v. Project Veritas Action Fund, opinion by Judge Reidinger, June 7, 2019.

munication such as propaganda, advertising, fiction, or entertainment."[212] Ida Tarbell was decades ahead of other journalists in adopting verification. She made a practice of checking affidavits from sources and only using sources that could be confirmed.

Going back to our friend Judge Reidinger, he addressed the knee-jerk, irrational objections that critics of undercover journalism often raise in a dress-down of Ms. Wells:

> So, again, the – here's the problem I'm having with what you're saying, Ms. Wells. You're saying, oh, it's the big picture. It's all the pieces together. And it seems like every piece that you point to is a piece that hurts your argument rather than helping it. And you can't have a bunch of minus ones and add it up to 20. It just doesn't – it's just not math…[213]

Unlike on cable news, in a federal court, critics are unable to throw mud. They have to accept their loss with dignity as Wells did in her response, "Sure. Thank you. Thank you, Your Honor, for letting me know where I stand."[214] Based on the evidence, Reidinger dismissed the case before it went to a jury. The cinéma vérité muckraker has little to fear in a court of law because if they fulfilled their work's virtues, it is one of the few places raw footage can be scrutinized by judicial authority for what it is: truth at twenty-four frames per second.

## REACTION AND THE DISTRIBUTED IDEA SUPPRESSION COMPLEX (DISC)

A thoughtful cultural critic, Eric Weinstein has introduced the concept he calls the "DISC," shorthand for "Distributed Idea Suppression Complex." The DISC "is a large collection of different structures, and it's not controlled in any one place. Many of these have emerged separately. But what makes an aspect of the DISC - what shows you a particular component - is that it protects institutions from individuals who are making valid and reasonable points."[215] DISC is used to suppress viewpoints and arguments that could oppose any selection of topics. Weinstein believes that the nation's institutions have been hastily built for growth, and this leaves them

212 Bill Kovach and Tom Rosenstiel, *The Elements of Journalism: What Newspeople Should Know and the Public Should Expect* (New York: Three Rivers Press, 2007).
213 Shirley Teter v. Project Veritas Action Fund, excerpt of proceedings, May 21, 2019.
214 Shirley Teter v. Project Veritas Action Fund, excerpt of proceedings, May 21, 2019.
215 Eric Weinstein, "Eric Weinstein (Solo), Ep. #018 of The Portal - Slipping the Disc: State of The Portal/Chapter 2020," February 13, 2020, YouTube video, 1:03:35.

vulnerable to attack. To protect themselves, they must tell untruths. The DISC, which is loosely assembled and under no central control, works to deny the citizenry access to those truths that would erode the power base of the nation's institutions. Weinstein is no pessimist. He believes the DISC can be slipped. "I want you to swing for the fucking fences w/ your research," he tweeted in January 2020. "I want you to remember that we need you to get out of our stagnation. I want you to believe pathologically in yourself."[216]

Andrew Breitbart was a born DISC slipper. He believed that the media could be more than just scooped. It could be hacked. "You can play the media. You can force them to cover things," Breitbart would say. "This is not just stenography. There's a performance art to it."[217] Saul Alinsky was a slipper of DISCs as well. In *Rules for Radicals*, Alinsky writes:

> The major premise for tactics is the development of operations that will maintain a constant pressure upon the opposition. It is this unceasing pressure that results in the reactions from the opposition that are essential for the success of the campaign. It should be remembered not only that the action is in the reaction but that action is itself the consequence of reaction and of reaction to the reaction, ad infinitum. The pressure produces the reaction, and constant pressure sustains action.[218]

### THE NATION'S INSTITUTIONS HAVE BEEN HASTILY BUILT FOR GROWTH, AND THIS LEAVES THEM VULNERABLE TO ATTACK.

It is through the honesty of his reporting that the muckraker produces the reaction necessary to slip the DISC. In February 2020, a Project Veritas journalist captured veteran ABC reporter David Wright sharing his opinions about the dynamics of his newsroom. "Commercial imperative is incompatible with news," the self-described "socialist" told the muckraker. "Like now you can't watch *Good Morning America* without there being a Disney princess or a Marvel Avenger appearing...It's all self-promotional." Wright also criticized ABC's vengeful, superficial coverage of Presi-

216 @EricRWeinstein, Twitter, January 16, 2020.
217 Noah Shachtman, "How Andrew Breitbart Hacked the Media," *Wired*, March 11, 2010.
218 Alinsky, *Rules for Radicals*, 129.

dent Trump, saying, "We don't give him credit for the things he does do." ABC responded to its reporter's truth-telling by punishing Wright. "David Wright has been suspended," said ABC News in a statement, "and to avoid any possible appearance of bias, he will be reassigned away from political coverage when he returns."[219]

The DISC self-activated at news of the suspension. Blue-check-marked journalist Melissa Ryan promptly wrote that the muckraker "potentially destroyed another person's life this week, and his employer helped." Curiously, she also conceded that the funding for Project Veritas might come from right-wing donors but that its power "comes from the companies and organizations responding to these videos."[220] Ryan was not alone in questioning Wright's suspension. "What really bothered me about this was that ABC gave into Project Veritas," said Northeastern's Dan Kennedy. "They just shouldn't have done it."[221] Here, Ryan and Kennedy both bemoan not so much the story itself, but the *reaction* to the story. They do what Weinstein anticipates they would do to protect the DISC. However, provoking this kind of reaction is essential if this DISC is to not just be slipped, but shattered.

219 Jamie Ross, "ABC News Suspends Correspondent David Wright Over Secret Video Footage: Report," *Daily Beast*, February 26, 2020.

220 Melissa Ryan, "Why James O'Keefe Still Has Power," Melissa Ryan blog on *Medium*, entry posted March 1, 2020.

221 GBH News, "Project Veritas Gets ABC Correspondent Suspended," February 28, 2020, originally broadcast by PBS *Beat the Press*, YouTube video, 5:35.

# CHAPTER 2
# IMAGE

## WORKS CITED

Alinsky, Saul D. *Rules for Radicals*. New York: Random House, 1971.

Bok, Sissela. *Secrets: On the Ethics of Concealment and Revelation*. New York: Random House, 1989.

Ettema, James S. and Theodore L. Glasser, *Custodians of Conscience: Investigative Journalism and Public Virtue*. New York: Columbia University Press, 1998.

Fuller, Jack. *News Values: Ideas for an Information Age*. Chicago: University of Chicago Press, 1997.

Godard, Jean Luc. *The Cinema Alone: Essays on the Work of Jean-Luc Godard 1985-2000*. Edited by Michael Temple and James S. Williams. Amsterdam: Amsterdam University Press, 2000.

Hodge, Roger. Introduction to *Submersion Journalism*. Edited by Bill Wasik. New York: New Press, 2008.

Kovach, Bill and Tom Rosenstiel. *The Elements of Journalism: What Newspeople Should Know and the Public Should Expect*. New York: Three Rivers Press, 2007.

Lesher, Stephen. *Media Unbound*. Boston: Houghton Mifflin Company, 1982.

Meyer, Philip. *Ethical Journalism: A Guide for Students, Practitioners, and Consumers*. Harlow, UK: Longman, 1987.

Ngo, Andy. *Unmasked: Inside Antifa's Radical Plan to Destroy Democracy*. New York: Hachette Book Group, 2021.

Nichols, Bill. *Representing Reality*. Indianapolis: Indiana University Press, 1991.

O'Neill, Kevin. "The Ambush Interview: A False Light Invasion of Privacy?" *Case Western Review Law Review*, Volume 34, Issue 1, 1983.

Sontag, Susan. "War and Photography," in *Human Rights, Human Wrongs: The Oxford Amnesty Lectures*. Edited by Nicholas Owen. Oxford: Oxford University Press, 2002.

Weston, Edward. *The Daybooks of Edward Weston*. New York: Aperture, 1990.

## JOURNAL ARTICLES

Barnett, Lyrissa C. "Intrusion and the Investigative Reporter." *Texas Law Review*, 1993.

Gaines, William. "The Lost Art of Infiltration." Written by William Gaines, Professor of Journalism at the University of Illinois. *SAGE Publications*, 2007.

O'Neill, Kevin. "The Ambush Interview: A False Light Invasion of Privacy?" *Case Western Review Law Review*, Volume 34, Issue 1, 1983.

Zimmerman, Diane Leenheer. "I Spy: The Newsgatherer Under Cover." *University of Richmond Law Review*, Volume 33, Issue 4, 2000.

## COURT CASES

Shirley Teter v. Project Veritas Action Fund, et al. United States District Court, Civil No: 1:17-cv-256 (2019).

St. Amant v. Thompson. 390 U.S. 727 (1968).

# CHAPTER 3

# DECEPTION

*If the use of undisclosed or false identities were per se wrongful as a form of fraud, then we'd have to be willing to allow restaurants to sue restaurant critics, landlords to sue fair housing testers, and stores to sue secret shoppers, who as it turns out, have no real intention to buy.*[222]

-Diane Leenheer Zimmerman, Professor, New York University School of Law

I f the American muckraker is free within reason to deceive his subject or source in order to extract information, he is *never* free to deceive the audience. It becomes a question of relative deception; either the muckraker deceives his audience, depriving the public of access to the truth, or he deceives the subject he is interviewing so that he can share the truth with the audience. If the objective is to always tell the truth to the audience, argues Gene Foreman in the *Ethical Journalist*, in some circumstances, a journalist has a "moral obligation" to deceive the subject, and a failure to do so could be morally wrong.[223]

## EVERY GOOD JOURNALIST IS A CONFIDENCE MAN

The first page of Janet Malcolm's book sent shockwaves through the media community three decades ago because she had the courage to call out the routine nature of journalistic deception: "[Every journalist] is a kind of confidence man, preying upon people's vanity, ignorance, or loneliness, gaining their trust and betraying them without remorse." Malcolm continues:

> The catastrophe suffered by the subject is no simple matter of an unflattering likeness or a misrepresentation of his views; what pains him, what rankles and sometimes drives him to extremes of vengefulness, is the deception that has been prac-

---

222  Diane L. Zimmerman, "I Spy: The Newsgatherer Under Cover," 33 *University of Richmond Law Review* 1185 (2000).

223  Gene Foreman, *The Ethical Journalist: Making Responsible Decisions in the Pursuit of News* (Oxford: Wiley-Blackwell, 2010), 286.

ticed on him. On reading the article or book in question, he has to face the fact that the journalist - who seemed so friendly and sympathetic, so keen to understand him fully, so remarkably attuned to his vision of things - never had the slightest intention of collaborating with him on his story but always intended to write a story of his own.[224]

## IN SOME CIRCUMSTANCES, A JOURNALIST HAS A "MORAL OBLIGATION" TO DECEIVE THE SUBJECT, AND A FAILURE TO DO SO COULD BE MORALLY WRONG.

To justify the morality of any type of deception in the abstract is a near impossibility. Said one veteran investigator, "That's like trying to invent dry water or fireproof coal."[225] To most elites in the journalism profession, as well as to the sanctimonious spectators on the sidelines, deception is deception, no matter how exalted the objective. An old joke often invoked by editors and occasionally attributed to others besides Winston Churchill illustrates their absolutist thinking.

> **Churchill:** Madam, would you sleep with me for five million pounds?
>
> **Socialite:** My goodness, Mr. Churchill…Well, I suppose… we would have to discuss terms, of course.
>
> **Churchill:** Would you sleep with me for five pounds?
>
> **Socialite:** Mr. Churchill, what kind of woman do you think I am?!
>
> **Churchill:** Madam, we've already established what you are. Now we are just haggling about the price.[226]

From the perspective of some editors, to deceive, even for a higher cause, establishes *what* a reporter is, and that is something other than a legitimate journalist. Conversely speaking, the American muckraker would say that to present deceptive information makes one something

---

224 Janet Malcolm, *The Journalist and The Murderer* (New York: Vintage Books, 1990), 3.

225 Those who justify undercover work argue that it represents *ethical deception,* but to others, the effort to justify it represents *deceptive ethics* and involves logically irreconcilable elements. Gary T. Marx, *Undercover: Police Surveillance in America* (Berkeley: University of California Press, 1988), 96.

226 John C. Havens, "The Price of Haggling for Your Personal Data," *Slate*, March 17, 2021.

other than a legitimate journalist. Michael Wolff came under fire for the way he gathered evidence for his anti-Trump book, *Fire and Fury*. Said Wolff, "I absolutely spoke to the President. Whether he realized it was an interview or not, I don't know, but it certainly was not off the record."[227] The real issue here should not have been the nature of the interview, but the accuracy of the report.

Serious students of journalism have been asking themselves about the ethics of deception in regards to interviewing a story's subject since the advent of journalism. Is it ethical, Jack Shafer asked in the *Columbia Journalism Review*, to project "a false impression with the clear intention to mislead, to deceive?" Here, Shafer was quoting Brooke Kroeger from her book, *Undercover Reporting: The Truth About Deception*. Although no fan of Project Veritas, Shafer, like Kroeger, acknowledged the legitimacy of the question. He added, "The 'deliberate projection of a false impression' is something reporters do almost daily" with their subjects.[228]

Ethicist Louis W. Hodges has expressed the moral quandary journalists face in these terms: "[D]eceit is morally wrong…but…circumstances can arise in which deceit is relatively less wrong than other possible courses of action."[229] Hodges goes so far as to say that in some "newsgathering" cases, "deceit is morally acceptable." Although the argument can be made that journalists ought not deceive unnecessarily and have a moral obligation to offer good reasons for deception, Hodges argues that a decision to deceive requires no justification.

Setting out deliberately to fool some of the people at least some of the time has repeatedly produced, important, compelling, and – this might be the key to the method's enduring popularity – often riveting results."[230]

### *"THE 'DELIBERATE PROJECTION OF A FALSE IMPRESSION' IS SOMETHING REPORTERS DO ALMOST DAILY" WITH THEIR SUBJECTS.*

---

227 Michael Wolff, "'Fire and Fury' author Michael Wolff: 'I absolutely' spoke to President Trump," originally broadcast by NBC, *The Today Show*, January 5, 2018.
228 Jack Shafer, "The Lying Game," *Columbia Journalism Review*, September/October 2012.
229 Foreman, *The Ethical Journalist*, 286.
230 Louis W. Hodges, "Undercover, masquerading, surreptitious taping," *Journal of Mass Media Ethics*, Fall 1988, 26–36.

This ethical dilemma has troubled mankind from the beginning but gained an audience of intellectual aristocrats during the Enlightenment. Eighteenth-century philosopher Immanuel Kant shed light not on journalism per se, but on the pursuit of any worthy cause:

> The *good will* is the only good without qualification. The *good will* is a will that acts for the sake of duty, as a "good-in-itself." If the purpose of life were just to achieve happiness, then we would all seek pleasure and gratification and hope that it would lead to happiness. The problem is that happiness is not totally within our power to achieve; to a large extent, happiness is a matter of luck.[231]

Ultimately, the decision to *not* suffer for the greater good and to *not* expose tyrannical forces is morally irresponsible. Had not Nellie Bly found the courage to infiltrate the Women's Lunatic Asylum in 1889, the women deemed insane for simply straying from social norms would have continued to endure their inhumane treatment, and the public would have remained unaware.[232] Legendary journalism changes systems.

## THE "LEAK"

Then there is the subject of leaks. The leak is essentially a press conference for the leaker. Means-ends moralists should express as much indignation and incredulity at the information being leaked, as they should undercover deceptions designed to give you firsthand observation. Leaks often go through several intermediaries because the information transmitted can undergo so many changes as to render the original message impossible to discern. In these cases, journalism creates misinformation, if not disinformation. Unfortunately, it is acceptable journalism to report someone else's assertions, whether or not that "someone" is identified and whether or not the underlying substance of the report resembles the truth.

Those who leak know that their message may be taken less seriously, as Sissela Bok has argued, precisely because its source remains concealed. And because those messages go through several filters before they appear in print, they may be so adulterated that they lose their point altogether.[233] According to Daniel Boorstin, the leak is the pseudo-event par excellence. "Now leaks are almost as well-organized and rigidly ruled by

231 Immanuel Kant, *The Doctrine of Virtue: Part II of the Metaphysics of Morals* (New York: Harper Torchbooks, 1964), 93.
232 Dr. Howard Markel, "How Nellie Bly went undercover to expose abuse of the mentally ill," PBS NewsHour, May 5, 2018.
233 Bok, *Secrets,* 223.

protocol as a formal press conference," writes Boorstin. "The institution-alized leak puts a greater burden on contrivance and pretense on both government officials and reporters."[234]

Government agents will almost never admit their mistakes at a press conference. In its own way, the leak from a government agent to a journal-ist is a very focused form of press release. It is unwise to expect that leak to be honest. Savvy investigative reporters know that the "leaked" informa-tion they acquire is only what the powers that be want them to discover.

## THE PARADOX OF RELATIVE DECEPTION APPLIED

CNN's Chris Cuomo once said of people caught unaware on a hot mic: "Sometimes that's when you're the most honest."[235] Cuomo was right. Peo-ple *are* more honest when off air than on. Consider the morally unambig-uous case of Amy Robach. On the set of *Good Morning America*, Robach stated on a hot mic between commercial breaks that her network spiked a bombshell interview she had done with Virginia Roberts Giuffre, a victim of influential pedophile Jeffrey Epstein:

> I've had the story for three years. I've had this interview with Virginia Roberts. We would not put it on the air. Um, first of all, I was told "Who's Jeffrey Epstein?" "No one knows who that is." "This is a stupid story." Then the Palace found out that we had her whole allegations about Prince Andrew and threatened us a million different ways. Um, we were so afraid we wouldn't be able to interview Kate and Will that we, that also quashed the story. And then, um, and then uh, Alan Der-showitz was also implicated in it cause of the planes. [Virgin-ia] told me everything. She had pictures. She had everything. She was in hiding for twelve years. We convinced her to come out. We convinced her to talk to us. Um, it was unbelievable what we had. [Bill] Clinton, we had everything. I tried for three years to get it on to no avail. And now it's all coming out, and it's like these new revelations, and I freaking had all of it. I – I'm so pissed right now. Like every day I get more and more pissed 'cause I'm just like, "oh my God, we - it was what, what we had was unreal." Other women backing it up. Hey. Yup. Brad Edwards, the attorney three years ago saying like, like we, "there will come a day," but we will realize Jeffrey Epstein was the most prolific pedophile this country has ever known, and I had it all three years ago.[236]

234 Boorstin, *The Image.*
235 CNN, "Chris Cuomo Defends James O'Keefe on CNN," May 17, 2015, ProjectVeritas.com, 0:13.
236 Project Veritas, "VIDEO: Leaked ABC News Insider Recording EXPOSES #EpsteinCoverup 'We had Clinton, We had Everything,'" November 5, 2019, YouTube video, 7:36.

The brave insider who gave us the recording of Robach's complaint felt *compelled* to practice the deception necessary toward his employer, ABC News, to capture the recording and share it with the world. While the insider wrestled with the decision to potentially risk everything, that insider admitted, "For me, there was no other option." This is a common refrain among those on the inside who use deception and make covert recordings. They think of their action as a "choiceless choice."[237]

Such is the paradox of relative deception that confronts anyone with a justice complex who is forced into a position of having to choose between 1) deceiving another subject in order to advance the public good by sharing the truth with the citizenry, or 2) being honest with the subject about your intentions to publicize what they're saying, therefore broadcasting potentially dishonest statements to the citizenry. The one morally defensible choice, sharing the video, is the much lesser of two evils. As a result of the Robach disclosures, ABC News eventually aired a documentary on Jeffrey Epstein, and it ignited a firestorm of #Epstein-Coverup tweets to ABC—as many as ten million—as well as letters to the network brass from numerous members of Congress.

The *deception* involved in taping Robach subverted the coercive power of ABC News. The network seemed intent on deceiving the public by depriving it of the information contained in the bombshell interview. In this case, the deception was clearly *less wrong* than ABC's cover-up. *Even more harm* would occur if nothing had been done, if the insider had chosen not to work with Project Veritas.

*"[BILL] CLINTON, WE HAD EVERYTHING. I TRIED FOR THREE YEARS TO GET IT ON TO NO AVAIL. AND NOW IT'S ALL COMING OUT, AND IT'S LIKE THESE NEW REVELATIONS, AND I FREAKING HAD ALL OF IT. I – I'M SO PISSED RIGHT NOW."*

---

237 C. Fred Alford, "Whistle-Blower Narratives: The Experience of Choiceless Choice," *Social Research* 74, no. 1 (2007): 223-48.

## ON MEANS AND ENDS: "THAT WHICH MAKES YOU FEEL BETTER THAN YOU WOULD OTHERWISE"

Literary tough guy Ernest Hemingway reduced morality to its starkest binary. "So far about morals," he once said, "I know only that what is moral is what you feel good after and what is immoral is what you feel bad after."[238] Novelist and early "new" journalist Thomas B. Morgan added some useful nuance. "Morally defensible journalism," he writes, "is rarely what you feel good about afterward; it is only that which makes you feel better than you would otherwise."[239]

Jessica Mitford, author of *Poison Penmanship: The Gentle Art of Muckraking*, wrote, "I make up ethics according to the situation." Says Mitford of the muckraker's decision-making: "It's inherently situational. It completely depends upon whether the audience thinks what you're exposing needs to be exposed…"[240]

Given the increasing dogma on both sides of any issue being exposed, the muckraker must not tailor his conscience to fit the opposition's expectations. Saul Alinksy's ninth rule of means and ends applies more consistently now than it did when he formulated it in *Rules for Radicals* fifty years ago. Writes Alinsky, "Any effective means is automatically judged by the opposition as being unethical."[241] In the way of example, many people see nothing wrong with Facebook censoring content and will judge anyone accused of violating Facebook's arbitrary rules as having crossed some ethical line.

Engaged in an electronic civil war, the American muckraker knows he cannot play by Facebook's rules. He judges his actions against the urgency of the circumstance and the compelling public interest of what is being exposed. He also knows that his critics will make it ostensibly about his methods and ethics, but in reality, it's about his *findings*, especially given the growing divide in American public opinion. As Holman Jenkins said of contemporary punditry in the *Wall Street Journal*, "Most of what people say isn't about true and false, but about self-protection and advancement."[242]

When it comes to evaluating the ethics of using an alias to draw someone in, the muckraker makes a subjective determination. He judg-

---

238 Ernest Hemingway, *Death in the Afternoon* (New York: Scribner, 1932), 13.
239 Martin Gottlieb, "Dangerous Liaisons? Journalists and their sources."
240 Jessica Mitford, *Poison Penmanship: The Gentle Art of Muckraking* (New York: New York Review of Books Classics, 1979).
241 Alinsky, *Rules for Radicals,* 35.
242 Jenkins, "How to Have More Police Shootings."

es the discomfort he and the subject will suffer against the story's newsworthiness and its benefit to the public interest. Largely indifferent, the legacy media ignores the skeletons in their own closets and in the closets of their allies. They worry far less about ethics than whose ox is being gored. To protect friendly oxen, they control the information flow narrowly and rigidly. Their power comes from controlling that flow, and it's all about raw power.

When an undercover reporter goes on a "date," it is impossible to evaluate the means in the abstract. Much is left to the undercover. She will allure the date, but not touch him. She will allow him to think there's a romantic spark, and take up several of his evenings, but will stop well short of a flame. The process is uncomfortable for her and will prove embarrassing for him, but she judges the results will most certainly be worth the pain.

Through the dating app Tinder, a Project Veritas undercover matched and met up with CNN technical director Charlie Chester. By the couple's fifth date, Chester was bragging that CNN engaged in "propaganda" and "got Trump out."[243] So powerful was the revelation that Project Veritas's critics could scarcely bring themselves to criticize the undercover journalist's technique. One sensed, perhaps, it may even signify the grudging respect for a job well done.

### *HE JUDGES THE DISCOMFORT HE AND THE SUBJECT WILL SUFFER AGAINST THE STORY'S NEWSWORTHINESS AND ITS BENEFIT TO THE PUBLIC INTEREST.*

Benny Thomas, Facebook's global creative director, proved equally susceptible to the charms of a Project Veritas muckraker. "Well, that, I um, work for a company that is doing a lot of damage in the world," Thomas told her on video. He compared the tech giant to the "[United States] Supreme Court." He even lobbied for the government to "break up Google and Facebook." He added, "I'll make less money, but it's a better thing for the world…It has to be stopped because it's not good for society."[244]

---

243 Project Veritas, "PART 1: CNN Director ADMITS Network Engaged in 'Propaganda' to Remove Trump from Presidency," April 13, 2021, YouTube video, 8:58.
244 Project Veritas, "Project Veritas | FB exec says Zuckerberg is too powerful," March 16, 2021, YouTube video, 2:02.

When the undercover journalist asked Thomas how much the public knew about these nefarious actions, he told her that Facebook's willingness to stay in the shadows—when combined with the apathy of the general public—created an atmosphere of ignorance, obfuscation, and obscurity. "No [the public doesn't know] because most people don't understand these things and most people don't think about them," Thomas told her. "Which is why a lot of shit goes down because a lot of people aren't paying attention." Thomas touched upon several other points of interest, including the idea of fact-checkers whose loyalty to Facebook and its preferred narrative overrides its concern for factual accuracy. Thomas also noted that Facebook has assumed a role not unlike that of a major country on the world stage. Given that power, Facebook wants, if anything, more control, more censorship. The Society of Professional Journalists offers two fundamental axioms as to when deception and undercover reporting are justified:

> When the information obtained is of profound importance. It must be of vital public interest, such as revealing great "system failure" at the top levels, or it must prevent profound harm to individuals.

> When all other alternatives for obtaining the same information have been exhausted.[245]

Following the Amy Robach/Jeffrey Epstein exposé, ABC News launched a brutal internal investigation to punish the leaker or leakers. The message that the Project Veritas insider sent to ABC speaks to both profound system failure and the exhaustion of all other alternatives:I sit right here with you all in complete shock. I, like many, are at a loss for words on how this has been handled. Instead of addressing this head-on like the company has in the past, it has spun into a mission of seek-and-destroy. Innocent people that have absolutely nothing to do with this are being hunted down as if we are all a sport. I challenge all of you to actually look inwards and remember why this company engages in journalism. We all hold the First Amendment at the foundation of this company, yet forget its history, its purpose, and its reasoning for even coming into existence to begin with. How lost we are…yearning to be found. I went to Project Veritas for the sole reason that any other media outlet would have probably shelved this as well.[246]

245 Society of Professional Journalists, "SPJ Code of Ethics", SPJ.org, revised September 6, 2014.
246 Emily Smith, "ABC Scrambles to Figure Out Identity of Amy Robach Leaker, Who Goes by 'Ignotus,'" *Page Six*, November 12, 2019.

# CHAPTER 3

# DECEPTION

## WORKS CITED

Bok, Sissela. *Secrets: On the Ethics of Concealment and Revelation*. New York: Random House, 1989.

Boorstin, Daniel J. *The Image: A Guide to Pseudo-Events in America*. New York: Vintage, 2012.

Foreman, Gene. *The Ethical Journalist: Making Responsible Decisions in the Pursuit of News*. Oxford: Wiley-Blackwell, 2010.

Hemingway, Ernest. *Death in the Afternoon*. New York: Scribner, 1932.

Kant, Immanuel. *Doctrine of Virtue: Part II of the Metaphysics of Morals*. New York: Harper Torchbooks, 1964.

Malcolm, Janet. *The Journalist and The Murderer*. New York: Vintage Books, 1990.

Marx, Gary T. *Undercover: Police Surveillance in America*. Berkeley: University of California Press, 1988.

Mitford, Jessica. *Poison Penmanship: The Gentle Art of Muckraking*. New York: New York Review of Books Classics, 1979.

## JOURNAL ARTICLES

Alford, C. Fred. "Whistle-Blower Narratives: The Experience of Choiceless Choice." *Social Research* 74, no. 1 (2007): 223-48.

Gottlieb, Martin. "Dangerous Liaisons? Journalists and their sources," *Columbia Journalism Review*, July 1989.

Hodges, Louis W. "Undercover, masquerading, surreptitious taping." *Journal of Mass Media Ethics*, Fall 1988.

Shafer, Jack. "The Lying Game." *Columbia Journalism Review*, September/October 2012.

Zimerman, Diane Leenheer. "I Spy: The Newsgatherer Under Cover." *University of Richmond Law Review*, Volume 33, Issue 4, 2000.

## DIGITAL DOCUMENTS

Society of Professional Journalists. "SPJ Code of Ethics." *SPJ.org*, September 6, 2014. Accessed September 1, 2021. https://www.spj.org/ethicscode. asp.

# CHAPTER 4
# SECRECY

*The work has to be done with such a degree of integrity in both law and ethics. My shorthand way of doing it is that we should do investigative reporting as if we were in a goldfish bowl, or as if there were 12 jurors looking over my shoulder at every stage.*[247]

-Paul Voakes; Dean of Journalism, University of Colorado Boulder

I n espionage, there are no rules. Anything goes.[248] A key distinguishing factor between the muckraking journalist and the spy, or political operative, is this: the journalist operates in the public interest and therefore must operate *with sufficient transparency* such that others can evaluate his methods. The *raison d'être* of the investigative reporter is to make public that which others seek to keep hidden, particularly information the public has a right to know. The muckraker must avoid violating his own stated mission by keeping unnecessary secrets about his methods. Activists and political operatives use information as currency in the marketplace of ideas. Spies and mercenaries take it one step further— weaponizing and leveraging information for state interest or private gain. Nineteenth-century writer and politician John Dalberg-Acton noted, "Everything secret degenerates, even the administration of justice; nothing is safe that does not show how it can bear discussion and publicity."[249] Nevertheless, deception and secrecy expert Sissela Bok observes, "While all deception requires secrecy, all secrecy is not meant to deceive."[250] The secrecy over muckraking operations must be limited to a few select issues that are morally indispensable and a necessity for the completion of the investigation. The muckraker must maintain secrecy in three ways: that of active investigations, the identity of donors, and the identity of insiders.

247 Paul Voakes, "What Were You Thinking? A Survey of Journalists who were Sued for Invasion of Privacy," *Journalism & Mass Communication Quarterly* 75, no. 2 (1998).
248 James Olson, *Fair Play: The Moral Dilemmas of Spying*, 1st ed. (Lincoln: Potomac Books, 2007).
249 Lord Acton, *The Correspondence of Lord Acton and Richard Simpson*, Letter to Richard Simpson, January 23, 1861, Volume III, ed. by Josef L. Althoiz, Damian McElrath and James C. Holland (Cambridge: Cambridge University Press, 1975).
250 Bok, *Secrets*, 31.

## THE SECRECY OF ACTIVE INVESTIGATIONS

The government often throws a veil of secrecy around "ongoing investigations," as does the muckraker. Revelation while in progress would be self-defeating. The harm of doing so is self-evident.[251] The muckraker doesn't discuss investigations, active or planned. Further, nearly every time an undercover investigation has been interrupted or compromised, those who seek the muckraker's demise jump to wild and erroneous conclusions about his intentions, objectives, and purpose. Here Bok speaks to the ethics of secrecy:

> Secrecy for plans is needed, not only to protect their formulation but also to develop them, perhaps to change them, at times to execute them, even to give them up. Imagine, for example, the pointlessness of the game of chess without secrecy on the part of the players. Secrecy guards projects that require creativity and prolonged work: the tentative and the fragile, unfinished tasks, probes and bargaining of all kinds."[252]

## THE SECRECY FOR INSIDERS

The need to protect sources is so codified in journalistic ethics that the subject would seem to need little discussion. The treatment of citizen journalists sometimes tests this understanding. Generally speaking, the reporter in his heart must be willing to protect a source at all costs, no matter what. Because the press has no subpoena power, sources are everything. As journalist Nicholas Gage writes, "Most important to an investigative reporter, ranking somewhere above his editor, newspaper, wife, and children, are his sources…They are to be protected above all else. He can always find another job, but if he betrays a source, he's through."[253]

---

251 When Pam Zekman did her famous Mirage investigation where a bar was purchased and run by the *Chicago Sun-Times* newsroom in order to secretly document conversations by city inspectors, Zekman was required to adopt compartmentalization of the newsroom within the *Chicago Sun-Times* so as not to compromise the investigation. Said Zekman, "Then there was the problem of money. Zekman's latest project estimate was $46,000. The *Sun-Times had planned on sharing this cost with television. Zekman and Recktenwald spent the next week trying to reorganize the project in ways to please the Sun-Times accounting department. The task was simple: Make half the budget disappear. This was one aspect of the newspaper business that Zekman had never seen dramatized in the movies.* " Zay Smith and Pamela Zekman, *The Mirage* (New York: Random House, 1979), 31.

252 Bok, *Secrets.*

253 Nicholas Gage, *The Mafia Is Not An Equal Opportunity Employer* (New York: McGraw Hill, 1971), 18–19.

## *TO MAKE PUBLIC THAT WHICH OTHERS SEEK TO KEEP HIDDEN, PARTICULARLY INFORMATION THE PUBLIC HAS A RIGHT TO KNOW.*

———

The legends of muckraking journalism consider the right to protect sources sacred and fundamental, as though inherent in natural law. Often called "Mr. Muckraker," Jack Anderson published sealed grand jury transcripts during Watergate. He insisted he had a constitutional right not to reveal his source. If the US Supreme Court were to order him to reveal his source, Anderson would have had to conclude the court was in error.[254]

Many journalists have gone to jail to protect their sources. One of those was then KMOL-TV San Antonio television reporter Brian Karem. In 1990, Karem began serving a six-month sentence for refusing to name three people who he says helped him get an interview with a jailed murder suspect. Said Karem from the Bexar County Jail, "I made a promise to someone, and I am not in the habit of breaking promises."[255]

A muckraking journalist must put this principle above politics. In the Trump era, this proved to be murky ground. Exactly two weeks before Donald Trump took the escalator ride to announce his presidential run in June 2015, Karem moderated a panel at a landmark event at the National Press Club. This was an event for journalists who spent time imprisoned by the State for doing their jobs.[256]

Like Karem, all of the journalists at the event were advocating for the enactment of a federal shield law. One issue with such laws is the difficulty in defining who qualifies as a journalist.[257] Drafts of such legislation typically leave noninstitutional media and citizen journalists outside the scope of protection.[258] The muckraker would argue that journalism is an activity, not just a profession. Judith Miller, a former *New York Times* reporter who spent eighty-five days in jail for failing to reveal her source, echoed this sentiment. Responding to a question of how broadly the privilege should be applied, Miller stated, "If you walk like a duck, quack like a duck, and write or broadcast like a duck, you're a duck."[259]

---

254 Dygert, *The Investigative Journalist,* 117.
255 Roberto Suro, "Texas Reporter Jailed for Withholding Names," *New York Times,* June 30, 1990.
256 Tom Molloy, "Brian J. Karem, Reporter Who Defied Team Trump, Went to Jail to Protect Sources," *The Wrap,* June 27, 2017.
257 William J. Olson, Herbert W. Titus, and Robert J. Olson, "Journalist Shield Laws: A Constitutional Conundrum," *American Thinker,* June 1, 2015.
258 Olson, Titus, and Olson.
259 Reporters Committee for Freedom of the Press, "Those who paid the price," rcfp.org.

### HE INSISTED HE HAD A CONSTITUTIONAL RIGHT NOT TO REVEAL HIS SOURCE.

———

Twenty-nine years after his release from jail, and four years after the event at the National Press Club, Karem, now *Playboy*'s White House correspondent and a CNN analyst, was in the press pool in the Rose Garden following a 2019 White House Social Media Summit. There, he had a famed dustup with Sebastian Gorka, former deputy assistant to the president.

"This is a group of people eager for demonic possession," Karem joked, referring to the social media representatives in attendance. One of whom was Karem. Another of whom was this muckraker.

"You're a journalist, right?" retorted Gorka, flashing mocking finger quotations.[260]

"Come over here and talk to me, brother," said Karem, who seemed eager for a fight. "We can go *outside* and have a long conversation."

"You're threatening me now in the White House. You're threatening me in the Rose Garden. You're not a journalist. You're a punk!" screamed Gorka in Karem's face. "You're a punk."

"Go home," said Karem, his hand wedged against his face to form one half of a megaphone. "Gorka, get a job!"

After witnessing the heated exchange, this muckraker walked to Karem, past the sea of journalists, their prying eyes watching me. Feeling a rush of adrenaline as I approached him in this different, totally different era from just a few years ago, I wondered what was to happen next. I extended my hand, and the words flowed out subconsciously:

> **O'Keefe:** I'm on the same team as you.
>
> **Karem:** Thank you!
>
> **O'Keefe:** We're both journalists, man. We're both investigative reporters. All I ask is do your job. Just don't attack the character of people who are trying to do their job.
>
> **Karem:** I'm not attacking anybody. I'm just asking questions.

260 Nicholas Ballasy, "Joy Villa and Sebastian Gorka Clash with Reporter in Rose Garden," July 11, 2019, YouTube video, 2:59.

**O'Keefe:** We're on the same team.

**Karem:** You don't have a disagreement with me.

**O'Keefe:** I respect you guys.

**Karem:** I respect what you do, I said that earlier.

Before this muckraker walked away, the only remaining thing he could think to say to him was one word: "Truth." With that, he left the White House.[261]

## THE SECRECY OF DONOR IDENTITIES

For the muckraker to accomplish his mission, the anonymity of donors is sacrosanct. There can be no freedom of association without it. Protecting associational privacy means allowing people to come together to support causes that may be controversial without destroying their livelihoods. Associational privacy is critical:

- It allows the public to focus on the message advocated by a group instead of personalities and people backing it.

- It serves to reinforce positive moral and religious norms.

- It allows for people to give without fear of being injured, harassed, or having their private lives made public.

Protecting the identity of financial contributors is the *sine qua non* of the muckraker's project. Today, that protection is even more critical. As a *Wall Street Journal* op-ed points out, "…in the blink of an eye an outed donor could face a Twitter mob that posts his address, email address, picture, place of business, kids' names and more."[262] Two particular incidents illustrate the need here for secrecy.

The following sequence of events began on January 29th, 2020 with a direct message Adam Goldman of the *New York Times* sent via Twitter to our Insiders Department Director Spencer Meads while he sat at his desk: "Hi Spencer. Do you have a minute to chat?" "What do you want to chat

261 Washington Post, "Gorka to Karem: 'You're not a journalist, you're a punk,'" July 11, 2019, You-Tube video, 2:34.
262 The Editorial Board, "Donor Disclosure at the Supreme Court," *Wall Street Journal,* April 23, 2021.

about," Spencer replied. "James O'Keefe is available to speak to you direct-ly." Several days later, on February 4, 2020, Mark Mazzetti, Washington investigative correspondent at the *Times* sent a message to Project Veritas's executive producer, Joe Halderman.

> "Hi Joe - It's Mark Mazzetti with the New York Times. Can we chat sometime? Thanks."

Joe assumed it was not a friendly request. In fact, he figured it was some type of "fishing expedition." Mazzetti apparently hoped Joe would speak off the record about Project Veritas. Within minutes of receiving the message, Joe alerted his fellow muckrakers to the contact and said he wanted to reply. He intended to see where this was going. There are very few leaks within Project Veritas because the employees actually believe in the mission. To "leak" would be a form of self-sabotage.

> "What would you like to talk about?" Joe responded.

> "Thanks. I'd like to talk about Project Veritas ??? Just want to meet and have an informal chat about various PV things. Ground [rules] would be up to you," replied Mazzetti.

Later that week, a series of mysterious things began to happen. A do-nor who had previously been stalwart in his support sent an email that appeared to be written by his board members or attorneys. The language was entirely uncharacteristic. It read as follows:

> Very quickly, I spoke with fellow trustees for ----------------- Foundation this morning. One trustee mentioned that my 2017 quote to the NYT was used by Project Veritas staff in a recent Daily Beast article. As you know, we have begun to support PV in an anonymous manner rather than directly. We have done this for the protection of our Foundation and all trustees involved in directing grants. Please direct your staff to not give out our name. Our name should be in a closed file and ESPECIALLY not used when talking with the media. I am certain that you understand the importance of my request for privacy. It is a shame that one has to worry about being a target of others opposed to our views and support.
>
> Keep up the fight and wishing you all the very best, --------

It's a shame that one has to worry about being a target of others opposed to our views and support. The donor's concern was understandable. Less clear, though, was this email's timing. It had been over two years since Lachlan Markay of the *Daily Beast* wrote a story about project Veritas's so-called "Big-Money Donors."[263] Our 990 tax returns were mistakenly unredacted and given to various secretary of state offices between 2011 and 2013. The states require an organization like Project Veritas to provide tax returns but allow for the redaction of names on the Schedule B filing. As a result of this error five years prior, a series of reporters began to dial up each and every one of the thirty-five individuals who donated at least $5,000 or more, the threshold for listing a contributor, during the two-year period in question.

The media complex has been obsessed with trying to uncover a non-existent sinister pattern among Project Veritas donors since the organization's inception over a decade ago. The ACORN investigation in 2009 began a natural chain reaction of DISC management among the media.[264] As such, they have been profoundly wrong in their reporting on this muckraker and his colleagues. After trying to plant a narrative of some great Republican plot, Pulitzer Prize-winner Carol Leonnig was reduced to having to report that the two young muckrakers had only spent $1,300 of their own money on the ACORN investigation. Impressively, the journalism that resulted moved Congress to defund a corrupt organization.[265] Leonnig also printed a front-page retraction for falsely claiming that the muckraker had racial motivations in going after ACORN, one of two front-page retractions the Pulitzer Prize winner would make in the course of five months.[266]

Years later, the *Washington Post* was still eager to even the score. To that end, Lachlan Markay and "White House reporter" Asawin Suebsaeng published a piece about a Project Veritas undercover reporter whom the *Post* burned after her failed attempt to covertly record anything useful in

---

263 Lachlan Markay and Asawain Suebsaeng, "James O'Keefe's Big-Money Donors Revealed," *Daily Beast*, December 8, 2017.
264 See Chapter 2: Image.
265 Defund ACORN Act of 2009, *House Resolution 3571*, September 15, 2009.
   Chris McGreal, "Congress cuts funding to embattled anti-poverty group Acorn," *The Guardian*, September 21, 2009.
266 "This article about the community organizing group ACORN incorrectly said that a conservative journalist targeted the organization for hidden-camera videos partly because its voter-registration drives bring Latinos and African Americans to the polls. Although ACORN registers people mostly from those groups, the maker of the videos, James E. O'Keefe, did not specifically mention them." Darryl Fears and Carol D. Leonnig, "Duo in ACORN Videos Say Effort Was Independent," *Washington Post*, September 18, 2009.

a covert meeting.[267] More on this failed sting later. Not all stings succeed; but, as was the norm, other media took this as an opportunity to remind Project Veritas that they were not "on the same team." The editor of the *Daily Beast*, Lloyd Grove, celebrated this tiny reversal of fortune as a "devastating exposé" of Project Veritas, an organization that in Grove's eyes was "impossible to shame."[268]

Grove's use of the word "shame" reveals his motive: to harm. He thought Project Veritas impossible to shame because virtually all calls by the media to donors fell on deaf ears. In fact, the media overreaction actually *emboldened* a few donors to give more, including one who gave ten times more. Not a single donor backed down from supporting our mission. Many supporters fully understood, by virtue of their participation with Project Veritas from the beginning, the small element of risk involved in supporting such an organization.

Frustrated by their inability to shame this muckraker out of existence, several in the media—*BuzzFeed*, the *New York Times*, and the *Daily News* among them—*desperately* sought something of any consequence to justify a headline that showed their power mattered more than the truth. Laura Loomer, a former muckraker at this organization, was solicited by Joe Bernstein, a senior technology reporter for *BuzzFeed*. He sent Loomer an SMS text message:

> **Bernstein:** If you have anything good on okeefe to share now would be the time.
>
> **Loomer:** I don't care if you gave me 10 MILLION DOLLARS, there is nothing in this world that would EVER compel me to say anything negative about James O'Keefe. He's an American hero, and I promise you, you're not going to find ANYTHING on him.

Loomer then tweeted a snapshot picture of her text message exchange with the reporter, writing, "A reporter from @Buzzfeed just tried to get me to speak negatively about @JamesOKeefeIII. I would give James O'Keefe my kidney if he needed it, because that's how much I respect him. If you come for O'Keefe, I will come for you. @Project_Veritas."[269]

---

267 Shawn Boburg, Aaron C. Davis, and Alice Crites, "A woman approached the Post with dramatic, and false, tale about Roy Moore. She appears to be part of undercover sting operation." *the Washington Post*, November 27, 2017.

268 Lloyd Grove, "It's Impossible To Shame James O'Keefe's Project Veritas," *Daily Beast*, December 2, 2017.

269 @LauraLoomer, Twitter, unknown date. Accessed before account suspension. Twitter's eagerness to

Project Veritas staff and friends are no shrinking violets when it comes to standing up to the media. The same goes for Veritas donors. In November 2017, while *BuzzFeed's* Bernstein was soliciting for dirt, the *New York Daily News* was receiving a letter leaked from the office of now disgraced former New York State attorney general Eric Schneiderman.[270] This letter was almost assuredly at the bidding of the equally disgraced governor, Andrew Cuomo. In the letter, Bureau Chief James G. Sheehan wrote the following:

> In response to question 14(B) of the URS, Project Veritas reported that none of its "officers, directors or principal executives [had] been convicted of a misdemeanor"...Project Veritas is directed to provide information showing why its response to Question 14(B) of the URS is not a violation of section 172-d(1) of New York Executive Law, which prohibits the making of any material statement which is untrue in an application for registration.[271]

This issue involved the most trivial of foul-ups, but it is worth exploring in some depth to understand the magnifying glass under which any serious muckraker works. In July 2011, the Project Veritas accountant had seemingly failed to checkmark a box on one of a thousand 501c3 forms a nonprofit is required to submit. The question was whether an officer or director ever had a misdemeanor conviction. This omission, though not intentional, quickly led to a coordinated series of events, the goal of which was to pressure politically motivated attorney generals to prevent Project Veritas from fundraising in their state.

## *"I WOULD GIVE JAMES O'KEEFE MY KIDNEY IF HE NEEDED IT, BECAUSE THAT'S HOW MUCH I RESPECT HIM. IF YOU COME FOR O'KEEFE, I WILL COME FOR YOU. @PROJECT_VERITAS."*

---

ban its users and delete their posts demonstrates the danger of referencing mutable, online content.

270 Denis Slattery, "Billionaire Robert Mercer donated $25G to James O'Keefe's nonprofit Project Veritas," *New York Daily News*, December 2, 2017.

271 Letter from James G. Sheehan to Project Veritas, November 29, 2017.

In an administrative telephonic hearing with the State of Utah attorney general's office in July 2013, the muckraker was asked about his title at the organization in 2011. The answer was "president." In fact, the muckraker did not become an official officer or director of the organization until a 2012 board meeting, but mistakenly thought he was president in 2011. It was truly his own "gotcha" moment. He was given no advance notice of this hearing and did not have a chance to prepare for questions related to the organization's inception.

In the beginning, well before he became chairman and CEO, he was an upstart videographer and had others set up the articles of incorporation and form a board, listing himself only as "founder." He did not have custody of funds or financial records. He had not even put himself on the board. Admittedly, his answer was wrong. He was not president in 2011. The muckraker did not do this intentionally. Rather, he was struggling to understand corporate governance at the organization's inception. Project Veritas lawyers would later piece the administrative puzzle pieces together, chalking it up to this muckraker's youth and inexperience. Therefore, in answering "no" to question 14(B) on the "URS" form in 2013, the accountant answered in a way that was indeed true and complete: in 2011, no *officer* was guilty of a misdemeanor, and there was no violation of New York's Executive Law.

### AT LEAST ONE NEW YORK CITY TABLOID PUT THE STORY ON ITS FRONT PAGE WITH THE HEADLINE "GOTCHA!"

But the slightest mistake in answering a question over the phone four years prior gave Utah and other states a reason to suspend Project Veritas's fundraising in those states. Some of the states requested Project Veritas remove the muckraker from the organization. The board opted instead to sign an affidavit saying Project Veritas would cease to fundraise in those states. This inadvertent mistake on a phone call in 2013 justified a tsunami of political pressure across the United States over a series of days.

White House reporters, allegedly tasked with speaking truth to power, made a bureaucratic miscue by making Project Veritas a top issue in many of the country's largest papers. At least one New York City tabloid put the story on its front page with the headline "Gotcha!"[272] America's reporters

272 Alexis de Tocqueville, *Democracy in America*, trans. Harvey C. Mansfield and Delba Winthrop (Chicago: University of Chicago Press, 2002).

inundated the New York attorney general's office, New Jersey's office, and various others to try to neutralize Project Veritas. In *Democracy in America*, written nearly two centuries prior, Alexis de Tocqueville smoked out the bureaucrat's eternal motivation. This routine harassment reminds us why even men of goodwill often do nothing:

> Subjection in minor affairs breaks out every day and is felt by the whole community indiscriminately. It does not drive men to resistance, but it crosses them at every turn, till they are led to surrender the exercise of their own will. Thus their spirit is gradually broken and their character enervated.[273]

Before the story broke, Shawn Boburg of the *Washington Post* sent Project Veritas a series of emails about the letter from the office of the New York State attorney general. Boburg had already received it by the time of his 4:05 p.m. email on November 30th, yet Project Veritas did not receive that same email from the Office of the Attorney General until 4:19! Then another publication, *Daily News*, reached out for comment. There was certainly a coordinated effort between the New York State attorney general, who reported to Andrew Cuomo, and the press.

Shawn Boburg gave Project Veritas a total of eleven minutes to respond before his story was filed at 4:30 p.m. He continued, "The State of Florida has told me Mr. O'Keefe is no longer permitted to solicit donations in that state because his conviction is disqualifying...Does Project Veritas want to comment on this?" Shawn Boburg even had a *copy* of the recording from the Utah interview in July 2013. Piecing some of this together to create some perception of impropriety, Boburg wrote, "A recording of James O'Keefe's testimony before Utah regulators contradicts your earlier assertion that Mr. O'Keefe was not president of the charity in 2010 and it could have a bearing on whether filings in several states were accurate." While Shawn Boburg was going back and forth with the Project Veritas communications director minutes before his story went live, the muckraker wondered anew how any independent journalist could survive what Chomsky described as the major media's "symbiotic relationship with powerful sources of information."[274]

Stopping for gas that evening, the muckraker caught a glimpse of the *Daily News* at a newsstand. The front-page image managed to both thrill him and punch him in the gut. It was an old Getty photo of the muckraker, looking befuddled, under the new headline "GOTCHA! O'Keefe Hides

273 Tocqueville, *Democracy in America*.
274 Herman and Chomsky, *Manufacturing Consent*, 77.

Criminal Conviction."[275] He had experienced the media *schadenfreude* before, especially after his arrest in New Orleans in 2010. He smiled in a bit of ironic exasperation. The media were not on his team. They never were. They were trying to crucify him and use the power of the State to shut down Project Veritas. These sham "Davids" were coordinating with the Goliaths to break this muckraker's will. In that moment, one foot up on the curb in front of that newsstand, the muckraker closed his eyes for a minute and wondered whether the enemy had finally succeeded.

If the *New York Daily News* had chosen a GOTCHA! stamp for its headline, the *Daily Beast* days later stamped its banner STUNG! in big red letters. The headline shouted that a "Failure to Disclose Criminal Record" had caused a donor to flee. At first glance, the story seemed troubling. "Project Veritas was de-registered as a charity in Mississippi," wrote Lachlan Markay. "Irrespective of other concerns, the Chisholm Foundation will not be supporting Project Veritas in the future because it does not meet this basic standard."[276]

The big "get" from the *Daily Beast* was that one out of the thousands of Project Veritas supporters pulled out. This donation, by the way, constituted a fraction of 1 percent of the 2017 annual budget. It turns out that the donor's family members had applied pressure to him after seeing the negative headlines. The donor in question, however, was truly supportive and would remain a friend of the cause:

> As I said in my earlier email, I received this from [the *New York Times* reporter] yesterday on LinkedIn and then I received a phone call and text today. This is such an obvious scare tactic, it's really aggravating. I thought my donations were private so I'm concerned as to how he gained access to it. This will not stop me from donating of course! Please let me know how I can help!

Another donor called the same day relaying that the manager of a donor-advised fund was being called by the *New York Times*, asking about its financial support of Project Veritas. Thinking back to the events of 2017, the muckraker realized *he had seen this movie before*. The next day he tried a new strategy: preempt the months-long sleuthing by the media and call the two *Times* reporters on their cell phones. Mark Mazzetti and Adam

275 Greg B. Smith, "Schemer behind Roy Moore setup of Washington Post hid criminal conviction in his N.Y. tax filings," *New York Daily News*, December 1, 2017.
276 Lachlan Markay, "James O'Keefe Donor Flees Over Failure to Disclose Criminal Record," *Daily Beast*, December 11, 2017.

Goldman both eagerly responded. They asked a series of probing questions about Project Veritas's financial supporters, the nuances of civil procedure in some of its cases, as well as names of former undercover reporters and employees. Then they shot over a list of questions that included the following:

> Last year PV received a $1 million contribution made through the firm --------------- & -----------. On whose behalf was that contribution made?

> Have you coordinated any of your activities with the White House or any Trump family members?

Exasperated, the muckraker responded within two hours, replying in part:

> The anonymity of donors to associate privately with organizations like the NAACP or Project Veritas is protected by the Supreme Court and intrinsic to the effective exercise of the 1st Amendment. It is exactly the same reason the New York Times is protected from revealing its sources, so that people can donate or talk without fear of retribution or attack.

Suffice it to say, the *Times* had no interest in publishing this defense of the First Amendment and printed only thirty words of the nearly seven-hundred-word statement provided to them:

> James O'Keefe, the head of Project Veritas, declined to answer detailed questions…but he called his group a "proud independent news organization" that is involved in dozens of investigations. He said that numerous sources were coming to the group "providing confidential documents, insights into internal processes and wearing hidden cameras to expose corruption and misconduct…No one tells Project Veritas who or what to investigate," he said.[277]

Literally *months* after these two Pulitzer Prize-winning reporters began their upriver fishing expedition, the *Times* eventually felt compelled to rush out a front page, above-the-fold article on Sunday, March 8, 2020. The *Times* omitted, or more accurately, "selectively edited" out of the article the comment about the importance of donor anonymity, choosing instead to print the following:

---

277 Mark Mazzetti and Adam Goldman, "Erik Prince Recruits Ex-Spies to Help Infiltrate Liberal Groups," *New York Times*, March 7, 2020.

Last year, the group received a $1 million contribution made through the law firm Alston & Bird, a financial document obtained by the New York Times showed. A spokesman for the firm said that Alston & Bird "has never contributed to Project Veritas on its own behalf, nor is it a client of ours." The spokesman declined to say on whose behalf the contribution was made.

The financial document also listed the names of others who gave much smaller amounts to Project Veritas last year. Several of them confirmed their donations.[278]

Ironically, they were forced to make two retractions in the botched attempt to damage our credibility. One retraction involved the age of the undercover journalist. Marisa was twenty-five at the time. They sloppily wrote her age as twenty-three because that's how old she was in the documents they had obtained two years prior.[279] The second retraction pertained to the sting operation she had been engaged in years prior. They wrote:

> [The former field director's] role in the teachers' union operation - detailed in internal Project Veritas emails that have emerged from the discovery process of a court battle between the group and the union - has not previously been reported..."[280]

Marisa was staking out the American Federation of Teachers (AFT) in Michigan, which resulted in a subsequent lawsuit. There was no possible way in which the *Times* received the Veritas emails referenced in their article from this muckraker or his associates. The second retraction stated, "The information came from source interviews, not documents in the lawsuit." There was only one way the *Times* acquired copies of these emails, the key portions of which were redacted. AFT-Michigan gave those emails to the *Times*. Clearly, the union executives did not like the optics of being known as the source of deposition transcripts or lawsuit emails. They may even have requested that retraction, however embarrassing for the *Times* to admit their error.

The meat of their argument had no relation to the AFT-Michigan portions of the article. It was that some nefarious connection existed between Donald Trump and Project Veritas. Wrote Goldman and Mazzetti, "Whether any Trump administration officials or advisers to the president were involved

---

278 Mazzetti and Goldman, "Erik Prince Recruits Ex-Spies."
279 Mazzetti and Goldman, "Erik Prince Recruits Ex-Spies."
280 Mazzetti and Goldman, "Erik Prince Recruits Ex-Spies."

in the operations, even tacitly, is unclear." With a subhead that reads, in part, "Mr. Prince, a contractor close to the Trump administration, contacted veteran spies for operations by Project Veritas." The editors insinuated there was a working relationship between Project Veritas and the White House.

However, there wasn't. Not even *tacitly*. For *Times* readers, the shadow on the wall of Plato's cave had become the substance. Writes Daniel Boorstin, "The power to make a reportable event is thus the power to make experience." In a way of example, Boorstin adds, "Saying the hotel is distinguished actually makes it one." In a similar vein, when the *Times* reports that someone is "close to the Trump administration" or asks whether some Trump official was "involved in the operations," those insinuations echo throughout the internet. Sympathetic reporters turn insinuation into fact, shadows into substance.

Consider this outraged tweet from MSNBC's Joe Scarborough: "The Education Secretary's brother has hired FOREIGN SPIES to target political rivals of Donald Trump. Disgusting."[281] All of that outrage hinges on the words "unclear." The muckraker could swear under oath that the statement is factually incorrect. The White House does not, and will never, instruct Project Veritas how to conduct its journalism, but the *Times'* insinuation would carry the day. This is how consent is manufactured. Unlucky for the *Times*, Project Veritas is willing to fight back; to throw a wrench in the machine's gears. The media complex is not used to that.

The experience above illustrates a profound point. Anonymous political speech played a defining role in founding the United States.[282] The right to associate privately and contribute anonymously is intrinsic to the effective exercise of the First Amendment.[283] The Constitution protects against compelled disclosure of political beliefs for a reason. "Anonymity is a shield from the tyranny of the majority," remarked the Supreme Court in the 1995 case, *McIntyre v. Ohio Elections Commission*.[284]

### *"SAYING THE HOTEL IS DISTINGUISHED ACTUALLY MAKES IT ONE."*

281 @JoeNBC, "The Education Secretary's brother has hired FOREIGN SPIES to target political rivals of Donald Trump. Disgusting." Twitter, March 7, 2020.
282 Benjamin Barr and Stephen R. Klein, "Publius Was Not a PAC: Reconciling Anonymous Political Speech, the First Amendment, and Campaign Finance Disclosure," *Wyoming Law Review* 14, no. 1 (2014).
283 Sean Parnell, "The Legal and Political Landscape of Donor Privacy," *Philanthropy*, Spring 2017.
284 Joseph McIntyre v. Ohio Elections Commission, 514 U.S. 334 (1995).

Although Project Veritas fights to disclose certain kinds of information, associational privacy is sacrosanct. It allows people to come together to support causes that may be controversial without destroying their livelihoods. Project Veritas may record someone at a bar bragging about which charities she supports, but that person chooses to share that information with a stranger in a location accessible to the public.

Society has a vested interest in keeping association information confidential. In entering the public arena, participants willingly sacrifice their anonymity. Their boosters should not have to. Those who wish to support a cause, but are in no position to act, can still make a mark. If respecting privacy seems to infringe on the right of an investigative reporter, the accuser might find it useful to revisit the civil rights era.

When the NAACP was working for equality in America in 1958, the Supreme Court realized that powerful state actors could do great damage to groups advocating for unpopular or controversial causes. In the 1958 case, *NAACP v. Alabama*, Supreme Court Justice John Marshall Harlan noted that allowing a local or state government to expose the NAACP's benefactors would subject them to "economic reprisals, loss of employment, threat of physical coercion, and other manifestations of physical hostilities."[285] The belief behind the First Amendment is that having more voices, more people, and more ideas clashing and interacting, is a net positive for society. To coerce Project Veritas or any comparable organization into releasing its donors would be to reduce its ability to report news and restrict a donor's right of free association.

As of July 1, 2021, the Supreme Court apparently agreed. The court opinion in *Americans For Prosperity Foundation v. Bonta* invalidated California's blatantly unconstitutional requirement that all charities operating in the state disclose the identity and address of their donors to the California attorney general.[286] The California attorney general policy has been antithetical to freedom of association and the rights of donors to remain anonymous, free to donate to causes they support without fear of "leaks" resulting in harassment and retaliation. Three states, in addition to the IRS, demand charities disclose the identity of their donors and the amount of their donations. Project Veritas will not comply with the state requirements. Nothing is more important to our mission than protecting our donors' identities. Each compelled unconstitutional disclosure risks our mission. We will protect our

---

285 NAACP v. Alabama, 357 U.S. 449 (1958).
286 Americans for Prosperity Foundation v. Bonta, 594 U.S. (2021).

donors' identities at all costs—our supporters must remain free to support us in the manner they deem appropriate, including anonymously, free from undue harassment and third-party retaliation.[287]

## *"THE DIFFERENCE BETWEEN YOU AND THEM IS THAT THEY WOULD NEVER COMPARE THEMSELVES TO YOU."*

This is, of course, precisely the aim of the opponents of free speech, including AFT-Michigan. In bringing suit against Project Veritas, David Hecker, president of the teachers' union, was unusually candid in stating his motive, specifically "in any way possible [to] stop Project Veritas from doing the kind of work that it...does."[288] This is why AFT-Michigan filed a restraining order in a failed effort to prevent Project Veritas from publishing a report. The muckraker explained his rationale to the AFT attorney in the deposition:

> Again, you guys are trying to halt us. Without us, no one would have known about [New Jersey school teacher] Alissa Ploshnick....[Project Veritas was] performing a public service by exposing the racial epithet used. But again, you guys have said on the record that you want to halt us, and I won't let that happen.

The attorney for AFT-Michigan, Mark Cousens, did not appreciate this response. Said Cousens, "You can mug for the camera all you want. What it comes down to is the truth." The muckraker agreed, "You brought me here against my will. You brought the cameras here. You are the one suing us. You are the ones admitting that you are using this as a device to stop us." Cousens switched tracks and attempted a futile request, "Are you willing to share the names of the sources?" The muckraker's retort, "I don't think a *New York Times* reporter or an NBC News reporter or a *60 Minutes* reporter would ever reveal their sources." Cousens shot back, "The difference between you and them is that they would never compare themselves to you."[289]

Another difference: Project Veritas has not been required to print more than three hundred retractions, as the mainstream media have been re-

---

287 Americans for Prosperity Foundation v. Bonta.
288 Project Veritas, "Project Veritas Legal Victories," ProjectVeritas.com, 2021.
289 American Federation of Teachers Michigan v. Project Veritas, et al., United States District Court, Civil No.: 17-cv-13292 (2017).

quired, in their reporting on a single topic; let alone a single non-profit. If the lawyers were interested in the "truth," as Cousens claimed, they would respect the fact that Project Veritas protects the anonymity of its sources and donors so people can talk freely. Those seeking a forcible disclosure of either donors or sources, including AFT-Michigan and its enablers at the *Times*, apparently want certain people to shut up.

Free speech protections have been an integral feature of the American tradition. Think about the writers who came together to pen the *Federalist Papers*. Not only were there three of them—John Jay, James Madison, and Alexander Hamilton—but all wrote anonymously under the pen name "Publius." At the time, advocating for a document as revolutionary as the US Constitution was dangerous. The anonymity of the authors also allowed the public to focus on the merits of the writers' arguments rather than on their public personalities.

Whether a group advocates on behalf of the LGBT community, or promotes gun rights, or does cutting edge investigative journalism, opponents should hesitate before attacking the protections afforded to these groups; protections that secure civil society in American life. Encouraging the government to use its tools to prevent people from coming together to support or fund causes only injures a free society. This is what Judge Learned Hand was hinting at in the 1943 case *United States v. Associated Press* when he wrote:

> The First Amendment…presupposes that right conclusions are more likely to be gathered out of a multitude of tongues, than through any kind of authoritative selection. To many this is, and will always be, folly; but we have staked upon it our all.[290]

---

290 United States v. Associated Press, 52 F. Supp. 362 S.D.N.Y. (1943), aff'd, 326 U.S. 1 (1945).

# CHAPTER 4
# SECRECY

## WORKS CITED

Acton, Lord. *The Correspondence of Lord Acton and Richard Simpson*, Letter to Richard Simpson January 23, 1861. Volume III. Edited by Josef L. Althoiz, Damian McElrath and James C. Holland. Cambridge: Cambridge University Press, 1975.

Bok, Sissela. *Secrets: On the Ethics of Concealment and Revelation*. New York: Random House, 1989.

Dygert, James H. *The Investigative Journalist: Folk Heroes of a New Era*.

Hoboken: Prentice-Hall, 1976.

Gage, Nicholas. *The Mafia Is Not An Equal Opportunity Employer*. New York: McGraw-Hill, 1971.

Herman, Edward S. and Noam Chomsky. *Manufacturing Consent: The Political Economy of the Mass Media*. New York: Knopf Doubleday Publishing Group, 2011.

Olson, James. *Fair Play: The Moral Dilemmas of Spying*. Washington DC: Potomac Books, 2007.

Smith, Zay and Pamela Zekman. *The Mirage*. New York: Random House, 1979.

Tocqueville, Alexis de. *Democracy in America*. Translated by Harvey C. Mansfield and Delba Winthrop. Chicago: University of Chicago Press, 2002.

## JOURNAL ARTICLES

Barr, Benjamin and Stephen R. Klein. "Publius Was Not a PAC: Reconciling Anonymous Political Speech, the First Amendment, and Campaign Finance Disclosure." *Wyoming Law Review*: Volume 14, No. 2, Article 9, 2014.

Parnell, Sean. "The Legal and Political Landscape of Donor Privacy." *Philanthropy*, Spring 2017.

Voakes, Paul. "What Were You Thinking? A Survey of Journalists Who Were Sued For Invasion of Privacy." *Journalism & Mass Communication Quarterly*, Volume 75, No. 2, 1998.

## COURT CASES

American Federation of Teachers Michigan v. Project Veritas, et al. United States District Court, Civil No.: 17-cv-13292 (2017).

Americans for Prosperity v. Bonta. 594 U.S. (2021).

Joseph McIntyre v. Ohio Elections Commission. 514 U.S. 334 (1995).

NAACP v. Alabama. 357 U.S. 449 (1958).

United States v. Associated Press. 52 Federal Supplement 362 (1943), 326 U.S. 1 (1945).

# CHAPTER 5
# CHARACTER

*From this point the roads go to the right and to the left. One of them will rise and the other will descend. If you go to the right - you lose your life, and if you go to the left - you lose your conscience.*[291]

-Aleksandr Solzhenitsyn; Soviet Dissident, *The Gulag Archipelago*

## TRULY OPERATING WITHOUT FEAR OR FAVOR

To quote Eric Cochran, the Pinterest engineer fired at age twenty-five for blowing the whistle on his employer's quiet ban of Bible verses, "In the end we'll fall to ashes. I want to mean something after I'm gone. Otherwise, what's the point?"[292]
Too many citizens live their lives trying to "survive at any price, adapting to anything."[293] The forces that hold society together include a willingness of most people to do anything except to be forsaken, to be sent, as Daniel Ellsberg noted, "space-walking."[294] The muckraker, however, has to put the ultimate target on his back and sacrifice his very well-being for his cause. In order to reach that point of consciousness, he is first required to sacrifice what Chris Hedges calls the "intoxicating embrace of comradeship,"[295] and give up the community he knows best. That first step is often the hardest of all. The American muckraker must school himself to operate without fear, to cease, as Solzhenitsyn reminds him, of being "afraid of threats." Having faced his fears, he enters the arena armed in virtue.

---

291 Aleksandr Solzhenitsyn, *The Gulag Archipelago*, vol. 2 (New York: Harper Perennial Modern Classics, 2007), 681. Volume 2 will be referenced in this chapter.
292 Project Veritas, "Project Veritas Features – Pinterest Insider Speaks Out: The tech companies can't fight us all," June 13, 2019, YouTube video, 19:33.
293 Solzhenitsyn, *The Gulag Archipelago*, 386.
294 C. Fred Alford, "Whistle-Blower Narratives: The Experience of Choiceless Choice," *Social Research* 74, no. 1 (2007).
295 Hedges, *Wages of Rebellion*, 61.

## *"IN THE END WE'LL FALL TO ASHES. I WANT TO MEAN SOMETHING AFTER I'M GONE. OTHERWISE, WHAT'S THE POINT?"*

The muckraker must be prepared to sacrifice, suffer, and endure to be effective. The temptation is to wait until it is "safe" to make a difference. We learn caution early on. Consider the college student who wants to speak truth to the professor but who reasons, "I won't get an A in class." Students are taught at a young age that boldness will somehow harm them in the long term, but whatever temporal gain they may accrue by getting a compliant A rather than a B+ with adventurous thought is offset by the damage done to their own soul. Upon graduation, they will reason, like Alinsky's imagined businessman, "First I'll make my million and after that I'll go for the real things in life." If only life were so simple. Adds Alinsky, "Unfortunately, one changes in many ways on the road to…the first million."[296] The muckraker forgets "the million." Their focus is on an obtainable, yet intangible goal: the truth.

Unlike reputation, however, integrity is not something his opponents can take from the muckraker. Integrity he has to give away. His capital is his integrity. He can only lose it once, and he can lose it privately just as easily as he can publicly. The system will hit him where it hurts and others will have a difficult time understanding what he is experiencing. The confusion among close friends and family will deter future action. It will also make whatever action he does pursue more difficult. As old-school muckraker Ralph Nader observed, "This unequal contest between the individual and the complex organization"[297] is due to the muckraker's own humanity.

In nontotalitarian societies, it is not one's life but one's livelihood that is at risk. A politician who follows his conscience risks his office. A journalist who follows her conscience risks her byline. A necessary product of being effective is to invite risk. The muckraker cannot effectively change anything and come away unscathed. To make a difference, he will take a knock or two upon his reputation. The oppressors will attack his integrity as well. As he ascends, resistance is a necessary part of the turbulence.

Promptly after assuming control of the *New York Times* in 1896, Adolph S. Ochs promised: "Give the news, all the news, in concise and attractive form, in language that is parliamentary in good society, and give it as early, if not earlier, than it can be learned through any other reliable

---

296 Alinsky, *Rules for Radicals*, 13.
297 Whiteside, *The Investigation of Ralph Nader*, 77.

medium; to give the news impartially, without fear or favor, regardless of party, sect, or interests involved."[298] This was a radical notion at the time. To this point in American history, most large newspapers were openly and rabidly partisan and not particularly reliable. Ochs offered something different. As Ashley Rindsberg observes in his account of the Gray Lady's fall from grace, the *Times* represented "the principle that despite every consideration of expedience and ideology, the truth must always win. Without this principle, which sits at the foundation of the proverbial fourth estate of governance – that is, a free press – liberty means nothing."[299] In that Ochs's heirs have since betrayed him, it falls to the muckraker to take up the mission. In order to succeed, the muckraker must heed Solzhenitsyn's warning to not go "chasing after rewards" and to continually remind himself of the attributes essential to his calling.

## CEASING TO BE AFRAID OF THREATS

---

### INCORRUPTIBLE

As Socrates assumes in Plato's *Republic*: "There are three kinds of people: lovers of wisdom, lovers of combat, and lovers of profit."[300] The American muckraker is a lover of wisdom. As such, he is incorruptible. The American muckraker feels burdened and even uncomfortable with the power, money, and responsibility that may accrue along his journey. He is naturally thrifty and can operate without resources if need be. He has come to understand the need to rebuild "with worn-out tools"[301] the things he has built, and others have destroyed. Saul Alinsky whispers in his ear, "Tactics means doing what you can with what you have."[302]

---

### IMPERVIOUS TO MANIPULATION

When the muckraker walks into a room, he does not scan the room looking for someone better to talk to. His vision is inquisitive; he has no interest in leveraging a situation for gain. In any room, there is always something to discover, to uncover, to expose. There is always a story to be told, and he ought not prejudge where he will find it. While a promising conversational lead may have run dry, an effective muckraker would only need to phrase the inquiry in a new way to loosen the tap of information.

---

298 Dunlap, "Looking Back: 1896 'Without Fear or Favor.'"
299 Rindsberg, *The Gray Lady Winked*, 223.
300 Plato, *The Republic* (Millis: Agora Publications, 2001), 347.
301 Kipling, *'If-' and other Poems.*
302 Alinsky, *Rules for Radicals,* 126.

## BOLD, YET BALANCED

The muckraker needs the prodigious ego required of those capable of convincing themselves they can find the truth. That said, he must be able to check his ego at the door without compromising his boldness of spirit. The muckraker lives with this internal dichotomy: his ego has been killed so many times, yet he will walk through a wall for a righteous mission without caring what others more powerful think or whether their value system matches his. Neither the muckraker, nor the truth, can survive too many kudos. He has to be aware that an increase in reputation often leads to a decrease in risk-taking. He must be prepared to walk through a wall for a righteous story regardless of the risks to his renown, his reputation, or even his relationships.

*THE AMERICAN MUCKRAKER FEELS BURDENED AND EVEN UNCOMFORTABLE WITH THE POWER, MONEY, AND RESPONSIBILITY THAT MAY ACCRUE ALONG HIS JOURNEY.*

## DRIVEN

A muckraker never gives up. "Making sense out of a chaos of information is a reporter's normal function. It's his job to separate wheat from chaff quickly, and tie several threads neatly into a concise, cogent communication," observes James Dygert.[303] "A man's ego," Ayn Rand instructs him, "is the fountainhead of human progress."[304] The muckraker harnesses the power of his ego, keeps it in check, monitors its usage like the throttle in a race car. Ego, individually and cumulatively, has driven Project Veritas from the beginning. Ego is a tool, one out of many, but indispensable just the same.

---

303 Dygert, *The Investigative Journalist*, 164.
304 Ayn Rand, *The Fountainhead* (New York: Penguin Publishing, 2005).

*Gradually it was disclosed to me that the line separating good and evil passes not through states, nor between classes, nor between political parties either—but right through every human heart—and through all human hearts.*[305]

Ego is a double-edged sword. It cuts both ways. The muckraker must operate with care. As Solzhenitsyn reminds him, the line separating good and evil passes through his own heart. The muckraker is his own worst critic. He knows the power of his ego and he strives to reinvest that power back into society for the betterment of mankind. The outcome will prove the difference between an ego channeled for the good and one channeled for evil. The results are easily judged, if not today, then perhaps tomorrow.

The *Fountainhead*'s Howard Roark refuses to submit to the forces of his day. Roark remains impervious to societal pressure and expectations in the face of the mob. His internal compass and self-confidence give Roark the ability to hold his bearings true north. For Roark, there is no other option. To submit would be to sell his soul. "His vision, his strength, his courage came from his own spirit," writes Rand. "A man's spirit, however, is his self. That entity which is his consciousness. To think, to feel, to judge, to act are functions of the ego."[306]

Roark is a builder. Project Veritas muckrakers are, in their own way, builders as well. On more than one occasion, others have compared the Veritas spirit to Roark's. Powered by this spirit, they have crafted many a media bombshell out of the materials at hand, sometimes with finesse, sometimes with a wrecking ball, always with passion. And, like all muckrakers, they have suffered for their craft.

**THE LINE SEPARATING GOOD AND EVIL PASSES THROUGH HIS OWN HEART.**

---

305 Solzhenitsyn, *The Gulag Archipelago*, 680.
306 Rand, *The Fountainhead*.

## NOT CHASING AFTER REWARDS

---

### SKEPTICISM

"Underlying the work is the belief that things are rarely as they seem, and seldom as they should be," writes CBS legend Mike Wallace. "The radicalism often associated with reporting stems from the perpetual search for root causes of events - and from a low tolerance for injustice."[307] Here, Wallace is on the money. "Judgment calls" shape the muckraker's craft. One of his core attributes must be discernment. He is stubborn, a natural skeptic, and especially so *vis-à-vis* entrenched power structures. The serious investigative reporter, observes Dygert, "is on the lookout for conspiracies and corruption almost everywhere."[308] The muckraker asks not whether a story fits the narrative but whether it's true. He questions whether the facts have been verified and, if so, whether a piece is worthy of the public. Now more than ever, the muckraker has a very nearly sacred duty to be accurate.

---

### POLITICAL DISINTEREST

Oddly, the American muckraker is not inherently political. Although possessed of his own value system, he operates with immunity from outside influences. In a sea of shifting political tides, external threats are the only constant. Doing good to one's friends and harm to one's enemies—the essence of political identity—is the opposite of how he behaves. Being apolitical does not mean his stories are not political. He usually meets his foes and finds his stories in the political arena.

The muckraker's discomfort with their inherent power, and that of others, stems from Pascal's axioms that power without justice leads to tyranny.[309] The muckraker is tyranny's enemy. Unmoved by money, power, or fame, the muckraker keeps an open mind when it comes to finding facts and following them wherever they may lead. "A reporter's zeal must be directed to uncovering and documenting facts, not to getting revenge or attracting attention," observes Wallace.[310]

The muckraker reports the facts and makes them understandable to the audience, *sans motif.* By being honest with his reporting, he stays true to his oath to inform the public. His motive is to seek truth and correct injustice, to inform the public as it has a right to know, and to inspire justice by keeping citizens informed.

---

307 Mike Wallace, foreword, David Weir and Dan Noyes, *Raising Hell: How the Center for Investigative Reporting Gets the Story* (New York: Addison-Wesley, 1983), 1.
308 Dygert, *The Investigative Journalist,* 149.
309 A. J. Beitzinger, "Pascal on Justice, Force, and Law," *The Review of Politics* 46, no. 2 (April, 1984): 212–243.
310 Mike Wallace, introduction, *Raising Hell.*

## INTERNAL SELF-MOTIVATION

The source of the muckraker's inspiration must be internal. All he endeavors must come from a deeply felt passion. Most people start a business or organization because they want to be financially successful and even perhaps change their social standing. The successful muckraker does not do things in order to amass an inventory of effects; money is not the motivator. The muckraker's only use for money is as a means. Resources are merely the tools he uses to complete the task at hand. It is the destination, the vision that drives him.

The ideal motivation comes from within, from his own human spirit. He has a perennial thirst for justice. He has a "justice complex," as it were. Pascal reminds him that truth is impotent without power. As uncomfortable as it makes him, the muckraker does not shy from assuming the responsibility associated with their power. He understands, as Alinsky did, that power "is the very essence, the dynamo of life."[311] He exercises it, however, with integrity and tenderness. "Power is not a means, it is an end,"[312] says the amoral despot O'Brien in *1984*, but for the muckraker, power, like money, is simply a means. It is not something that can be attained, for it is inherent in their work. He derives his power from his righteous and indefatigable spirit. Justice isn't just one profession among many, but, as Plato reminds him, it is a just man's only true calling.[313] In other words, responsibility is responding with ability. Assuming responsibility in response to injustice is to assume one's own power for the well-being of others.

## INSATIABLE CURIOSITY

The muckraker has the ability to probe not just both horizontally and vertically, but also in the Z-axis: depth. He efficiently "mines" information, not just data, and places it into a two-dimensional format that activates the viewer's interest. The muckraker never "turns off," not even when his day has been completed—the greater the curiosity, the greater the drive. "A good investigative reporter," veteran reporter Dan Thomasson observed, "must have an instinct for the jugular, yet can't be bloodthirsty or biased."[314] The muckraker's curiosity does not end at a story's completion. It carries through life and expresses itself in varieties of hobbies and passions. Remember, the muckraker's insatiable curiosity, coupled with a desire for a good and just world, oftentimes chooses their path for them. Only then, when all other qualities are aligned and well-attuned, Solzhenitsyn tells the muckraker that if he has "ceased to be afraid of threats," and is "not chasing after rewards," does he become "most dangerous."[315]

*"When you have ceased to be afraid of threats and are not chasing after rewards, you become the most dangerous man in the world."*[316]

---

311 Alinsky, *Rules for Radicals*, 51.

312 Orwell, *1984*, 267.

313 Plato, *The Republic*, 61.

314 Dygert, *The Investigative Journalist*, 83.

315 Solzhenitsyn, *The Gulag Archipelago*, 603.

316 Solzhenitsyn, *The Gulag Archipelago*, 603.

## PACK JOURNALISM

There is something about the media as a collective that evokes animal imagery. Senator Eugene McCarthy more than once likened the media to blackbirds on a telephone wire; journalists that come and go to a story in flocks.[317] Timothy Crouse, in his campaign classic, *Boys on the Bus*, compares the media to "a pack of hounds sicked on a fox."[318] David Halberstam has accused the media of minnow journalism, "changing direction 180 degrees instantly, and for no apparent purpose."[319] Stephan Lesher compares the eager reporter to a dog trained "to leap blindly toward whatever is held aloft."[320] In a similar vein, David Wright of ABC News told Christian Hartsock of Project Veritas: "In television, we've lost any sense of context and perspective, and it's just the urgent moment and the horse race and the outrage from Trump."[321]

Shane Smith, the founder of *Vice*, shifts metaphors but not meaning. He believes that "scrambling to keep up with the Jones's" has been the downfall of network news. "The problem with the news cycle today and the news media in general is that it's kindergarten [kids] playing soccer," said Smith. "The ball goes over here; everyone goes over here. The ball goes over there, everyone goes over there."[322] The muckraker's role at the soccer field in Smith's scenario is as a parent, ready to sound the alarm, upon witnessing the referee pocketing a bribe in a rigged game.

*IF HE HAS "CEASED TO BE AFRAID OF THREATS," AND IS "NOT CHASING AFTER REWARDS," DOES HE BECOME "MOST DANGEROUS."*

317 Eugene McCarthy, *The Year of the People* (New York: Doubleday, 1969).
318 Timothy Crouse, *Boys on the Bus* (New York: Random House, 2013).
319 Halberstam, *The Powers That Be*.
320 Lesher, *Media Unbound*, 30.
321 Project Veritas, "'Socialist' ABC Reporter Admits Bosses Spike News Important to Voters, 'Don't Give Trump Credit,'" February 26, 2020, YouTube video, 7:31.
322 Philip Lelyveld, "Vice's Shane Smith: 'Young people are leaving TV in droves,'" Philip Lelyveld's blog, entry posted March 2, 2014.

# CHAPTER 5
# CHARACTER

## WORKS CITED

Alinsky, Saul D. *Rules for Radicals*. New York: Random House, 1971.

Crouse, Timothy. *Boys on the Bus*. New York: Random House, 2013.

Dygert, James H. *The Investigative Journalist: Folk Heroes of a New Era*. Hoboken: Prentice-Hall, 1976.

Halberstam, David. *The Powers That Be*. Champaign, IL: University of Illinois Press, 2000.

Hedges, Chris. *Wages of Rebellion*. New York: Perseus Books Group, 2016.

Kipling, Rudyard. *'If-' and other Poems*. London: Michael O'Mara Books Limited, 2016.

Lesher, Stephen. *Media Unbound*. Boston: Houghton Mifflin Company, 1982.

McCarthy, Eugene. *The Year of the People*. New York: Doubleday, 1969.

Orwell, George. *1984*. New York: Signet Classics, 1950.

Plato. *The Republic*. Millis, MA: Agora Publications, 2001.

Rand, Ayn. *The Fountainhead* (New York: Penguin Publishing, 2005).

Rindsberg, Ashley. *The Gray Lady Winked: How the New York Times' Misreporting, Distortions and Fabrications Radically Altered History*. Monee, IL: Midnight Oil Publishers, 2021.

Solzhenitsyn, Aleksandr. The Gulag Archipelago, Volume 2. New York: Harper Perennial Modern Classics, 2007.

Wallace, Mike. Foreword by David Weir and Dan Noyes. *Raising Hell: How the Center for Investigative Reporting Gets the Story*. New York: Addison-Wesley, 1983.

Whiteside, Thomas. *The Investigation of Ralph Nader*. New York: Arbor House, 1972.

## JOURNAL ARTICLES

Alford, C. Fred. "Whistle-Blower Narratives: The Experience of Choiceless Choice." *Social Research* 74, no. 1 (2007).

Beitzinger, A.J. "Pascal on Justice, Force, and Law." *The Review of Politics*, Volume 46, Number 2 (April, 1984).

# CHAPTER 6

# INSIDERS

*To be a whistleblower is to step outside the great chain of being, to join not just another religion, but another world. Sometimes this other world is called the margins of society, but to the whistleblower it feels like outer space.*[323]

-C. Fred Alford; Professor of Government & Politics, University of Maryland

By far, the question the muckraker hears most is also the most critical question: "What can I do?" To that question, there is now a more challenging answer—you can wear a hidden camera and blow the whistle on a deserving employer through Project Veritas.

In effect, a "whistleblower" is a subset of "muckraker." He is to the muckraker what a guerilla fighter is to the allied commander. Wars can be won without partisan resistance, but success is much more likely for the side of justice with help from within. The relationship between whistleblower and muckraker is pure symbiosis. These anonymous, everyday people do not deserve to be targeted, but their low profile protects them from the flashy, ephemeral celebrity life that leads to self-delusion.

Writes Daniel Boorstin, "Topsy-turvily, these can remain heroes precisely because they remain unsung."[324] These heroes have the power to inform the public about the flaws in the system. From the inside, they can help the muckraker, observe Ettema and Glasser, "Decide what is, and what is not, an outrage to our sense of moral order and to consider our expectations for our officials, our institutions, and ultimately ourselves."[325]

Whistleblowing almost inevitably involves a crisis of conscience. Whistleblowers have to weigh their loyalty to the public interest against their loyalty to their organizations, and quite possibly to their own friends

---

323 C. Fred Alford, "Whistle-Blower Narratives: The Experience of Choiceless Choice," *Social Research* 74, no. 1 (2007), 6.
324 Daniel J. Boorstin, *The Image: A Guide to Pseudo-Events in America*, (New York: Vintage, 2012), 76.
325 James S. Ettema and Theodore L. Glasser, *Custodians of Conscience: Investigative Journalism and Public Virtue* (New York: Columbia University Press, 1998), 3.

and associates. On one hand, to follow one's conscience and take action against the forces of conformity and compliance puts the whistleblower at odds with the larger society, as well as with elements of the social contract. On the other hand, by acquiescing to an injustice instead of speaking up, "We raise the threshold of moral outrage."[326]

The insider represents "the presence of the outside, on the inside."[327] Traditionally, Americans are asked to work through existing avenues for change, but working inside can be as futile or cause a worse outcome. Whistleblowers throughout history have learned these unfortunate lessons. The problem for the heroic NSA whistleblowers Edward Snowden and Thomas Drake, for instance, was that their superiors were the very people who had put in place the surveillance systems on which they felt the need to alert the public. As such, they were not about to encourage whistleblowing. Congress proved no more helpful. It is almost impossible to make a substantial difference inside any major system. To be effective, one must work on the outside, but have *access* to the inside.

## WHISTLEBLOWING IN TOTALITARIAN SOCIETIES

A scene from Orwell's *1984* depicts protagonist Winston Smith being tortured in the "Ministry of Love." His torturer, O'Brien, tells him, "If you are a man, Winston, you are the last man. Your kind is extinct; we are the inheritors." O'Brien is emphasizing the control of the Party over humanity. Winston is the last to resist. O'Brien continues, "Posterity will never hear of you.... You will be annihilated in the past as well as in the future, you will never have existed."[328]

In the 2019 HBO series, *Chernobyl*, based on real-life events during the final days of the Soviet Union, the Communist chairman Charkov confronts truth-teller scientist Valery Alekseyevich Legasov. As a result of his investigation of a preventable accident at the Chernobyl Nuclear Power Plant, Legasov is dying slowly of radiation poisoning. In terms eerily close to O'Brien's, Charkov explains the facts of totalitarian life:

> **Charkov:** You're one of us, Legasov. I can do anything I want with you. But what I want most is for you to know that I know. You're not brave. You're not heroic. You're just a dying man who forgot himself.

326 Roberta Ann Johnson, *Whistleblowing: When it Works—and Why* (Boulder: Lynne Rienner Publishers, 2003), 25.

327 Alford, "Whistle-Blower Narratives," 23–24.

328 George Orwell, *1984* (New York: Signet Classics, 1950), 340.

**Legasov:** I know who I am, and I know what I've done. In a just world, I'd be shot for my lies, but not for this, not for the truth.

**Charkov:** Scientists…and your idiot obsessions with reasons. When the bullet hits your skull, what will it matter why? No one's getting shot, Legasov. The whole world saw you in Vienna; it would be embarrassing to kill you now. And for what? Your testimony today will not be accepted by the State. It will not be disseminated in the press. It never happened.[329]

The Soviet Union's experience showed that many millions of people proved, under duress, to be moral cowards. They lived their feckless lives as stool pigeons, ready to rat on each other in order to survive at any price. It was far easier and more rewarding to betray neighbors, friends, family, even parents, than to betray the state and its proxies. The "Lie" became a form of existence. People became systemically corrupt. Just about every conversation with almost any other person called for lies. "People had to decide, when raising children, whether to start them on lies instead of the truth so that it would be easier for them to live. The choice was really such that many chose not to have children."[330] The soul of the people was dying.

## WHISTLEBLOWING IN DEMOCRATIC SOCIETIES

In a society like the United States, unlike in the Soviet Union or the fictional Oceania of *1984*, dissidents remain in society, but their livelihoods may disappear. Historically, whistleblowing against the interests of the State or its allies has not been glamorous. "The majority of whistleblowers suffer in obscurity," argue the authors of *The Corporate Whistleblower's Survival Guide*, "frustrated by burned career bridges and vindication they will never be able to obtain. The prominent, lionized beacons of hope are rare exceptions, and even most of them pay a horrible price with lifelong scars."[331]

Even in a free society, the whistleblower faces considerable risk, especially if the enemy is powerful enough to neutralize the media. Jeffrey Wigand, the "Insider" who blew the whistle on Big Tobacco, learned the hard way:

---

329 *Chernobyl,* "Open Wide, O Earth," episode 3, originally aired on HBO May 20, 2019.

330 Aleksandr Solzhenitsyn, *The Gulag Archipelago 1918-1956 An Experiment in Literary Investigation*, trans. Thomas P. Whitney and Harry Willets, abr. Edward E. Ericson, Jr. (New York: HarperCollins Publishers, 2007).

331 Tom Devine and Tarek Maassarani, *The Corporate Whistleblower's Survival Guide: A Handbook for Committing the Truth* (San Francisco: Berrett-Koehler Publishers, 2011), 18.

My children's lives were threatened. My marriage ended. I was followed. I was subjected to a multimillion-dollar retaliatory investigation and was sued. I had to live 24/7 with armed security forces to protect my family, start my car, open my mail. I was threatened with criminal prosecution for revealing the truth. And this is all after I was fired! Despite being a high-level insider, I had no idea what I would be subjecting myself to when I exposed the lies concealing an industry's secret, indefensible culture. I knew it was going to be a tsunami of sorts and that the truth would win out in the end. My thoughts in the initial phases were of survival rather than a stellar victory.[332]

Wigand was hardly an outlier. C. Fred Alford, author of *Whistleblowers: Broken Lives and Organizational Power*, spoke with several dozen whistleblowers. "Not only do most whistleblowers get fired," writes Alford, "but they rarely get their jobs back. Most never work in the field again. In some tight-knit fields there is an informal blacklist."[333] This was whistleblowing in the twentieth century. In the twenty-first century, things would change.

> *"PEOPLE HAD TO DECIDE, WHEN RAISING CHILDREN, WHETHER TO START THEM ON LIES INSTEAD OF THE TRUTH SO THAT IT WOULD BE EASIER FOR THEM TO LIVE."*

## JULIAN ASSANGE, ED SNOWDEN, AND PROJECT VERITAS

In 2010, Julian Assange relayed through his longest-serving lawyer, Jennifer Robinson, "I've got 250,000 diplomatic cables and I am going to publish them…They are very well written and researched and the State Department comes off well - [but] that's not how they are going to see this."[334]

In December 2020, as this muckraker was writing the book you are reading, I received a message from an undisclosed source bringing an Assange audio tape to my attention. The tape was a recorded seventy-five-minute

---

332 Devine and Maassarani, *The Corporate Whistleblower's Survival Guide*, VIII.
333 Alford, "Whistle-Blower Narratives," 19.
334 Jane Croft, "Jennifer Robinson: 'Assange had information. That made him dangerous,'" *Financial Times*, January 8, 2021.

phone call between an attorney in Hillary Clinton's State Department and Julian Assange. In it, Julian Assange was warning the US Government of an imminent release of classified, unredacted information. Assange identified a rogue former employee who, said Assange, intended to release classified State Department cables without redactions or other precautions. The tape showed that Assange's objective was to try to prevent harm to individual US operatives working for the government. Assange and his team argued that they were trying to be responsible and careful with the material. His media partners corroborated that the full publication occurred only after it was available on hundreds of other websites.

The unredacted 250,000 cables were published online by Cryptome. org, the Pirate Bay, and other sites, none of which received a takedown notice or suffered a leadership indictment.[335] Assange faces fifty years of incarceration for receiving, possessing, and publishing this material.[336] Assange had tried to acquire an injunction against former employee Daniel Domscheit-Berg and German weekly *Der Freitag* but lacked standing.[337]

Under house arrest in the British countryside, Assange could not meet with officials in the US embassy in London. Otherwise stymied, he simply called the State Department and asked to speak with the highest ranking official. Said Assange to State Department lawyer Cliff Johnson in August 2011, "We have intelligence that the State Department Database Archive of 250,000 diplomatic cables…is being spread around and…within the next few days it will become public."[338] Assange recorded the conversation:

> **Johnson:** Who would be releasing these cables? Is this WikiLeaks?
>
> **Assange:** No, we would not be releasing them - this is Daniel Domscheit-Berg, a previous employee that we suspended last August.
>
> **Johnson:** And he apparently has access to the material that Wikileaks also has?

335 Cassandra Fairbanks, "BREAKING: Project Veritas Releases Shocking Never-Before-Heard Phone Call Between Julian Assange and Hillary Clinton's State Department," The Gateway Pundit, December 16, 2020.
336 Meredith Lee, "The charges against Julian Assange, explained," PBS NewsHour, April 11, 2019.
337 Fairbanks, "BREAKING: Project Veritas Releases Shocking Never-Before-Heard Phone Call."
338 "Assange's Call to the State Department," assangedefense.org, August 26, 2011.

**Assange:** Yes. That's correct.

**Johnson:** And he has access to everything you have is that right?

**Assange:** That's correct.

**Johnson:** OK. And that includes classified as well as the unclassified cables.

**Assange:** That's correct.

## "THE SOURCE OF A GIVEN PIECE OF INFORMATION IS A HELL OF A LOT LESS IMPORTANT THAN IF THAT INFORMATION IS TRUE."

After the conversational tape was revealed, Edward Snowden chimed in through Twitter:

> This extraordinary recording (which I had never heard before) confirms claims that @Wikileaks made for years, but its critics dismissed as lies.
>
> 1) Assange DID seek to minimize risks to individuals.
>
> 2) Bulk release of cables was forced, not intentional.[339]

After Project Veritas shared Snowden's tweet, an otherwise obscure "gaymer" named Kevin Johnson tweeted, "I don't think @Jamesokeefeiii should be used as a credible source of information." I doubt if Johnson expected a direct reply from Snowden, given Snowden's nearly five million followers, but he got one. Tweeted Snowden, "The source of a given piece of information is a hell of a lot less important than if that information is true."[340]

A New Jersey woman Julie O'Connor tweeted to Snowden, "Project Veritas? Really? So disappointed in you…" To which Snowden replied, "I don't care if James Clapper released it—I care if it is true…What matters most is the evidence."[341]

---

339 @Snowden, Twitter, December 16, 2020.
340 @Snowden, Twitter, December 16, 2020.
341 @DingoPrincess1, Twitter, December 16, 2020.

The muckraker tweeted back at Edward Snowden, "People come to @ Project_Veritas with recordings because there's nowhere else to go. Journalists™ are afraid to break new ground, afraid to be in an exposed position, and afraid to challenge the state's narrative."[342]

People tend to focus on the motives of the whistleblower. They shouldn't. As Snowden said, "What matters most is the evidence." Government officials lie under oath and get away it. When journalists fall into a symbiotic relationship with government, they become, as Sissela Bok observed, "willing if not enthusiastic collaborators."[343] Under these circumstances, actions like Snowden's become a moral imperative. "Certain outrages are so blatant, and certain dangers are so great," adds Bok, "that all who are in a position to warn the public have a prima facie obligation to do so."[344]

How deep was the deception to which Snowden responded? Consider the following exchange at a US Senate subcommittee hearing between Senator Ron Wyden and director of national intelligence James Clapper in March 2013:

> **Wyden:** Does the NSA collect any type of data at all on millions or hundreds of millions of Americans?

> **Clapper:** No, sir.

> **Wyden:** It does not?

> **Clapper:** Not wittingly. There are cases where they could, inadvertently perhaps, collect, but not wittingly.[345]

342 @jamesokeefeiii, Twitter, December 16, 2020, accessed before permanent suspension.
343 Sissela Bok, *Secrets: On the Ethics of Concealment and Revelation,* (New York: Random House, 1989), 217.
344 Bok, *Secrets,* 219.
345 Kara Brandeisky and Stephen Suen, "Has the Gov't Lied on Snooping? Let's Go to the Videotape," ProPublica, July 30, 2013.

**May 2019:** A victorious James O'Keefe and lawyer Jamie Dean pose for a candid photo on the steps of the U.S. District Court in Asheville, NC, after securing an extraordinary, directed verdict in Teter's defamation lawsuit. "I'm very concerned about making any ruling that is not only detrimental to the First Amendment but eviscerates the First Amendment.... If you made this argument against Mike Wallace, would everyone in the room laugh?" —U.S. District Court Judge Martin Reidinger, May 21, 2019.

**then I'll just fall to ashes.**

**2019:** Whistleblower Eric Cochran released source code showing how Pinterest was censoring Bible verses and pro-life messages on their platform. "To me there's no other option. Like, I can go through life, and I can live in the comforts of life, and I can go on for eighty years and then make money, do the formula of life, *and then I'll just fall to ashes*; and I think that's how a lot of people live their lives. This is something that no matter what happens, no matter what I lose, it'll mean something after I'm gone."

**February 2021:** James Golden aka Bo Snerdley, long-time producer of the Rush Limbaugh show, gives an impromptu speech at the Project Veritas CPAC after-party in Orlando, Florida, standing beside Project Veritas Insiders and James O'Keefe just nine days after Limbaugh's passing. Said Golden, "James O'Keefe is the reason that there was a Rush Limbaugh. Rush Limbaugh is the reason that there's a James O'Keefe."

Crowd favorite, Erie, Pa. USPS whistleblower Richard Hopkins joins James O'Keefe and the Project Veritas team at several events following the 2020 presidential election.

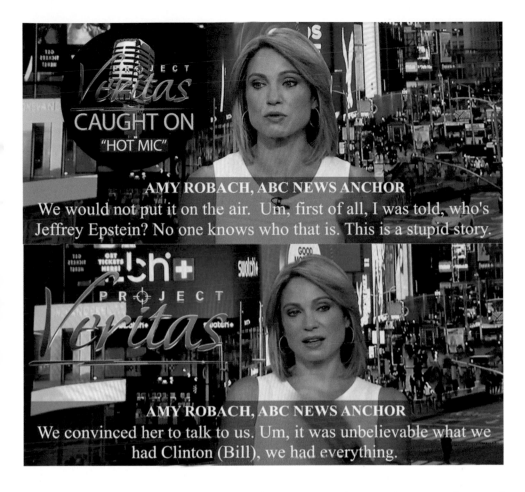

AMY ROBACH, ABC NEWS ANCHOR
We would not put it on the air. Um, first of all, I was told, who's Jeffrey Epstein? No one knows who that is. This is a stupid story.

AMY ROBACH, ABC NEWS ANCHOR
We convinced her to talk to us. Um, it was unbelievable what we had Clinton (Bill), we had everything.

Following CNN Insider Cary Poarch, a new media Insider came forward from within ABC News leaking this hot-mic moment of *Good Morning America* anchor Amy Robach detailing her network's efforts to spike the Jeffrey Epstein story for years. Said the anonymous ABC News Insider, "I came forward with this information bearing no motives other than to have this information public."

Fox 26 Insider Ivory Hecker surprises CBS 62 Insider April Moss follow-
ing an on-record emotional interview with Project Veritas founder James
O'Keefe. Moss was originally inspired to come to Veritas as a result of
Hecker's brave actions.

James O'Keefe pictured with CBS 62 Insider April Moss and family.

James O'Keefe questions *New York Times* Executive Editor Dean Baquet on the streets of Manhattan following a 2017 exposé into the *Times'* journalistic integrity and objectivity.

Somali American ballot harvester Liban Mohamed aka "KingLiban1" denied the evidence in his own Snapchats showing countless ballots in his car obtained only due to an extensive undercover investigation.

No. _____

———————◆———————

PROJECT VERITAS ACTION FUND,

*Petitioner,*

v.

RACHAEL S. ROLLINS, in her official capacity as District Attorney for Suffolk County, Massachusetts,

*Respondent.*

———————◆———————

## On Petition For Writ Of Certiorari To The United States Court Of Appeals For The First Circuit

———————◆———————

## PETITION FOR A WRIT OF CERTIORARI

———————◆———————

Project Veritas Action Fund's historic First Amendment case against Rachael Rollins heads to the United States Supreme Court via a *Petition For Writ Of Certiorari*.

James O'Keefe outside of the John Joseph Moakley United States Courthouse following an appeal in the PVA v. Rollins case in Boston, Massachusetts. Harvard law students attended the proceedings in this historic case.

CNN Technical Director Charlie Chester blasts his own network as "propaganda" and admits CNN pushes COVID-19 fear for ratings on undercover video.

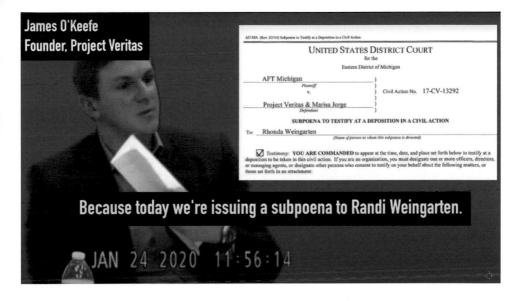

James O'Keefe presents a subpoena for American Federation of Teachers president Randi Weingarten during a videotaped deposition. O'Keefe, even on defense, goes on offense.

Undeterred by a days-long deposition in the *Teter v. Project Veritas* case, O'Keefe unleashes on politically tied Teter attorneys.

James O'Keefe pictured with US President Donald J. Trump following a Mar-a-Lago meeting. O'Keefe briefed Trump on Project Veritas' monumental legal victory on Motion to Dismiss in the defamation case against the *New York Times*.

James O'Keefe pictured with former *New York Times* Pulitzer Prize–winning reporter Judith Miller. Miller was jailed for eighty-five days for protecting the identity of her source in the Plame affair.

## *"ASSANGE HAD INFORMATION. THAT MADE HIM DANGEROUS."*

Not long afterwards, it was revealed that the NSA, in fact, does collect phone records on millions of Americans.[346] Once the truth came out, even the establishment media felt compelled to call Clapper out for lying. Unbothered, President Obama stood by Clapper until the end of his second term in January 2017, and CNN hired Clapper as a contributor when he stepped down.[347] In so doing, the network signed on to an unholy alliance with the permanent, unelected wing of the federal government. Not to be outmaneuvered, NBC and MSNBC promptly hired Obama's equally duplicitous CIA director, John Brennan. Worse than lying, the pair had worked covertly with Team Obama to undermine the Trump candidacy, a project fully enabled by Big Media. "Being on any team is a bad look for the press," said *Rolling Stone* reporter Matt Taibbi, "but the press being on team FBI/CIA is an atrocity, Trump or no Trump."[348]

Did blowing the whistle on the NSA make Snowden a hero or a traitor? For many people, his actions defy easy characterization. What is not arguable is that Snowden had "ceased to be afraid of threats," had stopped "chasing after rewards," and had access to truths that made him, by Solzhenitsyn standards, "most dangerous."[349] Attorney Jennifer Robinson said of her client, "Assange had information. That made him dangerous." Prosecuting him under the Espionage Act for relaying that information would set a "terrifying precedent" for whistleblowing activity essential to the checks and balances of the federal government and its activities.[350]

---

346 Brandeisky and Suen, "Has the Gov't Lied on Snooping?"

347 Jonathan Turley, "Clappers' actions sure do look like political manipulations," *The Hill*, April 28, 2018.

348 Matt Taibbi, *Hate Inc.: Why Today's Media Makes Us Despise One Another* (New York: OR Books, 2019), 262.

349 Solzhenitsyn, *The Gulag Archipelago*, vol. 2, 603.

350 Croft, "Jennifer Robinson: 'Assange had information.'"

## PROJECT VERITAS WHISTLEBLOWERS: A NEW WAY FORWARD

Would-be whistleblowers have an option they never had before. Many have become part of a vast new movement, the Veritas Army, whose motto, "Be Brave. Do Something," is inspiring citizens to become catalysts for reform. Project Veritas is, in a way, the modern incarnation of what muckraker Jack Anderson once described as "the Sirens of Greek mythology, who, by their seductive singing, enticed unknowing wayfarers to abandon the cramped boredom of safe passage for a hazardous try at strange excitements and gratifications."[351] Unlike the sirens, however, Project Veritas makes the abandonment of that safe passage worthwhile. Insiders-turned-whistleblowers are the beneficiaries of public donation campaigns, sponsored by Project Veritas, and conducted by GoFundMe competitor GiveSendGo to raise sums amounting to hundreds of thousands of dollars for those who risk their lives and careers in the pursuit of truth.

The whistleblowers in 2019–2020 for Project Veritas included two Google employees, three Facebook subcontractors, a Pinterest engineer, a CNN subcontractor, an ABC News insider, a CBS insider, and four United States Postal Workers. Many of them gave up their salaries and careers to ensure the public's right to know. Project Veritas had the privilege to recruit these brave souls. In coming out, they understood full well that an army of grateful citizens would stand behind them, as long as they followed their consciences. Their testimonies should warm those citizens' hearts:

> "The truth is more powerful than any NDA…" said Facebook whistleblower Zach McElroy.[352]

> "This was an act of atonement. An attempt to make my conscience clear," said Zach Vorhies, who leaked to Project Veritas the "Algorithmic Unfairness" document from within Google.[353]

> "Are we going to just let the biggest tech companies decide who wins every election from now on?" said Greg Coppola, who lost his job at Google after speaking out.[354]

---

351 Dygert, *The Investigative Journalist,* 95.
352 Project Veritas, "Facebook Content Moderator: 'If Someone's Wearing MAGA Hat, I'm Going to Delete Them for Terrorism,'" June 23, 2020, YouTube video, 19:55.
353 Project Veritas, "Google 'Machine Learning Fairness' Whistleblower Goes Public, says: 'burden lifted off of my soul,'" August 24, 2019, YouTube video, 19:34.
354 Project Veritas, "Current Sr. Google Engineer Goes Public on Camera: Tech is 'dangerous,' 'taking sides,'" July 24, 2019, YouTube video, 14:01.

"The things I found the company doing were appalling, and I felt the public had a right to know. Project Veritas just gave me the courage to do the right thing, even if it meant sacrificing my comfort," said Ryan Hartwig, the Facebook insider who was fired for leaking screenshots of their algorithms built to "deboost" posts and videos that were not aligned with their political agenda.[355]

"For me there was no other option," said Eric Cochran, the Pinterest engineer who was escorted out of the building after blowing the whistle on his employer.

Cochran's spontaneous testimony could serve as a whistleblower's manifesto:

I could go through life, and I could live in the comforts of life, and I could go on for eighty years, and then make money, do the formula of life, and then I'll just fall to ashes. And I think that's how a lot of people live their lives. This is something, no matter what happens, no matter what I lose, it'll mean something after I'm gone. What are you saving up your ammo for? This is the moment that matters. This is what I'm going to do with my life, this is how I make an impact on this world. I'm going to get ten more people to do what I did.[356]

It was destiny that the CNN wayfarer met the muckraker in the spring by happenstance, inspired by the actions of the others who came before. Said the insider, "I started at CNN with a dream to work in media, but my dream had become a nightmare."[357]

In the current media landscape, people are often famous simply for being famous. How else to explain the Kardashians or Paris what's-her-name? They are "influencers." Their names have become their brands. What they are not, are heroes.

355 Project Veritas, "Another Facebook Insider Details Political Censorship; Current HR Exec 'No One Has White Man's Back,'" June 25, 2020, YouTube video, 17:57.

356 Project Veritas, "Project Veritas Features - Pinterest Insider Speaks Out: "The tech companies can't fight us all," June 13, 2019, YouTube video, 19:33.

357 Project Veritas, "PART 1: CNN Insider Blows Whistle on Network President Jeff Zucker's Personal Vendetta Against POTUS," October 14, 2019, YouTube video, 19:50.

## MORAL COURAGE

Project Veritas has unearthed a new breed of genuine heroes—the sort that author Daniel Boorstin spoke of in his book, *The Image*: "In our world of big names, our true heroes tend to be anonymous," writes Boorstin. He continues:

> In this life of illusion and quasi-illusion, the person of solid virtues who can be admired for something more substantial than his well-knownness often proves to be the unsung hero: the teacher, the nurse, the mother, the honest cop, the hard worker at lonely, underpaid, unglamorous, unpublicized jobs.[358]

### *"IN OUR WORLD OF BIG NAMES, OUR TRUE HEROES TEND TO BE ANONYMOUS."*

These anonymous heroes become part of the Veritas army. Their revelations make their fellow citizens conscious of the world around them. Their words create sublime moments of awakening in a way little else can. They do not serve up "leaks" as commonly understood—manipulative, self-serving, partisan—but truths. These anonymous blue-collar heroes of solid virtue are the most reliable sources in all of journalism. Unlike "leakers," they have no friends in high places. These truth-tellers whose loyalty is to the public interest expect to pay a price for passing their information along, and usually do.

What shocks whistleblowers most is not the external reaction to their coming forward. That they anticipate. "The greatest shock," writes C. Fred Alford in *Whistleblowers*, "is what the whistleblower learns about the world as a result - that nothing he or she believed was true."[359]

### RICHARD HOPKINS: "I'D RATHER BE SHOT AT."

Of all the brave whistleblowers that have come to Project Veritas, Richard Hopkins stands out. His story of courage and resolve resonated with the entire Project Veritas staff, their audience, and this muckraker most of all. Hopkins is a Marine veteran and USPS worker from Erie, Pennsylvania. How his employers at the federal government turned on him should open the eyes of every American.

358 Boorstin, *The Image*, 76.
359 Alford, *Whistleblowers: Broken Lives and Organizational Power*, 20.

Hopkins is a man of extraordinary honesty and dignity, a patriot who sought nothing but the best for his country and his fellow citizens. Unfortunately, his sense of duty, forged by combat in Afghanistan, was not shared by his supervisors or the leadership of the US Postal Service (USPS).

## *"WHAT THE WHISTLEBLOWER LEARNS ABOUT THE WORLD AS A RESULT - THAT NOTHING HE OR SHE BELIEVED WAS TRUE."*

Two days after the November 3, 2020 national election, Hopkins reached out to Project Veritas to share the potential voter fraud he witnessed. Hopkins's testimony came the day after two other Post Office whistleblowers, both employed at a Traverse City, Michigan, post office, told Project Veritas about their experience. They claimed that during a pre-shift huddle the morning after the election, their supervisors instructed them to segregate all mail-in ballots they picked up on their routes. Then, when they arrived back at the post office, they were instructed to store the late ballots in special bins to be picked up by an overnight crew of postal clerks. Those clerks would then postmark the envelopes by hand for November 3, not November 4, the day they were actually received.[360] Remember, the postmark was the only way to determine if a mail-in ballot was returned on or before Election Day.

The Traverse City Post Office releases were huge news.[361] At the time, President Donald Trump was still ahead in key states that were continuing to count ballots.

The moral challenges legitimate whistleblowers face demands a muckraker's respect. In many circumstances, they need the courage to destroy their own careers for the greater good. Sometimes, when they can no longer abide the betrayal of their conscience, they are forced to betray their inner circle of friends, family, and co-workers.

As hard as the muckraker pressed the Traverse City whistleblowers to come forward, they would not. The first postal worker agreed to cooperate with his voice distorted, and the second would only confirm that his experience matched that of the first whistleblower.[362] Project Veritas issued a

360 Project Veritas, "Pennsylvania USPS Whistleblower Exposes Anti-Trump Postmaster's Illegal Order To Back-Date Ballots," November 5, 2020, YouTube video, 2:18.

361 Project Veritas, "MAIL FRAUD UPDATE: Federal investigators in Michigan investigating USPS after Veritas Whistleblower," November 5, 2020, YouTube video, 0:44.

362 Project Veritas, "Michigan USPS Whistleblower Details Directive From Superiors To Back-Date Late Mail-In-Ballots Nov 3," November 4, 2020, YouTube video, 2:19.

press release regarding these whistleblowers, in part because it was timely and spoke to people's real anxieties, and also to encourage others to come forward, especially from the Postal Service.[363]

To give some sense of scale to the broken electoral system in 2020, roughly 45 percent of 150 million ballots cast—some 67 million—were mailed in. This is the first time in American history that the Post Office has played such a significant role in choosing a president. Given the magnitude of the ballots going through the mail, the integrity of the election was directly tied to the integrity of the Postal Service. No one spoke to the Post Office's lack of integrity as boldly as Hopkins did. In the days following his courageous act, his fellow workers saw all too clearly how their employer treats truth-tellers.

The story began simply enough. On November 4, 2020, the day after Election Day, Hopkins was watching a YouTube livestream by journalist Tim Pool. Tim is fearless. He sees politics and media with the appropriately jaundiced eye. Tim started laying out the story about our Traverse City Post Office whistleblowers by showing a release from Project Veritas:

> BREAKING: Michigan USPS Whistleblower Details Directive from Superiors: Back-Date Late Mail-In-Ballots as Received November 3, 2020 So They Are Accepted. "Separate them from standard letter mail so they can hand stamp them with YESTERDAY'S DATE & put them through."[364]

Hopkins watched with great interest as Tim put his own unique spin on the news:

> I think this stuff should be investigated. That's about it. Investigate it. If it's true, we should take it seriously, and we should make sure we get to the bottom of it. I think we want to make sure whatever this election ends up being, for whoever it ends, we want to make sure it's clean, right? I think Democrats and Republicans alike will agree; we want the victory to be signed, stamped, you know, 'i's' dotted, 't's' crossed! If someone's saying, "Here's a guy coming out saying this," we look into it because I think every Democrat should accept: "Okay, we're going to debunk all your claims if they're lies and we're going to prove we won." They should

363 Project Veritas, "Project Veritas Offers $25K Reward for Tips Related to Election, Voter & Ballot Fraud in PA," November 9, 2020, YouTube video, 1:40.
364 Timcast IRL, "WaPo Says Postal Worker RECANTED Statement About Voter Fraud, He Did NOT, It's A CRAZY Story, November 11, 2020, YouTube video, 17:17.

want to do that, and they should be prepared for this. If they come out and say, "We refuse because we don't have to because they're stupid lies anyway." Then I'm going to be like, "Okay, you're scared."[365]

The following morning, November 5, Hopkins was the last postal worker sorting his mail for delivery. As he was wrapping up, he overheard his postmaster talking about how ballots processed after Election Day should be backdated in order to be counted in the 2020 election.[366] If proven true, this backdating would be an egregious act of illegal voter fraud in the pivotal swing state of Pennsylvania. Given what was known about Traverse City, this scheme might have been coordinated throughout the battleground states.

As hoped, the Traverse City Post Office whistleblower story brought Project Veritas more Postal Service whistleblowers, but none like Hopkins. Hopkins related that the Michigan whistleblowers' story inspired him to clear his conscience and reveal that he, too, had heard of such a scheme in his Post Office. His sense of duty prompted him to reach out to a trusted friend to ask for advice. His friend suggested he speak to a local investigator who was looking into voter fraud claims in Erie, but Hopkins thought this was much larger than a local story. He was right.

*HE OVERHEARD HIS POSTMASTER TALKING ABOUT HOW BALLOTS PROCESSED AFTER ELECTION DAY SHOULD BE BACKDATED IN ORDER TO BE COUNTED IN THE 2020 ELECTION.*

Hopkins then sent an encrypted message through the messaging app Signal to the Project Veritas "Insiders" team and shared his experience. He was shocked at how quickly the muckraking team responded. He was realizing how big his story would turn out to be. Project Veritas quickly scheduled a video interview with him via Zoom. At this point, Hopkins wanted to remain anonymous, so producers distorted his voice and blurred his face. He made the following statements during that interview:

---

365 Timcast IRL, "Postal Worker RECANTED."
366 Project Veritas, "Pennsylvania USPS Whistleblower."

This morning, I was casing my route and I saw the postmaster pull one of our supervisors to the side. He was pulling the supervisor, and it was really close to where my case was. So I was able to hear, listen in, and I heard him say to the supervisor that they messed up yesterday. He told the supervisor they had postmarked one of the ballots for the fourth [of November], instead of the third, because they were supposed to put them for the third.

I wasn't supposed to hear that -

I was one of the last carriers in the building. I don't even think he realized I was still there, you know what I'm saying? Backdating. All these ballots that were coming in - today, tomorrow, yesterday - are all supposed to be postmarked the third.[367]

The last thing Hopkins wanted from this interview was to be in the spotlight or have his face plastered all over the news. After his first anonymous interview went viral on social media, the muckraker pleaded with him to go public so that people could see the true face of courage. It was the one good choice he had to make. The muckraker even told Hopkins that thousands would donate to his cause, to which he responded:

**Hopkins:** Dude. It ain't about the money, bro.

**Muckraker:** Of course not; this is all bigger than us.

**Hopkins:** Fuck yeah it is. It's way bigger than all of us.

**Muckraker:** It's bigger than us. So, what do you say? I don't think they can fire you. There are whistleblower protections.

**Hopkins:** Yes, there is. But I mean, here's the thing. I think they're trying to [fire me] right now because they brought up a freakin' thing from months ago.

**Muckraker:** That's why you gotta go public. Because it will protect you. If they retaliate against you in this moment in time, it will just make the story bigger.

367 Project Veritas, "Pennsylvania USPS Whistleblower."

Hopkins had a lot to deal with. It is hard to imagine what was going through his mind, but the cause truly was larger than any he had ever faced:

> **Muckraker:** I know this is an awful situation to be in, and I can only imagine what's going through your heart and through your head in your life. But you are in a situation, right here and right now, where there's only two options: you do nothing, in which case they play games with you and they fuck with you; or you go public, and if they fuck with you, that's gonna be used against them. I can guarantee it.

Hopkins' actions were self-evident in that he never intended to go public. That reluctance refuted what federal agents would say later on. Hopkins was hesitant about his decision, but deep down he understood it was the right thing to do. He suspected that the USPS knew about his actions and was already planning to retaliate against him. This concern gave him even more of an incentive to go public as a way to defend himself.

As helpful as Hopkins's decision to go public was, Project Veritas was still competing against time. Hopkins was so conscientious, he did not want to exceed his lunch break even for a few minutes. This meant that the muckraking staff had to get to him before his lunch break was over. They would not offend this good man's dignity by asking him to miss work, especially considering that his world was about to be turned upside down.

### *HOPKINS WAS HESITANT ABOUT HIS DECISION, BUT DEEP DOWN HE UNDERSTOOD IT WAS THE RIGHT THING TO DO.*

---

It was now 1:37 p.m. and there was no guarantee that Jackson, our reporter in Erie, would be able to interview Hopkins once his lunch break was over. This was an opportunity that could not be missed, especially given the risk Hopkins had run and the work already done to convince him to go public. As all waited for Jackson to arrive, the muckraker asked Hopkins a few questions about how he was doing, now that the anonymous interview he had done the day before had gone viral:

> **Muckraker:** So, just before we get started, tell me again what you were saying earlier about what happened today. They [USPS] were retaliating against you? What happened?

**Hopkins:** I guess this morning; I ran a little bit late. They had a safety standout kind of thing and I get implied as being the one…

**Muckraker:** How did they imply that?

**Hopkins:** Haven't figured out. But the postal sweatshirt I was wearing yesterday [in the video] happened to be an old-school postal vest, and I am one of the few people who still wears those things.

It seemed entirely likely that Hopkins was burned. The USPS had to know he was the whistleblower.

**Muckraker:** Okay. What did they say to you? What did they do to you? What did they threaten you with?

**Hopkins:** Didn't threaten me with anything. But I know the union members all went to the back with the supervisors. One of the union reps came up to me and said, "I need you to write up the thing on what happened a few months ago." I said, "I gave that to you, I thought that was over and done with." You know?

**Muckraker:** Really?

**Hopkins:** Almost like they want to bring up some old shit to try and get rid of me.

In July 2020, Hopkins had received a warning from his superiors because a colleague objected to an amiable prank he had directed at her. These small pranks were commonplace in his USPS office. Hopkins heard no more about the incident until November. This maneuver by the government to strong-arm Hopkins infuriated everyone who sympathized with his story. One can only imagine what Hopkins must have felt. How treacherous of these postal union members to bring up a months-old story for no other purpose than to intimidate a colleague into silence. It should be noted that his union, the National Association of Letter Carriers, vigorously endorsed Joe Biden, telling its members that a Trump victory threatened the Post Office's survival.[368]

---

368 Sahil Kapur, "Postal carriers union endorses Biden, warns that 'survival' of USPS is at stake," NBC News, August 14, 2020, https://www.nbcnews.com/politics/2020-election/postal-workers-union-endorses-biden-warns-survival-usps-stake-n1236768.

Meanwhile, Hopkins was saying over the phone: "I'm so fucking nervous about this. I'm just smoking a shit ton of cigarettes." The muckraker reassured him that Project Veritas had his back, that he was doing the right thing. After a frantic miscommunication or two, Jackson caught sight of Hopkins, now on his route. Jackson was going to attempt to do something unanticipated, namely, interview Hopkins while he was delivering the mail.

**HE WAS A HUMBLE AND HONEST AMERICAN, A VETERAN, WHO JUST WANTED TO LIVE HIS LIFE AND DO THE RIGHT THING.**

After preparing several questions, this muckraker made his pitch to Hopkins to do the interview while he delivered the mail. For Hopkins, the request was almost as demanding as asking him to go public in the first place. Ultimately, he agreed:

> **Muckraker:** Okay, Richard. Do you have a couple minutes right now?
>
> **Hopkins:** Sure, I'm gonna be walking while I am doing this.
>
> **Muckraker:** Can we talk to you while you walk and do it?
>
> **Hopkins:** Sure.
>
> **Muckraker:** Okay. Great.[369]

The man was determined to do his job. He deserved respect for that. He was a humble and honest American, a veteran, who just wanted to live his life and do the right thing. The muckraker began interviewing him over the phone while Jackson recorded him from afar via his iPhone. Hopkins continued to deliver the mail, his back largely to the camera. Not ideal, but real, *cinéma vérité* at its purest.

---

369 Project Veritas, "BREAKING: PA USPS Whistleblower Richard Hopkins Goes Public; Confirms Federal Investigation," YouTube, November 6, 2020.

**Muckraker:** So, Richard, what happened today? Were you contacted by a federal agency?

**Hopkins:** Yes.

**Muckraker:** Who were you contacted by?

**Hopkins:** The postal inspectors.

More information was needed. It was important for the American public to understand why USPS officials were talking about backdating ballots and the ultimate goal of the USPS.

**Hopkins:** Well, I mean, the only purpose I can think of is that they want us to pick up these ballots, which seems odd already...the court said they can extend the count as long as all ballots that they receive are postmarked as the third. They cannot count anything that's received as the fourth or the sixth. Basically. You know what I'm saying?

It was entirely clear what he was saying. The muckraking continued:

**Muckraker:** Are you willing to testify? If you're subpoenaed, would you be willing to say under oath that what you heard the postmaster Robert tell Daryl is correct?

**Hopkins:** Yes.

**Muckraker:** That's illegal in Pennsylvania, to backdate a ballot from November fourth to November third. You're willing to testify under oath that what you saw is true?

**Hopkins:** Yes.

Hopkins was all in. He now had confirmed that he really meant business. It was important to understand what was going through his mind at this moment in time:

**Muckraker:** How are you feeling right now? You must be very afraid speaking on the record. The world is going to know. What do you feel right now?

**Hopkins:** Nerves. I'm nervous because this is a big deal. This could mean my job. I want to ensure that this election is done correctly. I don't care who wins, whoever wins in the end of the day, I'm going to laugh. Things are going to go south one way or the other...Whether Trump wins, we got crazy stuff happening in our country and they've been going on for a while. I'm going to laugh one way or the other.

Although Hopkins was understandably nervous, his sincerity was obvious. He had only one reason for risking his job. "I would like to see something like this [election] done properly and there's no tomfoolery," he said. "That's why I went and voted in person myself. Because I believe that is the safest [way to vote]...You know what I'm saying?" Yes, this was a patriot's response. He was a man with no partisan agenda who simply wanted a clean election. To assure clean elections in the future, he was willing to testify under oath about what he had heard. This could not have been an easy decision to make.

**Muckraker:** Since you did the interview with me yesterday, you've been spoken to by the union reps and the U.S. Postal Inspection Service. Have any other [USPS] employees witnessed what you heard, or feel the same way?

**Hopkins:** Um, there are [USPS] employees that feel the same way. They won't say anything. They contacted me actually and were like, 'that was badass,' and what not. They were glad that I did what I did. Nobody else witnessed what I did because I was one of the last people in the office at that point in time.

**Muckraker:** Nobody else witnessed what you witnessed, but you heard Robert tell Daryl to backdate those ballots? Wow. Do you believe the orders came from higher up beyond Rob's desk?

**Hopkins:** Oh yeah. I believe – I just think that they [Rob and Daryl] were doing what they were told. I think this comes from above. I just think they were doing what they were told.

**Muckraker:** Okay.

Those were strong claims Hopkins made. Orders coming from USPS and/or union leadership to backdate ballots shocked every patriotic American who heard Hopkins. As the interview was coming to an end, Hopkins introduced one critical subject:

**Hopkins:** I could probably lose my job over this.

**Muckraker:** Well, if you lose your job over telling the truth about fraud and backdating of ballots, that will create, in my opinion, a constitutional crisis.

**Hopkins:** Yeah.

**Muckraker:** We'll have your back. We'll handle your legal costs, whatever those may be. OK? We're going to get this [interview] produced and call you back.

**Hopkins:** Alright.

**Muckraker:** Alright. Thank you.

The Project Veritas team was relieved that the interview had worked out. This was a huge story. It was time to produce the video and release it that same evening, November 6.[370] The craziness would not end with the release. It would mark the beginning. For the Project Veritas team, it would be one more sleepless night in a season of sleeplessness. The journalistic non-profit had been breaking major stories exposing voter fraud across the country and the staff was running high on adrenaline. The week of the election was especially crazy. Millions of people were relying on them to expose election fraud. If not Project Veritas, who? Certainly not Big Media. Now, the people were counting on Hopkins.

Project Veritas's chief legal officer, Jered Ede, spoke to Hopkins about signing an affidavit attesting to the voter fraud scheme he overheard. Ede

---

370 Project Veritas, "BREAKING: PA USPS Whistleblower Richard Hopkins Goes Public; Confirms Federal Investigation," November 6, 2020, YouTube video, 2:19.

sent Jackson, still in Erie, a copy of the affidavit, and Hopkins signed it. Upon the affidavit being signed, Senator Lindsey Graham promised to use Hopkins' testimony in Senate hearings that would investigate voting irregularities in the 2020 election.[371]

Senator Graham's statement made news across the mainstream media, and every article cited Richard Hopkins by name.[372] As *Newsweek* noted on Sunday, November 8, Graham planned to call on the Department of Justice and the US Postal Service to investigate based on the "allegations from Richard Hopkins, a postal worker in Erie, Pennsylvania."[373] Project Veritas was making an impact, but it was Hopkins who was making a difference.

## "THE REASON THEY CALLED ME IN IS TO TRY TO HARNESS THAT STORM, TRY TO REEL IT BACK IN BEFORE IT GETS REALLY CRAZY."

After Senator Graham called on the DOJ and the USPS to investigate Hopkins's voter fraud claims, the levers of the unelected government decided it had had enough. It was time to send in the cavalry. A criminal investigator for the USPS Office of Inspector General, Russell Strasser—yes, *Casablanca* fans, the same name as the Nazi villain —was deployed from New York City to Erie. On Monday, November 9th, he interrogated Hopkins for nearly four hours under the pretense that he was sent to uncover voter fraud.[374] In reality, exposing fraud was the last thing on Strasser's agenda. He was actually sent to Pennsylvania to make sure the story was killed in the womb. He said as much himself.

"This storm is getting crazy, right?" Strasser said to Hopkins at the beginning of the interview. "It's out of a lot of people's control. And so, the reason they called me in is to try to harness that storm, try to reel it back in before it gets really crazy." No fool, Hopkins discreetly recorded the interrogation.[375]

371 Celeste Cannon, "Sen. Graham to follow-up on postal worker alleging some ballots were backdated," WACH FOX-57, November 7, 2020.
372 Kerry Picket, "Lindsey Graham calls for DOJ investigation after USPS whistleblower affidavit alleges ballot fraud," *Washington Examiner*, November 7, 2020.
373 Ewan Palmer, "Sen. Graham Silent on Biden Win after Trump Campaign Sends Affidavit from USPS Worker Citing 'Backdated Ballots,'" *Newsweek*, November 8, 2020.
374 Project Veritas, "RAW AUDIO: USPS Whistleblower Richard Hopkins FULL COERCIVE INTERROGATION By Federal Agents," November 11, 2020, YouTube video, 2:02:49.
375 Project Veritas, "INTERROGATION."

At the beginning, Strasser attempted to establish a bond with Hopkins. After all, both of them had served in the military. "I believe you," said Strasser. "I'm in your corner on this. I want to take care of you. Yes. You believe me on that? I mean, because that's why I'm here. There we go, okay?" As Strasser worked to gain Hopkins's trust, he tried to weaken his resolve by subtly threatening him. Strasser warned Hopkins that being a whistleblower could have significant consequences.[376] With our assistance, Hopkins had raised more than $100,000 on GoFundMe at this point.[377] The always helpful Strasser pointed out that by raising money, Hopkins could be seen as a profiteer instead of a whistleblower. Of course, that was never Hopkins's goal, and the thought of being branded that way disturbed him.

Strasser was very clear with Hopkins on this subject. "I am scaring you here, okay?" he connived. "If we are not a thousand percent accurate with our honesty, it can be argued that money was gained by – I'm going to say assumptions – they're going to say deceptions." Strasser wanted Hopkins to second-guess himself. This strategy became increasingly clear as the interrogation went on:

> I am actually, I am trying to twist you a little bit because in that, believe it or not, your mind will kick in. Okay? We like to control our mind. And when we do that, we can convince ourselves of a memory. But when you're under a little bit of stress, which is what I'm doing to you purposely, your mind can be a little bit clearer. And we're going to do a different exercise, too, to make your mind a little bit clearer.[378]

Strasser spoke of this five-day-old "memory"—a memory Hopkins shared with Project Veritas almost immediately—as though it were some dark secret Hopkins had repressed in his childhood. Strasser attempted to convince Hopkins that Project Veritas was not to be trusted and did not have his best interests at heart. Hopkins would later say that he never doubted Project Veritas. He knew the muckrakers had his back.

Hopkins had no lawyer present during the interviews and was prevented from leaving the room to talk to anyone. After hours of unrelenting interrogation, Strasser convinced Hopkins to "update his statement," the one he had made on the affidavit. Hopkins believed Strasser's claim

---

376 Project Veritas, "INTERROGATION."
377 Valerie Richardson, "Richard Hopkins, Pa. postal whistleblower placed on unpaid leave, raises $233,000 on crowdfunding," *The Washington Times*, November 17, 2020.
378 Project Veritas, "INTERROGATION."

that by signing, he would be safe from retaliation.[379] Hopkins never took back what he said in the affidavit, never agreed to "recant" anything.[380] He signed thinking the document would absolve him of any legal ramifications. Those in administrative power, of course, had other ideas. The day after Strasser promised to "take care" of Hopkins, November 10, Hopkins was notified by a "Stephanie Hetrick, Manager, Customer Service," that his services were no longer needed:

> This is written verification that you were placed in an off-duty/non-pay status effective November 10, 2020. You are placed in this off duty/non-pay status as per Article 16.7 of the Collective Bargaining Agreement.

> As per Article 16.7, an employee may be immediately placed on an off-duty status (without pay) by the Employer but remain on the rolls where the allegation involves intoxication (use of drugs or alcohol), pilferage, or failure to observe safety rules and regulations, or in cases where retaining the employee on duty may result in damage to U.S. Postal Service property, loss of mail or funds, or *where the employee may be injurious to self or others.*

> On November 5th and 6th, 2020, your actions may have placed employees and yourself as well as the reputation of the US Postal Service in harm's way.

> You are to remain off work until the completion of the OIG and internal investigation.

> You have the right to file a grievance under the Grievance/Arbitration procedures set forth in Article 15 of the National Agreement within 14 days of your receipt of this notice.[381]

Hopkins was now placed on unpaid leave, and this was just the beginning of their retaliation. On that same day, November 10th, the Project

---

379 Joe Walsh, "Mailman Recants Bogus Voter Fraud Allegation That Launched A GOP Conspiracy," *Forbes*, November 10, 2020.
380 Project Veritas, "USPS Whistleblower Richard Hopkins: 'I DID NOT RECANT,'" November 10, 2020, YouTube video, 0:46.
381 Letter from Stephanie Hetrick to Richard Hopkins, provided to Project Veritas by Richard Hopkins, November 10, 2020.

Veritas team was working on the numerous tips they had received from people who were alleging voter fraud when a Twitter notification popped up. The House Democrat Oversight Committee (@OversightDems) had sent out the following release:

> BREAKING NEWS: Erie, Pa. #USPS whistleblower completely RECANTED his allegations of a supervisor tampering with mail-in ballots after being questioned by investigators, according to IG.
>
> THREAD:
>
> Here are the facts: Richard Hopkins is a USPS employee in Erie, PA. He signed a sworn affidavit with allegations of ballot tampering/fraud and went public through Project Veritas.
>
> #USPS IG began investigating last week.
>
> #USPS IG investigators informed Committee staff today that they interviewed Hopkins on Friday, but that Hopkins RECANTED HIS ALLEGATIONS yesterday and did not explain why he signed a false affidavit.[382]

These people were insidious. They had weaseled what they passed off as a recantation out of Hopkins and then used that as a pretext to claim that his allegedly false witness had been "injurious to self or others." Project Veritas phones started buzzing with calls and messages from people asking what was going on. The White House chief of staff Mark Meadows even called in. It was chaos!

A quickly assembled Veritas team tackled this crisis head on. With the House Oversight Committee attacking this muckraker's credibility and White House officials raising questions, Veritas had to go on the offense immediately. This muckraker has learned one lesson time and again: when the truth is on your side, you don't back down.

The situation was about to become even more ominous. The *Washington Post* had just published an article headlined, "Postal worker recanted allegations of ballot tampering, officials say."[383] This was rich. The *Post* re-

382 @OversightDems, Twitter, November 10, 2020.
383 Sean Boburg and Jacob Bogage, "Postal worker recanted allegations of ballot tampering, officials say," *the Washington Post*, November 10, 2020.

fused to cover Hopkins's story when it broke. Apparently, the story only became newsworthy when it appeared to strengthen the fantasy that Biden won the election cleanly. This wasn't news. This was propaganda.

One passage in the Tuesday, November 10th, *Post* article revealed how the forces had aligned to humiliate Hopkins and thwart the truth: "Hopkins, 32, told investigators from the US Postal Service's Office of Inspector General that the allegations were not true, and he signed an affidavit recanting his claims, according to officials who spoke on the condition of anonymity to describe an ongoing investigation."[384]

"Officials who spoke on the condition of anonymity"? The only people in the room were the agents that Hopkins recorded, Strasser and Klein. Having listened to the recording, the Veritas team had much better insight into what actually happened than did the *Post*. Something really big was going on here. This orchestrated move by postal agents, the media, and Democrats in Congress confirmed everyone's worst fears. On full view was an unprecedented nexus among establishment forces. Working together, they had sabotaged an honest whistleblower and, by extension, an honest election.

The muckraker asked Hopkins to record a short video debunking the lies from the *Washington Post* while reaffirming that he stood by his original affidavit.[385] The video went viral on social media that very night and was tweeted out by President Trump himself.[386] The "journalists" behind the *Post*'s hit piece were Shawn Boburg and Jacob Bogage. CNN's Anderson Cooper invited the twenty-something Bogage on to his show as this drama was unfolding.[387] The November 11th interview should be placed in a time capsule to show just how corrupt journalism had become in the twenty-first century.

### THIS ORCHESTRATED MOVE BY POSTAL AGENTS, THE MEDIA, AND DEMOCRATS IN CONGRESS CONFIRMED EVERYONE'S WORST FEARS.

384 Boburg and Bogage, "Postal worker recanted."
385 Project Veritas, "USPS Whistleblower Richard Hopkins: "I DID NOT RECANT."
386 Geoff Earle, "Mailman who Donald Trump called 'a patriot' for claiming he heard possible election fraud told Postal Inspectors 'I didn't hear the whole story - my mind probably added the rest," *Daily Mail*, November 11, 2020.
387 Meredith Digital Staff, "Report: Postal worker recants claim of ballot-tampering," WFSB, November 11, 2020.

To begin, Bogage told Cooper that his writing partner, Boburg, "got a tip" that Hopkins had walked back his testimony.[388] That tip had to come Boburg's way immediately after Hopkins's interview on November 9th. The *Post* article was published November 10th based on what Bogage called "a combination of Postal sources and sources in Congress."[389] Bogage did not name these sources. He simply referred to them as "credible" multiple times, as though his saying "credible" would make them so. He had no document in hand, no evidence, just the word of the "credible sources," all of which had a powerful interest in seeing Hopkins discredited and Biden certified as president.

In addition to Hopkins's original affidavit, Project Veritas had recordings of multiple conversations with the man himself, including one in which he denied that he had recanted anything. Just as importantly, this muckraker had an audio copy of the postal inspector's Stasi-like interrogation of Hopkins. Bogage implied that none of this evidence ought to be taken seriously, as Project Veritas was no more than "a right-wing group that has tried to run sting operations against credible journalists and catch them in errors."[390] He had the nerve to use air quotes around "sting operations" to further diminish Project Veritas' credibility. It should be noted, too, that in media circles, "right-wing" is a synonym for journalists who try to report the truth.

For Bogage, at least, the comic highlight of this story came after he conceded that Hopkins had denied that he recanted anything. Hopkins's denial was not to be taken seriously, suggested Bogage, for one reason: "We also know through credible sources that he did the exact opposite with Inspector General agents."[391] For the record, Hopkins did not speak with an inspector general. He spoke with agents Strasser and Klein, neither of whom Bogage named.

There was something truly sad about Bogage's puffery about being a "credible journalist" with "credible sources." When it comes to journalistic credibility, Project Veritas has never settled a single slander or defamation lawsuit in its history. Can CNN or the *Washington Post* say the same? Didn't both of them have to settle lawsuits with Covington High School student Nick Sandmann for defaming him as a racist after the 2019 March for Life? Do these headlines ring a bell?

388 James O'Keefe, "#MailFraud," November 11, 2020, Facebook video, 3:19.
389 James O'Keefe, "#MailFraud."
390 Meredith Digital Staff, "Report: Postal worker recants."
391 Meredith Digital Staff, "Report: Postal worker recants."

"*Washington Post* settles lawsuit with family of Kentucky teenager"[392]

"CNN settles lawsuit with Nick Sandmann stemming from viral video controversy"[393]

The *Post* captioned the photo accompanying the article by Bogage and Boburg, "Despite being short staffed, overworked and receiving criticism from the president, poll officials were transparent throughout the process."[394] Like so much election coverage, this blanket statement was pure unverified propaganda. The article had nothing to do with "poll officials" and everything to do with postal inspectors who were not transparent at all. This one incident proved as much. Instead of all the subterfuge, Strasser might as well have just sat down with Bogage and dictated the story. The *Post* article was stenography at its finest.

Agent Strasser did not go to Erie to investigate the very real allegations of voter fraud; he admitted his motive was to "harness that storm and try to reel it back in before it gets really crazy." The very fact that the *Post* and the House Oversight Committee were able to leak information about Hopkins's interrogation before Hopkins ever saw the document he signed proves as much. Strasser was their operative, the *Post* their medium, and the House Oversight Committee their executioner. The fact that the *Post* reported on Hopkins's alleged recantation just one day after his interview suggests this coordination was approved, if not ordered, on high.

Things began to change for the powers that be when Project Veritas announced it was going to publish the full and unedited raw audio of Strasser's interrogation of Richard Hopkins. The muckraker also sat with Hopkins for an interview after he had been interrogated, in which he opened up about his ordeal. "They were grilling the hell out of me. I feel like I just got played," said the emotionally wracked Hopkins.

"I'm just doing my duty," he said when asked why he had come forward. "I honestly made an oath when I joined the Marine Corps from the get-go, and as most military guys say, it's a blank check. We never give up that check. We're going to protect our country and our Consti-

392 Paul Farhi, "Washington Post settles lawsuit with family of Kentucky teenager," *Washington Post*, July 24, 2020.
393 Oliver Darcy, "CNN settles lawsuit with Nick Sandmann stemming from viral video controversy." CNN Business, January 7, 2020.
394 Boburg and Bogage, "Postal worker recanted."

tution until the day we die. That's the point where that check is cashed in. And I've given that check and my heart to this country." More sobering still, Hopkins said he would "rather be out back in Afghanistan, getting shot at by Afghans, honest to God, than you know, having to be in this kind of position."[395] Like many whistleblowers before him, Hopkins was shocked to see up close just how corrupt were so many of the institutions in which he had previously put his faith.

Project Veritas published this interview along with the full raw audio of Hopkins being interrogated by Strasser. This evidence quickly put the mainstream media in panic mode. In an attempt to salvage their original lie, Bogage and his *Post* accomplices published a second article based on the audio that Project Veritas had posted online. Headlined, "Audio recording shows Pa. postal worker recanting ballot-tampering claim,"[396] the article doubled down on the "recanting" lie. To sell it, though, the three reporters had to avoid the most newsworthy element of the recording—Strasser's crude intimidation tactics. While establishment media wholeheartedly ignored the agent's methods, they did not go unnoticed by political commentator Mike Cernovich, who tweeted:

> Holy f*ck, this is an interrogation technique where the federal agent tries to use stress tactics to implant a false memory into the interview subject. You rarely get stuff like this on audio.[397]

Strasser had obviously received interrogation training, either in the Air Force or as a federal law enforcement officer. He used the "mild" variant of a technique called "Fear Up," the harsh variant of which is the technique often shown in TV cop shows: a detective screams at the suspect, pounds the table, and tells him he is going to fry in the electric chair if he doesn't fess up.

### HOPKINS SAID HE WOULD "RATHER BE OUT BACK IN AFGHANISTAN, GETTING SHOT AT BY AFGHANS, HONEST TO GOD, THAN YOU KNOW, HAVING TO BE IN THIS KIND OF POSITION."

---

395 Project Veritas, "USPS Whistleblower Richard Hopkins Gives New Interview Detailing Coercion Tactics Used By Fed Agents," November 11, 2020, YouTube video, 7:02.

396 Shawn Boburg, Jacob Bogage, and Dalton Bennett, "Audio recording shows Pa. postal worker recanting ballot-tampering claim," *Washington Post*, November 11, 2020.

397 @Cernovich, Twitter, November 10, 2020.

Fear Up Harsh is tough stuff, but it is really for beginners. The seasoned interrogator, such as Strasser, uses the Fear Up Mild approach. His attempt to mentally strong-arm Hopkins into capitulating was pure textbook. Intelligence manuals describe this approach as "a more correct form of blackmail when the circumstances indicate that the source does indeed have something to fear."[398] What Hopkins had to fear was losing his job. "The actual fear is increased," reads the manual, "by helping the source to realize the unpleasant consequences that the facts may cause and then presenting an alternative, which of course can be effected by answering some simple questions."[399] Once the target is fearful and disoriented, the interrogator offers the target a path to safety. In this case, Strasser told Hopkins that path was to "update his statement."[400]

When you hear Strasser, you hear a master manipulator at work. He praised Hopkins. He told Hopkins they shared a sense of duty from military service. All the while, he planted the seeds of confusion, doubt, anxiety, and finally fear. In the very beginning, Strasser told Hopkins he was under no obligation to stay, but at the end, when Hopkins asked for a smoke break, Strasser only allowed him to leave if he promised to speak to no one. After Hopkins agreed, Strasser had his agent partner tag along to escort him the whole time he was outside the bubble.

In contemporary America, the alternative media still have enough power to make the permanent administrative government at least appear to honor the United States Constitution. Several of the remaining honest journalists in the media started to pick up on the truth of what had happened to Hopkins. They were fascinated by the raw audio. There are very, very few audio recordings available of an actual federal agent aggressively interrogating a regular American for telling an inconvenient truth. It was not intended, but in a small way, the Hopkins release also exposed how the federal government treats a whistleblower. It was on tape, and it was undeniable. The *Washington Post* acknowledged its existence without, of course, admitting its implicit evil.

The *New York Post* saw things more clearly. Columnist Miranda Devine wrote a piece headlined, "FBI's failures to protect patriotic whistleblowers, then and now."[401] Devine explained how Hopkins was run through much the same gauntlet as Richard Jewell, the man who saved numerous lives from a bomb explosion during the 1996 Atlanta Olym-

---

398 "Appendix H: Approaches," Intelligence, GlobalSecurity.org, page last updated April 26, 2005.
399 Intelligence, GlobalSecurity.org.
400 Project Veritas, "Hopkins Gives New Interview Detailing Coercion Tactics."
401 Miranda Devine, "FBI's failures to protect patriotic whistleblowers, then and now," *New York Post*, November 11, 2020.

pics. Both Hopkins and Jewell trusted the authorities who interrogated them, and those same authorities would later leak lies to the media that would crush their respective reputations.[402]

Most importantly, the *Washington Post* and its allies lost control over this story. They thought their propaganda would be effective in quashing Hopkins, but they underestimated the power of *veritas*, truth. One can only imagine the lies the media would be publishing today about Hopkins if the interrogation recording did not exist. This was a lesson Project Veritas learned a long time ago: against foes as powerful as Big Media and Big Tech, the only way to be believed is through audio or video evidence. If it is your word against theirs, you're almost certainly doomed.

The hero of the story, of course, is Richard Hopkins. He had the courage to come forward with his story and the resourcefulness to tape the interview. Unlike so many of his fellow citizens, he has an inner strength and integrity that cannot be coerced away. He will always be a free man.

---

402 Kevin Sack, "Richard Jewell, 44, Hero of Atlanta Attack, Dies," *New York Times*, August 30, 2007.

# CHAPTER 6
# INSIDERS

## WORKS CITED

Alford, C. Fred. *Whistleblowers: Broken Lives and Organizational Power*. Ithaca and London: Cornell University Press, 2001.

Bok, Sissela. *Secrets: On the Ethics of Concealment and Revelation*. New York: Random House, 1989.

Boorstin, Daniel J. *The Image: A Guide to Pseudo-Events in America*. New York: Vintage, 2012.

Devine, Tom and Tarek Maassarani. *The Corporate Whistleblower's Survival Guide: A Handbook for Committing the Truth*. San Francisco: Berrett-Koehler Publishers, 2011.

Dygert, James H. *The Investigative Journalist: Folk Heroes of a New Era*. Hoboken: Prentice-Hall, 1976.

Ettema, James S. and Theodore L. Glasser. *Custodians of Conscience: Investigative Journalism and Public Virtue*. New York: Columbia University Press, 1998.

Johnson, Roberta Ann. *Whistleblowing: When it Works – and Why*. Boulder: Lynne Rienner Publishers, 2003).

Orwell, George. *1984*. New York: Signet Classics, 1950.

Solzhenitsyn, Aleksandr. *The Gulag Archipelago 1918-1956 An Experiment in Literary Investigation*. Translated by Thomas P. Whitney and Harry Willets. Abridged by Edward E. Ericson, Jr. New York: HarperCollins Publishers, 2007.

Solzhenitsyn, Aleksandr. *The Gulag Archipelago*, Volume 2. New York: Harper Perennial Modern Classics, 2007.

Taibbi, Matt. *Hate Inc.: Why Today's Media Makes Us Despise One Another*. New York: OR Books, 2019.

## JOURNAL ARTICLES

Alford, C. Fred. "Whistle-Blower Narratives: The Experience of Choiceless Choice." *Social Research* 74, no. 1 (2007).

# CHAPTER 7
# PRIVACY

*People committing malfeasance don't have any right to privacy... What are we saying - that Upton Sinclair shouldn't have smuggled his pencil in?*[403]

-Don Hewitt, CBS Executive Producer, *60 Minutes*

P roject Veritas reporters, like all honest muckrakers, work to expose the "human suffering hidden behind systemic failures."[404] It is very nearly impossible to expose this suffering without some collateral damage, especially to the privacy of the individuals responsible for the suffering. On this point all agree, but beyond this there is little in the way of consensus.

## THE TRUER IT IS, THE WORSE IT GETS

Said one observant military intelligence expert, "The less important the end to be desired, however, the more one can afford to engage in an ethical evaluation of the means."[405] By extension, when there is total consensus on the importance of the findings, there is very little debate about the harm done to an individual target. Assessing both harm and importance is inevitably subjective. The ethical judgment of the means used hinges on the politics of those doing the judging.

Often overlooked in the debate about the means used to gain access to a conversation is the *truthfulness* of the content. It is the power of the revelations on the video that makes people uncomfortable. The people who are harmed are victims of *telling the truth*. As Al Pacino, playing indignant CBS producer Lowell Bergman in the film *The Insider*, states, "Are we going to air it? Of course not. Why? Because he's not telling the truth? No. Because he is telling the truth. That's why we're not going to air it, and the more truth he tells, the worst it gets."[406]

403 Russ Baker, "Truth, Lies, and Videotape: 'PrimeTime Live' and the Hidden Camera," *Columbia Journalism Review* 32, no. 2 (July-August 1993): 27.
404 James Ettema, "Trying to stir public awareness," *The IRE Journal* (Summer 1989): 16.
405 Lieutenant Colonel Earl J. Boyce, "Dear Editor," *Military Intelligence: From the Home of Intelligence* 12, no. 4 (October-December 1986): 5.
406 *The Insider*, directed by Michael Mann, Touchstone Pictures, 1999.

Philip Meyer addresses this reality in *Ethical Journalism*: "A tape recorder's evidence is not easily denied...perhaps it is its *power* that makes some journalists uncomfortable?"[407] Meyer posits that discomfort is the "precise, immediate and incontestable" evidence itself, the inability for the source who is taped to lie in the future about what *has* occurred.

Because the "function of a tape recorder is to eliminate all doubt about what a person said,"[408] journalists no longer have the ability to give the subject *a way out*. Before the advent of recording devices, a favored president like FDR might simply deny that he was ever blasphemous, that he might ever say something such as, "This goddammed thing doesn't work."[409] Indulgent reporters may have thought that there was an immorality in *not* allowing the subject to lie. Raw truth shatters agendas. As Hunter S. Thompson neatly phrased it, "Absolute truth is a very rare and dangerous commodity in the context of professional journalism."[410]

In a 1997 ruling, an associate appeals court justice wrote of an unvarnished videotaped conversation: "These images gave a heft to defendants' broadcast that would otherwise have been lacking, just as they led to far greater embarrassment and distress for the plaintiff than he otherwise would have suffered."[411] As the judge suggested, to have written about the incident would have been less accurate than to have taped it.

## THE HIDDEN CAMERA AS AN EXTENSION OF MAN

Recording devices, argues Diane Leenheer Zimmerman in her book, *I Spy: The Newsgatherer Under Cover*, are "more than just sophisticated note-taking equipment. Their use can provide the press with content that can be communicated directly to the public." The ability to transmit directly, Zimmerman contends, "further complicates the question of whether video and audio recording ought to be treated as forms of speech activity or instead ancillary behaviors."[412] A Michigan appeals court argued in a 1982 case, "A recording made by a participant is nothing more than a more accurate record of what was said."[413]

---

407 Philip Meyer, *Ethical Journalism: A Guide for Students, Practitioners, and Consumers*, (Harlow: Longman, 1987).
408 Steven Perry, *Communications Lawyer* 14, no. 3 (Fall 1996): 20.
409 David Halberstam, *The Powers That Be* (Champaign: University of Illinois Press, 2000), 6.
410 "Hunter S. Thompson: in his own words; a selection of the best-remembered quotes from the master of the one-liner," *The Guardian*, February 21, 2005.
411 Sanders v. American Broadcasting Companies, Inc., 2d B094245 (Cal. Ct. App. 1997).
412 Diane L. Zimmerman, "I Spy: The Newsgatherer Under Cover," 33 *University of Richmond Law Review* 1185 (2000).
413 Sullivan v. Gray, 117 Mich. App. 476, 324 N.W.2d 58 (Mich. Ct. App. 1982).

The ability to record something is closely connected to the ability to write and speak. Legal scholar Laurence Tribe has argued that the public's right to know "means nothing more than a mirror of such a right to speak, a listener's right that government not interfere with a willing speaker's liberty."[414]

Few of the arguments made against the use of a recording device seem to involve *privacy*, but rather some mysterious notion about *dignity*. For instance, in a 1971 case involving two *Life* magazine reporters going undercover into a doctor's office, the judge ruled that to allow such reporting "could have a most pernicious effect on the dignity of man and it would surely lead to guarded conversations and conduct where candor is most valued."[415] In another case, a California judge said videotaping deprives a speaker of the "right to control the extent of his own firsthand dissemination."[416] This argument has been made in regard to just about every recording device, including the camera. To photograph people, writes Susan Sontag, "is to violate them, by seeing them as they never see themselves, by having knowledge of them they can never have; it turns people into objects that can be symbolically possessed."[417]

In evaluating the ethics of recording people in one-party consent scenarios, it's important to remember people may not know they are being recorded, but they do know they are being spoken to. Even in the most elaborate sting operations of a nongovernmental entity, as was the case with David Daleiden's sting of Planned Parenthood, staffers divulged information to people they scarcely knew.

Individuals are free to interact or not with other people as they see fit. People sitting at bars should observe the commonsense notion that what they say could easily be retold to countless others by any number of means. Whether at a bar or elsewhere, members of any given organization should be urged toward discretion. As a matter of course, the organization should instruct its members to be careful about those with whom they share sensitive information. No rules or laws can mandate discretion. An enlightened citizenry that practices basic concepts of self-governance should do the trick.

---

414 Sissela Bok, *Secrets: On the Ethics of Concealment and Revelation* (New York: Random House, 1989), 255.
415 Desnick v. American Broadcasting Companies, Inc., 44 F.3d 1345, 1995 U.S. App. 23 Media L. Rep. 1161.
416 Martinez v. Holmes, 4d E002917-AO (Cal. Ct. App. 1986).
417 Susan Sontag, *On Photography* (New York: Picador, 1977), 14.

### *THE PUBLIC'S RIGHT TO KNOW "MEANS NOTHING MORE THAN A MIRROR OF SUCH A RIGHT TO SPEAK, A LISTENER'S RIGHT THAT GOVERNMENT NOT INTERFERE WITH A WILLING SPEAKER'S LIBERTY."*

---

## WHAT IS "PRIVACY"?

In their famed 1890 *Harvard Law Review* article, Louis Brandeis and Samuel Warren invented a "right to privacy," broadly defined in the legal sense as "the right to be left alone." Publishing information that is "not of legitimate concern" qualifies, from their perspective, as a tort of intrusion. The two students continue, "The Press…is overstepping in every direction the obvious bounds of privacy and dignity." That said, they acknowledge that, "the right of privacy does not prohibit any publication of matter which is of public or general interest."[418]

To this day, however, the right to privacy remains amorphous, and few can agree on exactly what it means. First Amendment scholar Rodney Smolla argues broadly: "Laws protecting privacy are the means through which the collective acknowledges rules of civility that are designed to affirm human autonomy and dignity."[419] More specifically, MIT professor emeritus Gary Marx observes that undercover investigations impinge on people's freedom "to express themselves without suspiciousness or fear of others' ulterior motives."[420]

In that many covertly recorded exchanges take place in public settings, most discussions about the ethics of undercover work are not actually about privacy per se. Rather, they tend to focus on the individual's "ability to control information about the self."[421] This urge to manage one's self-image comes into direct conflict with the First Amendment. The argument states that covert reporting, or even overt reporting, in which the reporters fail to identify themselves—the *Washington Post*'s Pulitzer Prize winning story on Walter Reed Medical Center comes to mind—betrays primary relationships. Going well beyond mere betrayal, Gary Marx describes the seduction involved in covert operations as "the moral equivalent of rape because they both deny the dignity of the freedom of the individual."[422]

---

418 Samuel D. Warren and Louis D. Brandeis, "The Right to Privacy," *Harvard Law Review* 4, no. 5 (December 15, 1890): 193–220.

419 Rodney A. Smolla, *Free Speech in an Open Society* (New York: Vintage Books, 1992), 199.

420 Gary Marx, "Under-the-Covers Undercover Investigations: Some Reflections on the State's Use of Sex and Deception in Law Enforcement," 1999 revision of article in *Criminal Justice Ethics* 11, no. 1 (Winter/Spring 1992): 13–24.

421 Gary Marx, "Privacy and Technology," *Telektronik* (January 1996).

422 Marx, "Under-the-Covers Undercover Investigations," 13.

## THE CONSENT OF SPEAKING

As the experienced muckraker understands, the appropriate metaphor here is not rape, but consensual sex. That understanding, however, does not prevent the target from crying "rape." Consider the case of Passaic, New Jersey, schoolteacher Alissa Ploshnick. A Project Veritas reporter caught up with Ms. Ploshnick at a bar during a taxpayer-funded teachers' union bash. Boasting of her union's power, Ploshnick told the reporter, "It's impossible to fire a teacher. We had a case just recently, like someone said, 'you n\*\*ger!' The teacher has been demoted, and he is still teaching."[423] When Project Veritas went public with the tape, the state's leading newspaper, the *Star Ledger*, headlined the story, "Heroic N.J. teacher was sacrificed for political cause in hidden video," Ploshnick told the sympathetic reporter, "I felt like I was raped."[424]

In reporting on the incident, CNN's Anderson Cooper, in a segment ironically called "Keeping Them Honest," deflected from the broken tenure system and focused instead on Project Veritas's effort to keep the New Jersey Education Association honest. Cooper did say of Ploshnick, "She said some things [she] probably shouldn't have," but pivoted quickly to the supposed harm done to Ploshnick. "Civil libertarians would say this is a massive invasion of her privacy," said Cooper with a straight face. He ended the segment reporting that Ploshnick was considering legal action against the muckraker "for stalking and harassment."[425]

Cooper was all wrong. There is no civil right that protects someone like Ploshnick from having her open statement at a public bar reported. The right to record Ploshnick, explained further in the Privacy Chapter, is a First Amendment right that is closely tied to the listener's right to repeat what they have heard. Although there are a dozen states that prohibit secretly recording another, there is almost a universal exception when there is no expectation of privacy, and others nearby can overhear the conversation. Her urge to control her self-image comes into direct conflict with the rights of the stranger with whom she spoke. The muckraker possesses the right to speak his own mind as to what he heard. Neither was the muckraker reviewing written notes, nor reciting a recollection in newsprint. Their public experience was recorded with both audio and video.

423 Project Veritas, "Teachers Union Gone Wild–Volume I," October 25, 2010, YouTube video, 4:59.

424 Bob Braun, "Heroic N.J. teacher was sacrificed for political cause in hidden video," NJ.com, November 14, 2010.

425 Anderson Cooper, "Landmark Terror Trial; Palin Considering White House Run; Great Apes Raised with Language," *Anderson Cooper 360 Degrees* transcript, CNN, November 17, 2010.

It is one of the great ironies of the journalistic profession that reporters in the major media almost unilaterally argue *against* First Amendment rights in cases such as these. Nor is the phenomenon limited to the twenty-first century. The *Star-Ledger*, CNN, and the exposed teacher may think of the muckraker as a "rapist," but a century ago, Upton Sinclair was called worse. Not one to shirk a fight, Sinclair had a sexual metaphor of his own to describe the supine establishment reporters of his day. Writes Sinclair in *The Brass Check*, "The world lies just before you, and the gates to it are barred only by ignorance and prejudice, deliberately created and maintained by prostitute journalism."[426]

Schoolteachers are not the only Project Veritas subjects who have cried "rape." Lauren Windsor, an associate of Democratic dirty trickster Bob Creamer, was exposed by Project Veritas during the 2016 campaign. Creamer's operation, Democracy Partners, had contracted directly with Hillary Clinton and the Democratic National Committee in 2016 to incite violence at Trump rallies through a practice called "bird-dogging." Creamer sued Project Veritas for "trespass."[427] The lawsuit did not challenge the truthfulness of what was presented in the Project Veritas videos. Instead, Democracy Partners claimed that the Project Veritas journalist involved in the investigation, Allison Maass, broke laws while newsgathering.

As Windsor told Gizmodo, "A lot of people have described the experience [of being secretly captured on video] to me like psychological rape...they're destroying lives." Windsor supposedly heard from these "people" through a series of coordinated lawsuits launched after she helped encourage those "psychological rape victims" to sue Project Veritas.[428] One irony, of course, is that the plaintiffs, allegedly concerned about the invasion of their privacy, pursued actions that would bring them even more publicity through a lawsuit.

An even greater irony is that Windsor participated in an unseemly verbal "Gotcha, bitch" assault on the brave PV journalist Allison Maass, whose undercover work exposed the mischief of Windsor's associate Creamer. In the course of a Creamer lawsuit, Windsor herself was deposed.[429]

---

426 Upton Sinclair, *The Brass Check: A Study of American Journalism; Evidence and Reasons Behind the Media's Corruption* (Adansonia Press, First Published in 1919), 311.
427 Democracy Partners, et al. v. Project Veritas Action Fund, et al., United States District Court (D. D.C.), Civil No. 17-CV-1047; Memorandum Opinion - March 31, 2020 (19–21).
428 Project Veritas, "Dem Operative in Lawsuit Deposition Answer for "Gotcha B*tch" Attack & Their Selective Editing," April 15, 2020, YouTube video, 9:59.
429 Project Veritas, "Dem Operative in Lawsuit Deposition."

In the full video that Windsor's associates shot, she and partner Ryan Clayton can be seen screaming profanities at Maass on a Washington sidewalk. As Maass attempts to get in a cab to leave the scene, Clayton continues to follow her into the vehicle. Maass was only able to find safe refuge when entering the lobby of a hotel. Following this incident, Windsor and Clayton went on to publish only parts of the encounter to construct a false narrative about what took place. In one of the depositions in this lawsuit, Windsor was questioned about her behavior toward Maass. Depositions are useful tools. Under oath, Windsor had to admit she doctored the video. What follows is the exchange between the attorney for Project Veritas Action (PVA), Paul Calli, and Windsor:

> **PVA:** So, you edited out these parts where, these first two parts where you and Mr. Clayton were confronting Ms. Maass? You didn't include those?

> **Windsor:** I object to your characterization of my actions.

> **PVA:** Okay. You're not a lawyer so your lawyer is here, and he'll object for you so what I am asking you is…

> **Windsor:** Well, I disagree with your characterization of my actions.

> **PVA:** Which part? Which part?

> **Windsor:** That I edited anything out.

> **PVA:** Oh, okay. So, what did you do that these parts didn't make the video?

> **Windsor:** Well, so, it's called editing. And it's what your client engages in when he makes videos.

> **PVA:** Okay, same exhibit. (*Plays Clayton clip*) Is that Mr. Clayton again?

**Windsor:** It is.

**PVA:** And just play to 9:26, please. (*Plays clip*) Did those last two statements make your published final version of this confrontation with Ms. Maass?

**Windsor:** I don't believe so.

**PVA:** Why not?

**Windsor:** We chose not to publish any video from that.

**PVA:** Why not?

**Windsor:** Because it wasn't necessary in the narrative that we were trying to produce.[430]

## *"OH, OKAY. SO, WHAT DID YOU DO THAT THESE PARTS DIDN'T MAKE THE VIDEO?"*

---

## *"WELL, SO, IT'S CALLED EDITING."*

---

While investigating Democracy Partners, Allison Maass was following a proud muckraking tradition of undercover journalists who expose corruption wherever found. It took true courage for Maass to infiltrate Democracy Partners and uncover the malfeasance orchestrated by that organization. True to form, Windsor and her associates freely resorted to the deceptive editing tactics that Project Veritas is routinely, and falsely, accused of deploying. This is what happens when Project Veritas deposes someone who thinks they're too smart to get caught. Oh, by the way, Creamer's accusation of "trespass" was thrown out of court before trial.

430 Democracy Partners, et al. v. Project Veritas Action Fund, et al.

## ONE-PARTY CONSENT RECORDINGS AND HARM

In gathering truthful information in the course of his duties, the muckraker will affect certain individuals in a negative way. In pursuing the greater good—namely, the public's right to know—this is almost inevitable. As former *Washington Post* editor Leonard Downie writes in *The New Muckrakers*, "The investigative reporter must face the fact that his stories will hurt people."[431]

What must never be forgotten, however, is that, in a democratic republic, protecting the people's right to know is necessary if citizens are to make informed decisions. Without the ability to make such decisions, the public is vulnerable to the wiles of those who control the information flow. Our Founding Fathers did not draft the First Amendment to benefit publishers, but to preserve democracy and ensure liberty. An informed populace is as necessary today for the intelligent exercise of democratic rights and duties as it was then.

The journalist must find a balance between the very real importance of the information to be shared and the potential harm done to an individual. Until the early twentieth century, this balancing act was largely limited to the printed word. Radio broadcasts became commonplace in the 1920s and the television became the living room's centerpiece by the late 1950s. Each medium introduced a new level of immediacy. The advent of hidden camera technology and internet-connected desktop computers in the dawning of the twenty-first century democratized the ability to transmit information about anyone or anything instantly. In this brave new world, with a brand-new genre, finding a balance became all the more difficult but all the more imperative.

*IN A DEMOCRATIC REPUBLIC, PROTECTING THE PEOPLE'S RIGHT TO KNOW IS NECESSARY IF CITIZENS ARE TO MAKE INFORMED DECISIONS.*

In one-party consent scenarios, the muckraker has to evaluate the methods of recording people. He must set aside the assumption that critiques of his work are about his methods. In reality, they will be about his *findings*. As Alinsky notes, "The less important the end that is desired

---

431 Leonard Downie, *The New Muckrakers: An Inside Look at America's Investigative Reporters* (Washington: New Republic Book Company, 1976), 12.

the more one can engage in ethical evaluations of the means."[432] When there is total consensus on the importance of the findings, there is no debate about harm. Then, too, the judgment on the ethics of means depends upon the political positions of those judging. However, in real life situations, he assesses not so much the *falsity* of the means of deception so much as the *truthfulness* of the information acquired. It is not really the means that worries the subjects of an investigation and their allies. It is the power of audio and video and the revelations that make them uncomfortable. The subjects in question are harmed only by *telling the truth* about themselves.

In a world where CNN is streamed at airports, in a world where CNN has the power to intimidate all three branches of government, CNN's Patrick Davis became an unwitting whistleblower. He told a colleague on camera, "I hate seeing what we were and what we could be and what we've become." Davis had a good job. He had children. His income from CNN supported his mortgage. So why didn't the muckraker protect his identity and obscure his face? The muckraker made the utilitarian decision that the benefit of the information shared is greater than the harm done to the one who unknowingly shared it. Although he might have had an awkward time of it at work, Davis had no reason to be embarrassed by what he said.

"A tape recorder's evidence is not easily denied," writes Philip Meyer in *Ethical Journalism*. This power denies the person who has been taped the ability to lie in the future about what *has*, in fact, occurred.[433] The argument contends that journalists ought to give the subject *a way out*, that there is an immorality in not allowing that subject to lie. In a successful 1997 appeal brought by ABC, the court spoke to the power of videotape in capturing the words and gestures of the subject being taped: "These images gave a heft to defendants' broadcast that would otherwise have been lacking, just as they led to far greater embarrassment and distress for plaintiff than he otherwise would have suffered."[434]

The media would not have been as quick in their attacks on Project Veritas had they consulted with journalism scholars such as Theodore L Glasser. Glasser has vigorously defended the use of the concealed tape recorder:

---

432 Saul D. Alinsky, *Rules for Radicals* (New York: Random House, 1971), 34.
433 Meyer, *Ethical Journalism*, 82.
434 Sanders v. American Broadcasting Companies, Inc.

The use of a concealed tape recorder, at least when one party is present, is not nearly the moral quandary its opponents would have us believe: it is not an invasion of privacy, it is not an act of deception, it is not a form of eavesdropping, and it does not constitute entrapment.[435]

## THIS POWER DENIES THE PERSON WHO HAS BEEN TAPED THE ABILITY TO LIE IN THE FUTURE ABOUT WHAT HAS, IN FACT, OCCURRED.

Indeed, writes Glasser, "Recording Devices are just sophisticated note-taking equipment. This latter reason to use recording devices further complicates the question of whether video and audio recording ought to be treated as forms of speech activity or instead ancillary behaviors."[436]

Such recording techniques have their critics. The attorneys for A. A. Dietemann in his case against Time, Inc. argued that undercover journalism "could have a most pernicious effect on the dignity of man and it would surely lead to guarded conversations and conduct where candor is most valued."[437] Among the more interesting legal ramifications of the 1994 murders of Ronald Goldman and Nicole Brown Simpson was the civil case *Beverly Deteresa v. American Broadcasting Companies, Inc.* Deteresa was an American Airlines flight attendant who worked the flight on which O. J. Simpson departed Los Angeles for Chicago. Without her consent, an ABC producer secretly recorded a conversation he had with Deteresa while a colleague discreetly videotaped the interaction from afar. Although Deteresa proved unwilling to speak on the record, the producer identified himself and had a genuinely pleasant exchange with the woman.

In a split decision, a panel of the Ninth Circuit Court of Appeals sided with ABC, arguing that Deteresa had no reasonable expectation that a conversation with a journalist would be kept confidential. A dissenting judge, however, insisted that the speaker, not the journalist doing the recording, should have the "right to control the extent of his own firsthand dissemination."[438]

---

435 Theodore Glasser, "On the Morality of Secretly Taped Interviews," *Nieman Reports* 39, no. 1 (Spring 1985): 19.
436 Glasser, "On the Morality of Secretly Taped Interviews."
437 Dietemann v. Time, Incorporated, 284 F. Supp. 925 (C.D. Cal. 1968).
438 Deteresa v. American Broadcasting Companies, Inc, No. 95-56748, 9d U.S. App. 1997.

# "ANY EFFECTIVE MEANS IS AUTOMATICALLY JUDGED BY THE OPPOSITION AS BEING UNETHICAL."

The unanswered question, though, was how does hidden camera footage "damage" or "hurt" someone? Why is the truth more harmful than a less accurate version of the events in question? Had the ABC producer been taking written notes, even mental notes, rather than recording Deteresa, why would that have been more acceptable? Although many critics object to a surreptitious taping only when it works against their candidate or cause, some critics seem motivated more by dissatisfaction with the truth rather than with the findings or with the methodology of newsgathering.

Just as the telephone and the telegraph aroused critics jealous of their privacy in their day, so, too, does undercover video. As Alinsky noted, "Any effective means is automatically judged by the opposition as being unethical."[439] The muckraker knows from experience, however, that restrictive laws on the use of hidden cameras work almost always to protect the powerful, especially those who have something to hide.

In all such cases, there is a necessary balancing act. In the final analysis, however, the muckraker understands that society places little value on "protecting an individual's reputation, dignity or emotional security from the assaults from true disclosures,"[440] if the truth revealed warrants those assaults. In all of the privacy cases brought against Project Veritas, neither the facts nor the law supported those who had been damaged. The belief that the use of video was more destructive than the taking of notes was proved to be little more than an "emotional response to a new technology."[441]

## THE FREEDOM TO RECORD IS FREEDOM OF SPEECH

The right to record is closely tied to the right to speak, or even to take contemporaneous notes about what one sees and hears. Historically, Americans have treasured freedom of speech above all other freedoms. In the famous "Pentagon Papers" case, *New York Times Co. v. United States*, Justice Hugo Black argued with the majority that "only a free and unrestrained press can effectively expose deception in government."[442]

---

439 Alinsky, *Rules for Radicals*, 35.
440 Diane L. Zimmerman, "Requiem for a Heavyweight: A Farewell to Warren and Brandeis's Privacy Tort," *Cornell Law Review* 68, no. 3, 1983.
441 Meyer, *Ethical Journalism*.
442 The New York Times Company v. The Washington Post Company, 403 U.S. 1971.

What must never be forgotten is that in a democratic republic, government officials are mere agents of the people. Legitimate governments, the Declaration of Independence insists, "deriv[e] their just powers from the consent of the governed."[443] If that consent is lacking, a government has no "just powers." The Declaration's principal author, Thomas Jefferson, stated in a letter to a colleague, "...were it left to me to decide whether we should have a government without newspapers or newspapers without a government, I should not hesitate a moment to prefer the latter."[444]

There is near consensus that an informed populace is necessary for the intelligent exercise of democratic rights and duties. In the sentence following his defense of newspapers, Jefferson added, "But I should mean that every man should receive those papers & be capable of reading them." As Jefferson suggested, the consent must be informed, and *not* manufactured. Indeed, all serious theories of democracy, including the economic theory, hinge on the notion that voters have reliable access to the information that will enable rational decision-making on the basis of self-interest.[445]

What has changed since the days of Jefferson is not ideology so much as technology. The concept of informed consent has evolved from the social contract theory of John Locke, through the originating documents of the Founding Fathers, to the street wisdom of the late Andrew Breitbart, who famously stated, "Politics is downstream from culture."[446] What Breitbart meant was simply that the information people absorb from the media, political and cultural, will sooner or later translate into votes. This concept is one the Big Tech and Big Media cabal understands implicitly, which helps explain why America's most beautiful and stylish First Lady never made it to a magazine cover. Politics, for the ruling elite, is simply public relations.[447]

Throughout the first century and a half of America's existence, dueling political camps warred with print to sway public sentiment, which, as Abraham Lincoln observed, was "everything."[448] The early

443 Thomas Jefferson, *The United States Declaration of Independence*, July 4, 1776.
For more on how the *New York Times* has ignored these issues, see Alexander Meiklejohn, *Political Freedom*, 1961.
444 Thomas Jefferson, "Letter to Edward Carrington," ed. Stephen D. Solomon, FirstAmendmentWatch.org, November 27, 2017.
445 Jason Stanley, *How Propaganda Works* (Princeton: Princeton University Press, 2015), 82.
446 Daniel M. Rothschild, "Policy Is Also Downstream of Culture," *Discourse Magazine*, June 3, 2021.
447 Chris Hedges, *Wages of Rebellion* (New York: Perseus Books Group, 2016), 56.
448 Allen C. Guelzo, "'Public Sentiment Is Everything': Abraham Lincoln and the Power of Public Opinion," Lincoln and Liberty: Wisdom for the Ages, ed. Lucas E. Morel (Lexington: University

great muckrakers—Bly, Sinclair, Tarbell—were all print warriors. They swayed public sentiment.

As technology evolved in the mid-twentieth century, it centralized. By the 1940s, FDR was going to the media rather than to Congress, and he put more energy into his press relations than into his congressional ones.[449] It is well enough known that the power of television fused with that of the federal government by the 1960s. It is not well established that for years, independent muckrakers were forced to contest this enormous broadcast power only with print. With the advent of the internet and enhanced video technology, Project Veritas and others were able to begin to redress this staggering imbalance of power. Not everyone was pleased.

## *"POLITICS IS DOWNSTREAM FROM CULTURE."*

Now exposed to unwelcome audio and visual imagery, opponents demanded "privacy." This argument was disingenuous. In the 2001 case, *Bartnicki v. Vopper*, Justice John Paul Stevens argued that the First Amendment provided protection, even to speech that disclosed the contents of an illegally intercepted communication. Wrote Stevens for the majority: "Exposure of self to others in varying degrees is a concomitant of life in a civilized community. The risk of this exposure is an essential incident of life in a society which places a *primary value* on freedom of speech and the press."[450] A citizen of the United States who chooses to be an active participant in American society cannot simply ignore this "primary value." Among the truths the nation holds to be self-evident are the freedoms of speech and press. Historically, no other country has cherished these values as has America. One cannot wish them away.

The First Amendment makes all rights in our society possible. Supreme Court Justice Stanley Reed affirmed this in the unanimously decided 1946 case *Pennekamp v. Florida*, writing, "Free discussion of the problems of society is a cardinal principle of Americanism."[451] The technology has changed since 1946, but the primacy of free speech has not. Whether it is Upton Sinclair using his pencil or a Project Veritas journalist using a button camera, the muckraker honors a tradition as old as the republic itself.

---

Press of Kentucky, 2014), 171-190.
449 Halberstam, *The Powers That Be*, 13.
450 Bartnicki v. Vopper, 532 U.S. 514 (2001).
451 Pennekamp v. Florida, 328 U.S. 331 (1946).

Nevertheless, as Justice Reed also noted, "Freedom of discussion should be given the widest range compatible with the essential requirement of the fair and orderly administration of justice." To abide by a fair and orderly exercise of the First Amendment, the muckraker must at least try to balance so-called "privacy" concerns with the public interest.

## THE DILEMMA OF RECORDING THE UNWITTING WHISTLEBLOWER

The issue at hand is the recording of "innocent" people working for a corrupt institution. The first question to ask is whether these people are *innocent*. The second is whether the *damage* done to them is actually harmful.

Throughout the twentieth century, investigative reporters typically picked stories highlighting what Ettema and Glasser call the "machinations of villains and the plight of victims."[452] Pam Zekman, preeminent undercover reporter of 1970s for the *Chicago Sun-Times*, echoes that sentiment: "I pick subjects for the villains and heroes."[453] Project Veritas does much the same and, in accordance with law, the recordings are made in public places where the target has no expectation of privacy.

For the muckraker, there are weightier issues than the damage done to an unwitting truth-teller who works for an arguably villainous organization. If the truths revealed in these secretly recorded conversations need to be shared for the sake of the public interest, it would be immoral not to share them. If the individual sharing the truth is "damaged" by that truth, it is likely that a larger damage is being inflicted by the organization trying to conceal it. Much depends upon the particular circumstances, but the muckraker can make some general observations about the legitimacy of his targeting.

### *"I PICK SUBJECTS FOR THE VILLAINS AND HEROES."*

In societies that practice overt propaganda, like modern North Korea and China or the historical Soviet Union and Nazi Germany, the State control is such that leadership can afford to parade truth-tellers and publicly humiliate them. Recall that in *1984*'s Oceania, the "party" exposed Winston's *forbidden diary*. In covert propaganda societies, however, the State has an interest in *not* exposing forbidden diaries or their media equivalent.

452 James S. Ettema and Theodore L. Glasser, "Narrative Form and Moral Force: The Realization of Innocence and Guilt Through Investigative Journalism," *Journal of Communication* 38, no. 3 (Summer 1988).
453 Zay Smith and Pamela Zekman, *The Mirage* (New York: Random House, 1979).

In America, for instance, media titans have seemingly convinced themselves of their own virtue and are unwilling to confess the flaws in their own methodology. Given the symbiotic relationship between Big Media and Big Tech, conventional journalists are hesitant to challenge the prevailing narrative, certainly not in public. Holes in that narrative, however, are not hard to identify. To cast a Project Veritas camera in any random direction within the Big Media/Big Tech empire is to find a story that contradicts the abundance of media lies.

In private, lower ranking employees at Big Tech and Big Media combines are much freer with the truth. In order to highlight the machinations of villains, it becomes necessary to record the truthful statements of nonvillains about the companies and institutions for which they work. In 2019, for instance, CNN insider Cary Poarch recorded the unguarded comments of several of his colleagues about the network that had sadly abandoned its "facts first" mission. Here are a few of them:

> "We could be so much better than what we are."
>
> -Patrick Davis, Manager of Field Operations.

> "They sold themselves to the devil. It's sad."
>
> -Mike Brevna, Floor Manager.

> "We used to cover news. We used to go out and do stories."
>
> -Scott Garber, Senior Field Engineer.[454]

In explaining why he chose to covertly record his colleagues, Poarch told Project Veritas, "I want CNN and any other outlet to basically return to what they once were, where hey, we tune in to get our facts...I don't want anyone to basically, you know, be spun into believing or programmed into believing one way or the other."[455] Poarch came forward knowing there would be collateral damage, not just to his colleagues but to himself as well.

Shining a light on good people within corrupt institutions is crucial work. There are many who are sufficiently uncomfortable that the field has been left to Project Veritas. The major media are in no position to police

454 Project Veritas, "PART 3: CNN Field Manager: Zucker's 9am Calls 'BS;' "...Totally Left-Leaning...Don't Want to Admit it," October 17, 2019, YouTube video, 15:48.
455 Project Veritas, "PART 3: CNN Field Manager."

themselves. Nor does it serve the public interest for Project Veritas to report what a CEO claims, since media CEOs habitually convince themselves of their own lies. Preferring to perpetuate the illusion of a free and objective press, they routinely turn a blind eye to Project Veritas reports. They don't want to hear the truth, cover it, or lend it credibility, even if the Project Veritas target is a "rival."

David Wright and Amy Robach, who unintentionally blew open ABC's cover-up of the Jeffrey Epstein case, are indeed known, with Robach moderately well-known. That said, neither were in a position of ultimate authority or anything close to it. They did not make major network decisions or practice corporate governance, but in what Boorstin called "this life of illusion and quasi-illusion,"[456] Robach and Wright showed the "solid virtues" necessary to "fill our void" with the truth. By illuminating them in their natural habitats and *not* pixelating their faces or distorting their voices, Project Veritas gave them the power to break through a web of lies—whether they intended to or not.

Some believed that Robach was more upset that she didn't get a byline than that her network participated in a pedophilia cover-up. Whatever Robach's motives, her passion was real enough to spark outrage. Had Project Veritas blurred her face or distorted her voice, that passion would have been lost. Such editing would have also given critics an opportunity to attack the credibility of the report as a "deep-fake" video or a "deceptively edited" video, rather than address its substance.

Given the urgency of the issues a major network covers—or doesn't cover—employees of these companies subject themselves to the possibility of being recorded by strangers in public spaces. In the case of the Amy Robach tape, CBS News and ABC News colluded to find and fire the leaker. To offset that power imbalance, journalists need not consider undercover reporting a "method of last resort." The media has no self-policing mechanism. "The real need of the press is self-examination and a degree of open-mindedness to the criticisms which are leveled against it," said Senator J. William Fulbright in the wake of Watergate. "Journalists bear an exceedingly important responsibility for keeping office holders honest."[457] In the past sixty years, that need has only grown more pressing. As the events of the Amy Robach incident suggest, the media are at least as inclined to cover up their own failings as was the Nixon White House, likely more so given their near immunity from external scrutiny.

---

456 Daniel J. Boorstin, *The Image: A Guide to Pseudo-Events in America* (New York: Vintage, 2012).
457 J. William Fulbright, "Fulbright on the Press," *Columbia Journalism Review* 40, no. 4, (November/December 1975).

This is a long-standing problem. Supreme Court Justice Felix Frankfurter said in a concurring opinion in a 1946 case on the First Amendment: "[B]ecause the press cannot and should not be restrained from outside, it bears a special responsibility for restraining itself…"[458] Solzhenitsyn reinforced this sentiment more than thirty years later in his famed Harvard address, asking, "What sort of responsibility does a journalist or a newspaper have to his readers, or to his history - or to history?"[459]

> If they have misled public opinion by inaccurate information or wrong conclusions…do we know of any cases of open regret voiced by the same journalist or the same newspaper? No, this would damage sales.[460]

Short of libel law, it seems clear that citizens need new counterweights to hold the media to the same level of scrutiny that the media hold other institutions. As political scientist Larry Sabato asks, "Must the price of a free press be so high?"[461]

The ABC insider who recorded Robach apologized to her for reasons unrelated to collateral damage. "To Amy Robach: You are the only person deserving of an apology. I am most certainly sorry," said the insider. "I cannot imagine doing all the hard work to only have it shelved."[462] Robach was not willing to say out loud what she said in between commercial breaks on a hot mic. After the story broke, she proved equally unwilling to say publicly what one might have hoped she would say. Like the subject of a Maoist exercise in self-abasement, she more or less recanted. In a statement given to Project Veritas from ABC News top brass, Robach was quoted as saying, "I was caught in a private moment of frustration," before adding, "The interview itself [with Virginia Roberts Giuffre] didn't meet our standards. In the years since no one ever told me or the team to stop reporting on Jeffrey Epstein, and we have continued to aggressively pursue this."[463] As pundit Jesse Watters noted, "The statement reads like she had a gun to her head."[464]

---

458 Fulbright, "Fulbright on the Press."

459 Solzhenitsyn Center, "Harvard Address," April 12, 2013, YouTube video, 1:02:29.

460 Solzhenitsyn Center, "Harvard Address."

461 Larry Sabato, *Feeding Frenzy: Attack Journalism and American Politics* (Baltimore: Lanahan Publishers, 2000).

462 Ignotus was the codename for the ABC insider and provided their Robach email to Project Veritas.

463 Claudia Harmata, "Amy Robach Walks Back Leaked Video Claiming ABC 'Quashed' Jeffrey Epstein Story: 'I Was Upset,'" People.com, November 5, 2019.

464 Aiden Jackson, "Asking the Question: What ARE ABC's Editorial Standards?" Newsbusters.org, November 11, 2019.

In this sorry bit of corporate *newspeak*, Amy contradicted her unscripted comments on the hot mic. Her backpedaling further validated the reason *not to blur* the subject's face. If the individual is not fully shown and named, her comments can easily be shoved down a memory hole. As has become evident over the years, media brass will use any means necessary to dismiss or bury reporting that has been shown to be true. The greater the truth, the greater the need to bury. Not surprisingly, the people at the executive level of ABC News had *convinced* themselves they had done no wrong. They had *no choice* but to tell themselves that it was Robach who was in the wrong. Those higher up the chain of command than the employee at the anchor desk were not about to confess to a systemic failure.

Amy Robach's public statement, given to Project Veritas exclusively via the top brass of ABC News, contradicted ABC's own editorial guidelines. The notion that the Virginia Robert Giuffre allegations "did not meet our standards for air," begged the question of what ABC editorial standards actually are, especially in light of the fact that the network aired allegations against Justice Brett Kavanaugh that were clearly less substantiated than those against Epstein.

Project Veritas reporters find success in unearthing the human drama lurking below the surface of systemic failure. Someone has to look. Jeff Zucker, president of CNN, seems to have abdicated the authority to investigate his own newsroom. He publicly claims to have been "unconcerned" about the rot the Veritas tapes revealed. Similarly, executive editor of the *New York Times* Dean Baquet brushed off a Project Veritas reporter, saying of the tapes showing his employees violating ethical standards, "I will deal with that." To maintain the upper hand, he added, "[Project Veritas's] sin was greater."[465]

In their own way, Amy Robach, David Wright, and Patrick Davis were all channeling Winston's forbidden diary from *1984*. Each was speaking truths they knew were not supposed to be said aloud. The difference was that Winston's overlord, O'Brien, had an interest in exposing what Winston was privately saying in order to crush Winston publicly, and to confirm his own power by so doing. The American Pravda have an interest in making sure that the forbidden diaries of those working for such "free" institutions never see the light of day. In this Manichean political environment, the moral calculus will inevitably depend upon the political implications of the findings.

---

465 mmatters2, "Dean Baquet On O'Keefe And Sin – 101217," October 12, 2017, YouTube video, 2:31.

## *"IF CITIZENS AND THE MEDIA ARE HANDCUFFED BY A FEAR OF LIABILITY, THAT'S DETRIMENTAL TO POLITICAL DISCOURSE, IT IS DETRIMENTAL TO SOCIETY AS A WHOLE, AND IT IS DETRIMENTAL, REALLY, TO OUR FUNDAMENTAL FREEDOM."*

Here, it might be useful to review the case referred to earlier involving Shirley Teter, a plaintiff who sued Project Veritas. Creamer associate Scott Foval described Teter as "one of our activists who had been trained up to birddog." Foval made this claim in a hotel lobby to a Project Veritas undercover journalist. Consider the statement of Federal Judge Reidinger in an extraordinary Rule 50 hearing dismissing the case immediately before the jury was to issue its verdict:[466]

> I believe the First Amendment implications also extend to a greater degree in a case like this because the court is being asked to walk a very fine line. On the one hand, the free exchange of ideas requires a very broad latitude for the media, and for private citizens alike, to be able to express their opinions, to express their views, to say what they feel needs to be said, particularly on issues of great public importance. And at the top of the list of issues of great public importance would be an issue regarding who should be elected as our president. Therefore, if citizens and the media are handcuffed by a fear of liability, that's detrimental to political discourse, it is detrimental to society as a whole, and it is detrimental, really, to our fundamental freedom.[466]

This federal judge put his thumb on the "public importance" side of the scale, arguing that almost nothing could be more politically important than electing a president. That established, covertly filming a campaign manager or political consultant was invariably going to be legally and morally justified under the theory of the public's right to know. Nevertheless, the judge added that the reporter has "a degree of responsibility," especially given that, "in our current situation, as we have it today, the media is trusted by the public on par with a used car salesmen and Congress."[467]

---

466 Shirley Teter v. Project Veritas Action Fund, et al., United States District Court (W.D.N.C. - Asheville), Civil No: 1:17-CV-256; Excerpt of Proceedings - May 21, 2019.
467 Shirley Teter v. Project Veritas Action Fund, et al.

The issue then shifts to the accuracy of the medium itself and the means used to obtain the information. As veteran journalist James Reston writes, "All cameras tend to corrupt, and television cameras corrupt absolutely."[468] Cameras corrupt because they give the illusion of reality, but the imagery obtained can be manipulated as easily as print. Images captured on hidden camera technology and spread on the internet can be manipulated just as readily as the TV networks manipulate theirs. Aware of this brutal new reality, Project Veritas, when helpful, posts the raw unedited video for the world to judge the fairness of its edits. The networks never do that. The immediacy, the accuracy, and the honesty of this new video genre confront and shatter illusions the way network television never could. The only recourse for the networks and their print allies is to cry foul or, worse, "rape."

## WHEN PUBLIC ACCOUNTABILITY REPLACES CIVILITY

To insist on all-party consent before a reporter can engage a subject in conversation smacks of Big Brother. In 2018, Project Veritas found a chink in Big Brother's armor in a Massachusetts court and made First Amendment history when Chief United States District Judge Patti Saris argued in Project Veritas's favor. She ruled that secretly recording a public official was a fundamental human right. Specifically, Saris ruled that Massachusetts statutes "may not constitutionally prohibit the secret recording of government officials, including law enforcement officials, performing their duties in public spaces, subject to reasonable time, manner and place restrictions."[469]

In the Shirley Teter "bird-dogging" case referred to earlier, Judge Reidinger also made the case for covert recording. In a rare "direct verdict," Reidinger pointed out to plaintiff's attorney Dixie Wells that there was a distinction without a difference between a recording and say, the taking of notes:

> **Judge:** [The muckraker] says we go out there, we interview people, we find what the facts are, and we report the facts that we learn. We don't have an obligation to then go beyond what we learned in our investigation.

---

468 Mitchell Stephens, *The Rise of the Image, the Fall of the Word* (Oxford: Oxford University Press, 1998).

469 Philip Marcelo, "Court weighs ban on secret recordings of public officials," *AP News*, January 8, 2020.

...

> **Wells:** Your Honor, you've called it an interview, and I may
> have slipped and called it that as well. This was taped at a bar,
> and different places, where the person did not know that they
> were being, "interviewed."

> **Judge:** He knew he was being asked questions.[470]

Or consider another example, Kim Koerber. Koerber sent a "cease and desist" letter to Breitbart.com to remove a Project Veritas video in which she was "videotaped without [her] knowledge." Speaking in her capacity as former sales rep for Pearson textbook publishing, Koerber stated on video:

> I did a presentation for AP history and the AP US history
> agenda was set, until [the State of] Texas got upset about it,
> and they wanted to have their founders. They wanted their
> founders in it. And it's like come on, the dead white guys did
> not create this country.[471]

Project Veritas released the video in January 2016, and more than 120,000 people viewed it on YouTube alone. Koerber was speaking face to face with two journalists during a first meeting at the outside patio of a Starbucks. The music was loud enough to be heard in the background, and surrounding voices threatened to drown out Koerber's own. Koerber's lawsuit against Project Veritas read in part:

> The private conversation which occurred was one in which
> my comments expressed only my personal beliefs. The con-
> versation was not structured or formal and I made varied re-
> marks, ranging from opinion and belief to sarcasm and jest.[472]

Koerber added, "At no time was I aware I was being recorded...I did not intend for my comments to be used other than as anonymous research to assist Kamala Harris in formulating policy."[473] The trial court cut short

---

470 Shirley Teter v. Project Veritas Action Fund, et al.
471 Project Veritas, "Undercover Common II: Another Top Publishing Exec: 'It's never about the kids,'" January 14, 2016, YouTube video, 4:46.
472 Kimberly Koerber v. Project Veritas, B291770 (Cal. Ct. App. Sep. 29, 2020).
473 Kimberly Koerber v. Cengage Learning, Inc., et al., Case No.: BC649878, Superior Court of Cal-ifornia, Los Angeles County; (Declaration of Plaintiff in Opposition to Defendant Project Veritas' Special Motion to Strike, November 21, 2017).

Koerber's lawsuit, finding it was an attempt to punish Project Veritas for exercising its First Amendment right of newsgathering. In that, Koerber had no dispute with the relevant facts that would be brought before a jury. The trial court awarded Project Veritas $63,000 for attorneys' fees.[474] Koerber appealed that decision, and the court of appeal said the trial court decision was correct.[475] She then petitioned the California Supreme Court to review her case, and the court declined.[476] Koerber's statement that "the content of the photographs, audio…my name and likeness are offensive to me" is absurd on its face; she chose to speak in the manner she did.

Another executive caught on Project Veritas cameras was Dianne Barrow, a strategic account manager in Houghton Mifflin Harcourt's early childhood schoolbooks division. Barrow was hired to sell books in a thirteen-state territory. At a Starbucks, she explained to two Project Veritas reporters the way the system works:

> **Barrow:** You don't think the educational publishing companies are in it for education do you. No, they're in it for the money. [laughing] The fact that they have to align the educational standards is what they have to do to sell the books.
>
> **Veritas:** So, it's really about the money and not really about the kids.
>
> **Barrow:** You think?
>
> …
>
> **Veritas:** You seem like you're in it for the kids, though, you seem like you know-
>
> **Barrow:** No, I hate kids, [laughter]. I'm in it to sell books, don't even kid yourself for a heartbeat.[477]

Barrow was promptly fired. The publisher promptly released an exculpatory statement: "Houghton Mifflin Harcourt is as appalled by these comments as we expect readers will be…These statements in no way re-

---

474 Kimberly Koerber v. Project Veritas, (Attorney Fees Motion, December 19, 2019).
475 Kimberly Koerber v. Project Veritas, (Second Appeal, January 7, 2020).
476 Kimberly Koerber v. Project Veritas, (Third Appeal, September 29, 2020).
477 Project Veritas, "Undercover Common Core Vid: Exec Says 'I hate kids…it's all about the money,'" January 12, 2016, YouTube video, 7:49.

flect the views of HMH and the commitment of our over 4,000 employees who dedicate their lives to serving teachers and students every day."[478] Barrow sued. Her lawsuit was dismissed and Project Veritas was awarded $73,000 in legal fees.[479]

The *public interest served / harm done* equation clearly favors the former. The way in which millions of children are taught has "profound public importance" and constitutes an overriding public interest. Although Barrow was harmed, it was largely a self-inflicted wound from which it would not have been too hard to recover.

To assess the harm done to the individual, it is useful to assess boundary management and explore arguments for two-party consent laws that prohibit publishing what someone voluntarily tells you. In Project Veritas's appellate brief before the First Circuit Court of Appeals to overturn the Two-Party Consent Law in Massachusetts, the Project Veritas attorney stated:

> All these arguments make a radical claim - that everyone, everywhere enjoys a right to be notified that they will be recorded... This position stands contrary to common law, developed standards of privacy law, because when an individual stands, walks or transacts activities in public places, he knowingly and voluntarily exposes his presence, actions and associates to being viewed and recorded by others...[480]

This principle of boundary management forms the foundation for most privacy analyses today. On one hand, "There are private and personal spaces that are beyond official reach...when the public-private boundary can be transgressed at will, whether through deception or coercion and force, liberty is impossible."[481] It would be strange to claim that the individual had a right not to be photographed at Boston Common or Fenway Park, or even on a patio outside a Starbucks in California. In reality, whenever people step out into the public square, into the "concomitant of life," they voluntarily expose themselves to others.

---

478 Matthew Renda, "Publishing Exec Blames Firing on Right-Wing Sting," Courthouse News Service, June 23, 2017.

479 Project Veritas, "Project Veritas Legal Victories: Dismissal Dianne Barrow v. Project Veritas," ProjectVeritas.com.

480 Project Veritas Action Fund v. Rachael S. Rollins, 19-1640 1d, (U.S. Ct. App. Dec. 15, 2020).

481 Gary Marx, "Ethics of Undercover Investigations," *Encyclopedia of Applied Ethics*, 2ed, 2012: 442-451.

*"WHEN AN INDIVIDUAL STANDS, WALKS OR TRANSACTS ACTIVITIES IN PUBLIC PLACES, HE KNOWINGLY AND VOLUNTARILY EXPOSES HIS PRESENCE, ACTIONS AND ASSOCIATES TO BEING VIEWED AND RECORDED BY OTHERS."*

━━━━━━━

At the heart of this issue is something deeper than recording human interaction. That something predates modern technology and is as old as human interaction itself—*social trust issues*. Individuals discriminate as to whom they choose to trust. There is no formal duty to keep confidential what someone voluntarily shares. False friends, moles, and spies have a well-documented existence—"Et tu, Brute?"—long before the advent of recording devices.[482] Prior to electronic recording, conversations could be transcribed or jotted down in the reporter's notebook or even recollected after the fact. A California court acknowledged in a 1968 case against *Time* magazine that the "successful practice" of investigative reporting "long antecedes the invention of miniature cameras and electronic devices."[483]

The risk of betrayal and exposure, a trust risk, has not choked off all social exchange. Rather, from time immemorial, individuals gauged relationship strength before deciding whether and how much information to disclose to another. In most such cases, it is against one's own self-interest to betray the confidence of another. As Judas can attest, an act of betrayal likely harms the person doing the betraying as much as it does the person "betrayed."

As the muckraker can attest, the betrayal of trust, even to advance the public interest, comes at a cost. Project Veritas, for instance, recently had to spend $350,000 in legal fees on just one frivolous lawsuit to defend its right to publish what a subject willingly shared. Whistleblowers, especially those without the advantage of a hidden recording device, often pay an even greater cost. For violating their nondisclosure agreements and exposing the bad behavior of their employers, they routinely lose their jobs, their homes, their bank accounts, their families.

---

482 Project Veritas Action Fund v. Rachael S. Rollins.
483 Dietemann v. Time, Incorporated.

Gifted with a "messianic sense of purpose," Upton Sinclair infiltrated Chicago's packing houses, "memorializing details of what he saw, then rushing back to his room to write everything down."[484] The result was the 1906 muckraking classic *The Jungle*, a book that led to sweeping reforms in the food industry. Sinclair, like contemporary Jacob Riis who wrote about the jarring conditions of immigration slums, felt he had a right to shout from the rooftops what someone told him.

> *TO BAN SURREPTITIOUS AUDIO AND VIDEO RE-CORDINGS ENTIRELY WOULD ONLY REMOVE INFORMA-TION FROM THE PUBLIC SPHERE THAT OFFERS A MUCH MORE ACCURATE DEPICTION OF A GIVEN INCIDENT.*

Without a recording device, however, the facts sometimes got distorted. In a 1906 magazine article titled, "Is the Jungle True," Sinclair conceded that he had presented a selected version of the truth, having "reserved the right to 'dramatize' and 'interpret' what he reported."[485] With video, the speaker's cadence, inflection, and tonality, as well as other important context captured in a recording, limits the investigator's ability to "interpret." To ban surreptitious audio and video recordings entirely would only remove information from the public sphere that offers a much more accurate depiction of a given incident.[486] Surely, as the Louisiana Supreme Court has held, "Society would not consider reasonable an expectation of privacy which would result in a *more inaccurate version* of the events in question."[487]

## THE CAMERA'S PERNICIOUS EFFECT ON DIGNITY

As Dylan suggested in the song, "Dignity," the nature of a recording of any sort often comes into conflict with a person's sense of being worthy of esteem or respect. If a photograph troubles some, more advanced technology troubles others even more. A federal appeals court judge said that to

---

484 Anthony Arthur, *Radical Innocent: Upton Sinclair* (New York: Random House, 2006), 49.
485 Arthur, *Radical Innocent*, 79.
486 Project Veritas Action Fund v. Rachael S. Rollins.
487 State of Louisiana v. Charles W. Reeves, 427 So. 2d 403, 418 (Supreme Court of Louisiana. 1982).

allow images of people to be broadcast "in full living color and hi-fi to the public" could have the "most pernicious effect on the dignity of man."[488]

When publisher rep Kim Koerber said in regard to "the content" captured by Project Veritas that "my name and likeness are offensive to me," she was not talking about privacy. She was talking about her *dignity*. As legal scholar Dorothy Glancy observes, individuals have an innate sense of psychological integrity and a natural urge to "exercise control over information which both reflected and affected that individual's personality.[489]

"I did not intend for my comments to be used," Kim Koerber told the court. She wasn't the first person to make the argument that published revelations varied from how the individual wanted to be perceived. Although it is generally accepted that people are primarily concerned about how they will be portrayed to people who know them, they are often more honest with the people who *don't* know them, even with strangers. This can result in more far-reaching harm to the individual. So believed Justice Brandeis. He subscribed to "the principle that each of us should be able to control the circles within which details about our lives are disseminated.[490]

The fact that a story raises a "legitimate public concern" matters little to a person whose sense of dignity has been breached. Legal scholars have been all over this issue, but few deny that an affront to privacy robs the individual of his individuality[491] or that there is an inevitable tension between public accountability and civility.[492] Everyone in the public eye knows from experience that public scrutiny can be destructive to a sense of dignity.

## THE RIGHT TO CONTROL FIRSTHAND DISSEMINATION

In one 1998 California case, Justice Brandeis's sentiments were much cited. *Emergency Response*, a TV program that followed the real-life experiences of emergency rescue teams, recorded Ruth Shulman and her son at the scene of an accident. Mercy Air, an operator of rescue helicopters,

---

488 Dietemann v. Time, Incorporated.
489 Dorothy J. Glancy, "The Invention of the Right to Privacy," *Arizona Law Review* 21, January 1, 1979.
490 Diane L. Zimmerman, "Requiem for a Heavyweight."
491 Edward J. Bloustein, "Privacy as an Aspect of Human Dignity: An Answer to Dean Prosser," *N.Y.U. Law Review* 962, 1964.
492 Robert C. Post, "The Social Foundations of Privacy: Community and Self in the Common Law Tort," *California Law Review*, October 1989.

transported Shulman to the hospital. Paralyzed from the waist down, Shulman told her rescuer, "I just want to die." The helicopter pilot responded, "You don't want to die, Ma'am." In the grisly episode packaged by Group W Productions, Shulman was never identified, but she argued, eventually successfully, that she had lost the right to control the dissemination of her own image.[493]

What Shulman—and Koerber in the Project Veritas case—truly sought was the "ability to control the use of [their] image on TV," or in Koerber's case, YouTube. An unwilling loss of privacy can result in the victim feeling shamed, legal scholar Hyman Gross argues, "not because of what others learn, but because they and not he, may then determine who else shall know it and what use shall be made of it."[494]

Over the years, the privacy issue has been decided in a variety of ways by well-meaning judges, but the reality is that an independent press cannot function if the subjects of news stories are able to control their own portrayal. As to the harm done to the subject, there are those who insist that hidden camera footage is somehow more harmful, but this position would seem to hold that the truth is more harmful than a less accurate version of the events. Why is it, then, that recording someone harms them more than writing down what they say? Critics of surreptitious taping seem more troubled by the *medium* than with the findings. Video can be unflattering, but then again, so can be the truth.

## THE BOUNDARIES OF PRIVACY

In their 1890 *Harvard Law Review* article, "The Right to Privacy," Warren and Brandeis warn that new "mechanical devices" would assure a future in which, "What was whispered in the closet shall be proclaimed from the house-tops."[495]

Project Veritas leaves the closets unopened and avoids as much as possible what legal scholars call, "the sphere…characterized by intimacy and trust,"[496] or what Sissela Bok calls the "sanctuary of retreat."[497] Even public figures keep some aspects of their lives private; as well they should. Project

---

493 Shulman v. Group W Productions Inc, 2d B081390 (Cal. Ct. App. 1996).
494 Hyman Gross, "Privacy and Autonomy," in *Privacy and Personality*, ed. James Roland Pennock and John Chapman (London: Aldine Transaction, 2009), 177.
495 Warren and Brandeis, "The Right to Privacy."
496 Lyrissa Barnett Lidsky, "Intrusion and the Investigative Reporter," *Texas Law Review* 71, no. 433 (1992-1993).
497 Bok, *Secrets*.

Veritas respects that right. Not unlike the *Washington Post*, Project Veritas draws a distinction between recording information and publishing it. "There are things we don't publish. Lots of them, all the time,"[498] said *Post* managing editor Len Downie.

When Project Veritas caught a Teachers Union official proposing a threesome with two undercover reporters—"Let's go up to a bar and engage in ménage à trois"—Project Veritas omitted this angle from the story, "Teachers Unions Gone Wild." The revelation did not speak to the abuse of public funds or to the concealment of inappropriate classroom behavior. When it comes to undercover reporting, there are some secrets that ought to remain secret, especially those that "accompany human intimacy."[499] The revelation of such secrets rarely serves a legitimate public interest. The State has a vested interest in enforcing these boundaries.

The behavior of the powerful, however, even the intimate behavior, can become an issue of public interest. Many of the Founding Fathers, Sam Adams among them, thought that the public had a right to investigate the personal morals of public figures. His cousin President John Adams made a strong case for the primacy of public integrity:

> Public virtue is the only foundation of republics. There must be a positive passion for the public good, the public interest, honour, power and glory, established in the minds of the people, or there can be no republican government, nor any real liberty: and this public passion must be superiour to all private passions.[500]

## "INVESTIGATIVE REPORTERS… ARE THE GUARD DOGS OF SOCIETY, BUT THE TROUBLE WITH GUARD DOGS IS THAT THEY SOMETIMES ATTACK WITH EQUAL FERVOR THE MIDNIGHT BURGLAR AND THE MIDDAY MAILMAN."

---

498 Downie, *The New Muckrakers*.
499 Bok, *Secrets*, 252.
500 Letter from John Adams to Mercy Otis Warren, April 16, 1776, Founders Online, Archives.gov.

The question the muckraker must ask is whether the infidelity of a politician is a public integrity issue. During FDR's presidency, the media honored the Rooseveltian rule of coverage that the private life of any public figure was nobody's business but his or her own, unless it impinged upon public performance. JFK lived under the same rules. His brother Ted rendered that rule obsolete when in 1969 he allowed his young female companion to drown at Chappaquiddick in a vain attempt to protect his career options.[501] At that point, the personal became political. In the years since, there have been any number of high-profile cases of sexual misconduct that had genuine public interest ramifications, perhaps none higher than the one that led to President Bill Clinton's 1998 impeachment or, more recently, the indiscretions of Hunter Biden that almost cost his father the presidency.

The muckraker believes that "with great power comes great responsibility." What does this mean? As television critic Michael Arlen has argued, "Investigative reporters... are the guard dogs of society, but the trouble with guard dogs is that they sometimes attack with equal fervor the midnight burglar and the midday mailman."[502] The responsible muckraker recognizes the difference.

## FALSE CLAIMS REGARDING PRIVACY AND CONFIDENTIALITY.

As Sissela Bok writes, "[I]t would be wrong to conclude that journalists ought to write only about persons who have given their consent... [Those] who use secrecy to cover up for abuses often resort to spurious claims of privacy, confidentiality, or national security. It is important for reporters not to take those claims at face value."[503]

Consider the case of AFT Michigan. This teachers' union sued Project Veritas after it exposed the union for negotiating a $50,000 payoff for a teacher fired on the offense of sexually molesting a ten-year-old. David Hecker, the President of AFT Michigan, was not shy about sharing his ambitious motives for filing the lawsuit against Project Veritas. When asked by Paul Mersino, Project Veritas attorney, why he pursued this action, Hecker did not hold back:

---

501 Josh Sanburn, "'The Kennedy Machine Buried What Really Happened': Revisiting Chappaquiddick, 50 Years Later," *Vanity Fair Magazine*, July 17, 2019.
502 Michael J. Arlen, "The Prosecutor," in *New Challenges for Documentary*, ed. Alan Rosenthal (Berkeley: University of California Press, 1988), 328.
503 Bok, *Secrets*.

To have the lawsuit in - in any way possible stop Project Veritas from doing the kind of work that it - it does, and to, as part of that, to compensate AFT Michigan for damages…If the result of it was also in some way slowing down or limiting what Project Veritas does, that would have been a great outcome as well, or will be a great outcome as well.[504]

## THE MUCKRAKER WILL INEVITABLY DAMAGE CERTAIN INDIVIDUALS. NEVERTHELESS, THE PUBLIC'S RIGHT TO KNOW IS PARAMOUNT.

The American Federation of Teachers Michigan was shockingly frank about its efforts to squelch free speech. In a press release, the organization boasted, "A Federal judge has issued a crucial ruling allowing AFT to gather information on conservative hit group Project Veritas, as legal and financial pressure on the embattled outfit mounts."[505] The celebration did not last long. Judge Linda V. Parker overturned the restraining order shortly thereafter in a strong defense of First Amendment rights:

> For cases involving prior restraint, courts must consider if the publication "threaten[s] an interest more fundamental than the First Amendment itself and to forego the prerequisites from the realm of everyday resolution of civil disputes governed by the Federal Rules. Only if a plaintiff can meet this substantially higher standard can a court issue an injunction prohibiting publication of pure speech." Plaintiff has not persuaded the Court that its commercial interests are more fundamental than the Defendants' First Amendment right.[506]

In sum, by gathering truthful information in the pursuit of the public good, the muckraker will inevitably damage certain individuals. Nevertheless, the public's right to know is paramount. For every individual damaged, many more individuals will be spared damage if the information gathered is accurate and compelling.

---

504 Project Veritas, "PV Releases Deposition Tapes Showing American Federation of Teachers Wants to Bleed Us Dry," January 24, 2020, YouTube video, 5:27.
505 Andrew Crook, "Judge Allows AFT to Examine Project Veritas Documents," AFT Press Release, aft.org, July 20, 2018.
506 AFT Michigan v. Project Veritas, Civil Case No. 17-cv-13292 (E.D. Mich. Dec. 27, 2017).

## PRIVATE COMMUNICATIONS

One of the most ambitious undercover investigations ever undertaken by a newspaper took place in Chicago in 1977. That year, the *Chicago Sun-Times* purchased a bar and used it to attract Chicago's predictably shady politicians. Reporters actually ran the tavern—aptly named "Mirage"—and documented a series of crooked deals orchestrated by their politician customers using hidden cameras.[507] Unfortunately, when the Mirage story was denied the Pulitzer Prize, undercover journalism fell out of favor.

Benjamin Bradlee of the *Post* and Eugene Patterson of the *St. Petersburg Times* argued that the reporters could have simply interviewed those who were being shaken down, but as the *Sun-Times* reporters noted, this was impossible. "Nobody wanted to go on record. Everyone was afraid of city hall."[508] *The fear* of city hall meant there was no other way to get at the truth.

Business owners were not willing to go on the record in the 1970s for much the same reason that today, individuals and businesses fear blowing the whistle on those who control the reigning progressive narrative. Due to the recent strong-arming by Big Tech, apps like Telegram have become popular for the simple reason that their encrypted platforms allow users to "bypass authorities."[509]

Although terrorists, in some cases, use these same Telegram channels to purchase guns and arrange rendezvous, Telegram and other encrypted channels also allow those whose voices may have been censored by the powers that be to organize protests throughout the world. As the *Financial Times* reported, "Thanks to Telegram's technology, the app was soon the key source of information on the protests for Belarusians."[510] Today's political refugees, in fact, are dependent upon encrypted messaging apps to continue their fight. "The authorities had no means of shutting them down," added the *Financial Times*, "and that was something people could see."[511]

"How do you fight back against Telegram channels? Do you have the ability to block them?" asked Belarus president Alexander Lukashenko. "Even if you get rid of the internet today, those Telegram channels will

---

507 Michael Miner, "To Investigate and Advocate," *Chicago Reader,* July 15, 2010.

508 Miner, "To Investigate and Advocate."

509 Ruth Fogarty, "French journalist goes undercover with Islamic State terror cell," ABC News, July 11, 2016.

510 James Shotter and Max Seddon, "How Belarus's protesters staged a digital revolution," *Financial Times,* February 27, 2021.

511 Shotter and Seddon, "How Belarus's protesters staged a digital revolution."

keep working from Poland. So don't let your guard down."[512] Nevertheless, Telegram and encrypted applications that allow for information to flow freely have been, and will be, under attack by those who wish to control the narrative. The muckraker has to rely on these often-criticized methods to gain access to subjects who are, for the most part, inaccessible. He lives with the knowledge that his access to sources is precarious.

---

512 Shotter and Seddon, "How Belarus's protesters staged a digital revolution."

# CHAPTER 7
# PRIVACY

## WORKS CITED

Alinsky, Saul D. *Rules for Radicals*. New York: Random House, 1971.

Arlen, Michael J. "The Prosecutor," in *New Challenges for Documentary*. Edited by Alan Rosenthal. Berkeley: University of California Press, 1988.

Arthur, Anthony. *Radical Innocent: Upton Sinclair*. New York: Random House, 2006.

Bok, Sissela. *Secrets: On the Ethics of Concealment and Revelation*. New York: Random House, 1989.

Boorstin, Daniel J. *The Image: A Guide to Pseudo-Events in America*. New York: Vintage, 2012.

Downie, Leonard. *The New Muckrakers: An Inside Look at America's Investigative Reporters*. Washington: New Republic Book Company, 1976.

Gross, Hyman. "Privacy and Autonomy," in *Privacy and Personality*, ed. James Roland Pennock and John Chapman. London: Aldine Transaction, 2009.

Halberstam, David. *The Powers That Be*. Champaign, IL: University of Illinois Press, 2000.

Hedges, Chris. *Wages of Rebellion*. New York: Perseus Books Group, 2016.

Jefferson, Thomas. *The United States Declaration of Independence*. July 4, 1776.

Meyer, Philip. *Ethical Journalism: A Guide for Students, Practitioners, and Consumers*. Harlow: Longman, 1987.

Sabato, Larry. *Feeding Frenzy: Attack Journalism and American Politics*. Baltimore: Lanahan Publishers, 2000.

Sinclair, Upton. *The Brass Check: A Study of American Journalism; Evidence and Reasons Behind the Media's Corruption*. Adansonia Press, First Published in 1919.

Smith, Zay and Pamela Zekman. *The Mirage*. New York: Random House, 1979.

Smolla, Rodney A. *Free Speech in an Open Society*. New York: Vintage Books, 1992.

Sontag, Susan. *On Photography*. New York: Picador, 1977.

Stanley, Jason. *How Propaganda Works*. Princeton: Princeton University Press, 2015.

Stephens, Mitchell. *The Rise of the Image, the Fall of the World*. Oxford: Oxford University Press, 1998.

## JOURNAL ARTICLES

Baker, Russ. "Truth, Lies, and Videotape: 'PrimeTime Live' and the Hidden Camera." *Columbia Journalism Review* 32, no. 2 (July-August 1993).

Bloustein, Edward J. "Privacy as an Aspect of Human Dignity: An Answer to Dean Prosser." *N.Y.U. Law Review* 962, 1964.

Boyce, Lieutenant Colonel Earl J. "Dear Editor." *Military Intelligence: From the Home of Intelligence* 12, no. 4 (October-December 1986).

Ettema, James. "Trying to stir public awareness." *The IRE Journal* (Summer 1989).

Ettema, James S. and Theodore L. Glasser. "Narrative Form and Moral Force: The Realization of Innocence and Guilt Through Investigative Journalism." *Journal of Communication* 38, no. 3 (Summer 1988).

Fulbright, J. William. "Fulbright on the Press." *Columbia Journalism Review* 40, no. 4 (November/December, 1975).

Glasser, Theodore. "On the Morality of Secretly Taped Interviews." *Nieman Reports* 39, no. 1 (Spring 1985).

Glancy, Dorothy J. "The Invention of the Right to Privacy." *Arizona Law Review* 21, January 1, 1979.

Guelzo, Allen C. "Public Sentiment Is Everything: Abraham Lincoln and the Power of Public Opinion." Lincoln and Liberty: Wisdom for the Ages. Edited by Lucas E. Morel (Lexington: University Press of Kentucky, 2014).

Lidsky, Lyrissa Barnett. "Intrusion and the Investigative Reporter." *Texas Law Review* 71, no. 433 (1992-1993).

Marx, Gary. "Ethics of Undercover Investigations." *Encyclopedia of Applied Ethics*, 2ed, 2012: 442-451.

Marx, Gary. "Privacy and Technology." *Telektronik* (January 1996).

Marx, Gary. "Under-the-Covers Undercover Investigations: Some Reflections on the State's Use of Sex and Deception in Law Enforcement." *Criminal Justice Ethics* 11, no. 1 (Winter/Spring 1992).

Perry, Steven. *Communications Lawyer* 14, no. 3 (Fall 1996).

Post, Robert C. "The Social Foundations of Privacy: Community and Self in the Common Law Tort." *California Law Review* (October 1989).

Warren, Samuel D. and Louis D. Brandeis. "The Right to Privacy." *Harvard Law Review* 4, no. 5 (December 15, 1890).

Zimmerman, Diane L. "Requiem for a Heavyweight: A Farewell to Warren and Brandeis's Privacy Tort." *Cornell Law Review* 68, no. 3 (1983).

Zimmerman, Diane L. "I Spy: The Newsgatherer Under Cover." *University of Richmond Law Review* 33, no. 1185 (2000).

## COURT CASES

AFT Michigan v. Project Veritas, Civil Case No. 17-cv-13292 (E.D. Mich. Dec. 27, 2017).

Bartnicki v. Vopper. 532 U.S. 514 (2001).

Democracy Partners, et al. v. Project Veritas Action Fund, et al., United States District Court (D. D.C.), Civil No. 17-CV-1047; Memorandum Opinion - March 31, 2020 (19–21).

Desnick v. American Broadcasting Companies, Inc. 44 F.3d 1345, 1995 U.S. App. 23 Media L. Rep. 1161.

Detresa v. American Broadcasting Companies, Inc. No. 95-56748, 9d (U.S. App. 1997).

Dietemann v. Time, Incorporated. 284 F. Supp. 925 (C.D. Cal. 1968).

Kimberly Koerber v. Cengage Learning, Inc., et al., Case No. BC649878, Superior Court of California, Los Angeles County; (Declaration of Plaintiff in Opposition to Defendant Project Veritas' Special Motion to Strike, November 21, 2017).

Kimberly Koerber v. Project Veritas, B291770 (Cal. Ct. App. Sep. 29, 2020).

Martinez v. Holmes, 4d E002917-AO (Cal. Ct. App. 1986).

Pennekamp v. Florida. 328 U.S. 331 (1946).

Project Veritas Action Fund v. Rachael S. Rollins, 19-1640 1d, (U.S. Ct. App. Dec. 15, 2020).

Sanders v. American Broadcasting Companies, Inc. 2d B094245 (Cal. Ct. App. 1997).

Shirley Teter v. Project Veritas Action Fund, et al. United States District Court, Civil No: 1:17-cv-256 (2019).

Ruth Shulman v. Group W Productions Inc. 2d B081390 (Cal. Ct. App. 1996).

State of Louisiana v. Charles W. Reeves, 427 So. 2d 403, 418 (Supreme Court of Louisiana, 1982).

Sullivan v. Gray, 117 Mich. App. 476, 324 N.W. 2d 58 (Mich. Ct. App. 1982).

The New York Times Company v. The Washington Post Company. 403 U.S. (1971).

# CHAPTER 8
# POWER

*The party seeks power entirely for its own sake...Power is not a means, it is an end.... The object of power is power.*[513]

-George Orwell, *1984*

hat do people lie about most? A good candidate is power. Power is the one language those in industry and government best understand. It is fundamentally coercive and manipulative and potentially destructive. In an unjust society, it can be measured by one's ability to lie and get away with it. To maintain such power, as Orwell understood, "one must be able to dislocate the sense of reality."[514] Elaborates Chris Hedges, "The vast distance between the perceived reality and the actual version of reality is characteristic of totalitarian systems."[515]

The muckraker returns reality to its proper place. He is a journalistic pugilist, one who leaves the ring, climbs into the mezzanine, and punches straight the contorted faces of those sitting in the VIP section. You're not supposed to do that, he is told. It's against the rules, but he can't fight by Queensbury rules when the opposition is armed and dangerous. The muckraker fractures not only the narrative, but the means of the message. He tears people away from believing that the legacy media, for example, is credible at all. He doesn't put that message on ABC News or in the *New York Times*. He transcends both.

The Project Veritas exposé of the "#EpsteinCoverup" at ABC News in November 2019 sent shockwaves through the organization. The *New York Post* reported that internal investigations "report[ed] back up the very highest levels of human resources and ABC's parent company Disney," and that Disney was forced into rifling "through staff emails and news logs and grilling staffers" to try to identify the employee who blew the whistle on a pedophilia cover-up. [516]

---

513 George Orwell, *1984* (New York: Signet Classics, 1950), 332.
514 Orwell, *1984*, 271.
515 Chris Hedges, *Wages of Rebellion* (New York: Perseus Books Group, 2016), 55.
516 Emily Smith, "ABC Scrambles to Figure Out Identity of Amy Robach Leaker, Who Goes by 'Ignotus,'" *Page Six*, November 12, 2019.

Nine years prior, ABC's George Stephanopoulos dared to insinuate that the muckraker was a white supremacist on live television, a lie that circulated wildly through the blogosphere. Afterward, Andrew Breitbart pulled the neophyte aside. "You thought you were playing ball before," Andrew chided him. "This is fucking Disney. This is the big leagues."

Said Günter Wallraff, "Our task is to deceive in order not to be deceived, to break the rules of the game to disclose the secret rules of powers." For what the muckraker does is a necessity. Günter Wallraff knew from experience what the muckraker faced:

> [His] opponents are so powerful and so closely linked in a vast conspiracy with state, industry and the military, no alternative method, according to this argument, can succeed. Anyone who is serious about the mission of unmasking must therefore use disguise and deceit to "break through the palace guard."[517]

Don Hewitt, executive producer for *60 Minutes*, has said in defense of muckraking, "It's the small crime versus the greater good…If you catch someone violating, 'Thou shall not steal' by your violating 'Thou shalt not lie,' that's a pretty good trade-off."[518]

*ANDREW BREITBART PULLED THE NEOPHYTE ASIDE. "YOU THOUGHT YOU WERE PLAYING BALL BEFORE," ANDREW CHIDED HIM. "THIS IS FUCKING DISNEY. THIS IS THE BIG LEAGUES."*

## DOUBLETHINK

In *1984*, the protagonist Winston Smith learns of a book authored by the legendary dissident, Emmanuel Goldstein, called "The Theory and Practice of Oligarchical Collectivism." In it is explained the theory of *doublethink*, a concept "indispensably necessary" and "essential" to the functioning of this nightmarish collectivist state:

---

517 Gunter Wallraff, *The Undesirable Journalist* (Woodstock: The Overlook Press, 1979).
518 Howard Kurtz, "Hidden Network Cameras: A Troubling Trend? Critics Complain of Deception as Dramatic Footage Yields High Ratings," *Washington Post*, November 30, 1992.

> …To tell deliberate lies while genuinely believing in them, to
> forget any fact that has become inconvenient, and then, when
> it becomes necessary again, to draw it back from oblivion for
> just so long as it is needed, to deny the existence of objective
> reality and all the while to take account of the reality which
> one denies…Even in using the word DOUBLETHINK it
> is necessary to exercise DOUBLETHINK. For by using the
> word one admits that one is tampering with reality…[519]

To justify his inaction, Brian Stelter was forced to embrace doublethink. He purposely ignored what even Warzel of the *Times* called "a
huge story on half the internet"[520] and, in the process, he created a news
vacuum. This was not unusual. CNN routinely ignores stories that do not
serve to manufacture consent across the progressive spectrum.

One prominent example, while mentioned in depth in the previous
chapter, was the refusal to cover the airing of the hot mic "Jeffrey Epstein"
rant in November 2019 by ABC News anchor Amy Robach. The video's
impact as it unleashed a sensational viral web across the internet was undeniable. Congress sent a letter to ABC News president, James Goldston,
demanding clarification. Millions of Americans saw the video, and yet it
received no mention on CNN or at the *New York Times*. Brian Stelter mentioned the story only in a newsletter and only in passing. Refusing to cite
Project Veritas by name, he traced the source of the video to "a right-wing,
pro-Trump activist group." His summary:

> Nonetheless, Tuesday's video clip caused widespread outrage,
> particularly on the right, with many commenters using it
> to stoke hatred of the media writ large. Personally, the most
> troubling part to me is Epstein's usage of high-profile, high-
> priced lawyers to intimidate news outlets…[521]

Stetler refused to mention Project Veritas in any context until February 26, 2020, when he tweeted:

> Per @farhip ABC News has suspended correspondent David
> Wright "for unguarded remarks he made in a video by opera-
> tives of Project Veritas." The video hasn't been released yet.[522]

519 Orwell, *1984*, 270.
520 @cwarzel, Twitter, June 24, 2019.
521 The Right Scoop, "CNN's Brian Stelter writes about the REAL villains of ABC News spiking the
   Epstein story," therightscoop.com, November 6, 2019.
522 @brianstelter, Twitter, February 26, 2020.

As another example, one can see doublethink at work in an interview with Dean Baquet, the executive editor of the *New York Times*. He was explaining to *Times* media reporter Ben Smith why they reported accusations against then Supreme Court nominee Brett Kavanaugh made forty years prior. The *Times* had reported the forty-year-old allegations on the same day they surfaced, but waited nineteen days to mention Tara Reade's allegations from 1993. Ms. Reade's allegations? Candidate Joe Biden had "pinned her to a wall in a Senate building, reached under her clothing and penetrated her with his fingers."[523] Said Baquet:

> Kavanaugh was already in a public forum in a large way. Kavanaugh's status as a Supreme Court justice was in question because of a very serious allegation. And when I say in a public way, I don't mean in the public way of Tara Reade's. If you ask the average person in America, they didn't know about the Tara Reade case.[524]

Baquet's circular reasoning comes right out of Orwell. As aware as Winston Smith is of the disinformation shaping his thoughts, writes Orwell, "An elaborate mental training, undergone in childhood and grouping itself round the Newspeak words CRIMESTOP, BLACKWHITE, and DOUBLETHINK, makes him unwilling and unable to think *too deeply* on any subject whatever." Citizen awareness is the enemy of state control. As Nazi minister of information Joseph Goebbels reportedly said, "Propaganda loses its power as soon as it becomes apparent."[525] For this reason, as the fictional Goldstein points out, "moment-to-moment flexibility in the treatment of facts"[526] is essential for the state to keep its citizens ignorant. Over time, Baquet has proved flexible enough to at least keep his own audiences ignorant.

For one, the "average person" cannot know about an allegation unless the media inform him or her about it in the first place. Commonly held opinions prevail due to the fact that pundits have commonly held opinions. In the "age of the expert," as Henry Kissinger pointed out, the "constituency" of that expert is simply "those who have a vested interest in commonly held opinions; elaborating and defining its consensus at a high level has, after all,

523 Ben Smith, "The Times Took 19 Days to Report an Accusation Against Biden. Here's Why," *New York Times*, April 13, 2020.
524 Smith, "The Times Took 19 Days."
525 Hans Speier, "Nazi Propaganda and Its Decline," *Social Research* 10, no. 3 (September 1943): 358–377.
526 Orwell, *1984*, 266–267.

made him an expert."[527] For the *Times* editor to say that the Reade incident is not a story makes it not a story in much the way, as Boorstin observes, "Saying the hotel is distinguished, actually makes it one."[528]

For another, the executive editor of the *Times* is able to play judge and jury about what is newsworthy and what is not, stemming, as Ettema and Glasser would say, "not so much from right and wrong as important or unimportant."[529] Baquet pretends he is not making moral judgments by merely reporting what is newsworthy. But, as one communications scholar notes, "News judgment *is* moral judgment."[530] Determining what is newsworthy inevitably requires making a moral judgment. In a display of what Orwell would call "protective stupidity,"[531] Baquet is unable to explain to Ben Smith the difference in the *Times'* treatment of Kavanaugh and Biden:

> Having gone through Harvey Weinstein and all of them, you make these judgments. It's very subjective. It has to be. You just gotta add up all the pieces and talk to as many people as possible and then do a gut check. There's no magic formula.[532]

Magical isn't exactly the right word to describe *Washington Post* columnist Callum Borchers's approach to the news. Ideological would be closer to the truth. In a series of columns, Borchers attempted to assess whether the events described in Michael Wolff's anti-Trump book *Fire and Fury* occurred as Wolff claimed they did. A tabloid author who used no recording device, Wolff stood accused of recreating scenes and events from conversations with people in Trump's orbit much too creatively. Particularly troubling, even to sympathetic journalists, was his use of an admitted off-the-record conversation with Fox News honcho Roger Ailes after Ailes had died.[533] Borchers defended Wolff, saying, "There is no evidence that Ailes did not say the things attributed to him in *Fire and Fury*."[534] Ailes was hardly in a position to protest.

527 Edward S. Herman and Noam Chomsky, *Manufacturing Consent: The Political Economy of the Mass Media* (New York: Knopf Doubleday Publishing Group, 2011), 23.
528 Daniel J. Boorstin, *The Image: A Guide to Pseudo-Events in America* (New York: Vintage, 2012).
529 James S. Ettema and Theodore L. Glasser, *Custodians of Conscience: Investigative Journalism and Public Virtue* (New York: Columbia University Press, 1998), 8.
530 Mark Lisheron, "Lying to Get the Truth," *American Journalism Review* (October/November, 2007).
531 Orwell, *1984*, 267.
532 Ben Smith, "The Times Took 19 Days."
533 Eun Kyung Kim, "Michael Wolff says he 'absolutely' spoke to President Trump for his tell-all book," Today.com, January 5, 2018.
534 Callum Borchers, "It's almost as though Michael Wolff is trying to make journalists look bad," *Washington Post*, January 10, 2018.

Borchers's pretzel-like locution, "no evidence he did *not* say the things attributed to him," is, of course, a logical fallacy. No one can prove a negative, especially from a dead person. Suggesting that an individual prove he didn't say something violates basic standards of due process and common sense. It does, however, recall Orwell's notion of "CRIMESTOP." Writes Orwell, "Orthodoxy in the full sense demands a control over one's own mental processes as complete as that of a contortionist over his own body."[535] To justify the political implications of the story, Borchers was prepared to contort it to the breaking point.

## THE FAITH OF COMMUNISTS

Why do the violent mobs, the cancel culture cliques, and the anti-First Amendment crowd seem to be winning? Because they believe. Because they have faith. Because their faith is not lukewarm as is the faith of many old-line liberals and tepid conservatives. In the 1953 classic account of his struggle against Communists in America, *Witness*, former Communist Whittaker Chambers spoke to the power of faith, even faith in an evil cause. Chambers argued that neither power nor money moved Communists; nor was adventure a factor for them. It was faith that moved them. In the final conflict, he believed, only equal faith could overcome them. Republicans may be unwilling to ask themselves which hill they are willing to die on, but the hard left has no such hesitance.

The revolutionary heart of communism, writes Chambers, is "the power to hold convictions and act on them. It is the power that moves mountains; it is also an unfailing power to move men. Communists bear witness to their faith. It is a simple, rational faith that inspires men to live or die for their faith."[536]

Unfortunately, it is safe to say that Communists believe more in their faith than most Christians do in theirs. Communists perform their services as an obligation, as a witness, and as a sacrifice. The Communist will suffer, or inflict, almost any degree of injustice for the cause he serves. Observes Chambers, "He will not act openly against his cause. For to do so would be to breach discipline. And discipline to this great secular faith is what discipline is to an army. It is also what piety is to a church. To a Communist, a deliberate breach of discipline is an act of blasphemy."[537]

---

535 Orwell, *1984*, 267.
536 Whittaker Chambers, *Witness* (Washington: Regnery Publishing, 1969).
537 Chambers, *Witness*.

A true witness, writes Chambers, "is a man whose life and faith are so completely one that when the challenge comes to step out and testify for his faith, he does so, disregarding all risks, accepting all consequences.[538]

## IT'S NOT ABOUT POLITICS. IT'S ABOUT POWER.

Arguments against muckraking are rarely about the truth or falsity of the reporting. Serious arguments are fundamentally about power. The straw man in David Halberstam's book about the evolution of the media, *The Powers That Be*, obsesses over the character and the politics of the individual under scrutiny with little consideration given to the facts of the story. If in the twentieth century, the medium was the message, in the twenty-first century, the medium would seem to be the messenger. For example, Eric Weinstein, a mathematician and managing director of Thiel Capital, claims that Project Veritas reporters are "tinged" with ideology. "If you could just get your politics out of it," Weinstein implores. But there are, in fact, fewer politics involved in the art form of *cinéma vérité* than in any other type of reporting.

The best muckrakers—Upton Sinclair and Günter Wallraff come quickly to mind—were political animals. There was inevitably an ideological "tinge" to their reporting. But that tinge didn't matter as long as the facts they were reporting were true. Some of these muckrakers even expressed frustration that the audience missed the ideology by focusing on the facts!

Sinclair was disappointed by the impact of *The Jungle*. At the time, he expressed dismay that his muckraking exposé had "failed in its purpose." He wrote the book to protest what he saw as the barbarities of capitalism. His goal was to help meatpacking workers, not to improve the quality of meat. "I aimed for the public's heart," Sinclair wrote, "and by accident hit it in the stomach."[539] Sinclair had less interest in the killing of animals for food than in the "distortion of the industrial system, the warping of the machine, caused by the uncontrolled desire for profit."[540] History remembers Sinclair for the facts he exposed, not the ideology he professed. Would Weinstein have gone after Upton Sinclair to get his socialist politics out of *The Jungle*? "Why did you go after ACORN?" Weinstein protested.[541] If the facts are straight, the motivation of the report does not matter, and it never has.

---

538 Chambers, *Witness*.
539 Upton Sinclair, "What Life Means to Me," *The Cosmopolitan*, October 31, 1906: 591-595.
540 Leon A. Harris, *Upton Sinclair: American Rebel* (New York: Thomas Y. Crowell Company, 1975).
541 Eric Weinstein, "James O'Keefe on The Portal, Ep. #026 (w E Weinstein) – What is (and isn't) Journalism in the 21stC.," April 20, 2020, YouTube video, 2:25:27.

In fact, to underscore the irony of Weinstein's plea to "keep your politics out of it," consider the response to the exposure by Project Veritas of the politics of ABC News Correspondent David Wright. On camera, Wright admitted he was a socialist. Wright wasn't taken to task, but Project Veritas was vilified for including his ideology in its report even though the revelation of his ideology made the report newsworthy.

> **Veritas:** Would you consider yourself a Democratic Socialist?

> **Wright:** More than that, I would consider myself a socialist.[542]

What sunk Wright at ABC was that he is an honest socialist. He suggested that his view was sufficiently widespread at his network to skew its reporting. "I think that we don't have the bandwidth to give everybody a fair shot. And we should…" he told Project Veritas's undercover journalist. He added, perhaps fatally for his career, that ABC does not "give Trump credit for what things he does do." ABC couldn't handle the truth. Its public relations flack, aptly cut down to the simplistic "PR" logline, responded promptly:

> …any action that damages our reputation for fairness and impartiality or gives the appearance of compromising it, harms ABC News and the individuals involved. David Wright has been suspended, and to avoid any possible appearance of bias, he will be reassigned away from political coverage when he returns.[543]

Given ABC's reaction—exactly the response a muckraker would hope for—it seems all the more absurd that critics would take issue with Project Veritas for sharing Wright's honest admission of his socialism. Of course, that admission was newsworthy. The blue checkmarks on Twitter claimed the issue was about exposing a person's politics. No, they never would have protested had an undercover journalist exposed a Fox News producer admitting he was a fascist. The issue was about having the *correct* political viewpoints, nothing more, nothing less.

---

542 Project Veritas, "'Socialist' ABC Reporter Admits Bosses Spike News Important to Voters, 'Don't Give Trump credit,'" February 26, 2021, YouTube video, 7:31.

543 Paul Farhi, "ABC News suspends correspondent David Wright after comments about Trump coverage, socialism, in Project Veritas sting," *Washington Post*, February 26, 2020.

# ABC DOES NOT "GIVE TRUMP CREDIT FOR WHAT THINGS HE DOES DO."

"This is fucking infuriating," tweeted the *Intercept*'s Aida Chavez. "ABC News suspended David Wright for telling an undercover right-wing operative that he considers himself a socialist…But Capitalists in media are completely neutral, unbiased beacons of light, right?[544] Even Ezra Klein made comment: "If there is a problem with Wright's work - if it was false or wrong or misleading - he should be fired. The idea that he shouldn't have, or on his own time, express, personal views is absurd."[545]

The good news is that Goliath will always fear David more than David fears Goliath. When you're up close and personal with these people, you can see the fear in their eyes. The muckraker knows. He has seen them look away when he has tried to shake their hands.

## A RENDEZVOUS WITH THE EXECUTIVE EDITOR OF THE *NYT*

In autumn 2017, Project Veritas released a four-part investigation into the *New York Times*. This investigation uncovered a *Times* audience strategy editor, Nick Dudich, admitting his reporting wasn't objective. "I will be objective. No, I'm not," the twenty-nine-year-old stated sarcastically, unaware he was being recorded by a button camera on the blouse of a Veritas journalist.

Bizarrely, Dudich then claimed that James Comey was his godfather. His sensational claim proved not to be true. He informed the undercover reporter to "keep it hush-hush" because his "friends curate the front page" of YouTube.[546] It turned out Dudich was very close friends with Earnest Pettie, the brand and diversity curation lead at YouTube. Dudich admitted, "I can put that program at, a time of the day where I knew it'd get killed… We actually just did a video about Facebook negatively, and I chose to put it in a spot that I knew wouldn't do well."

Pettie would later admit to an undercover muckraker that, yes, in certain instances, YouTube employees intervene to make certain items trend: "…in those cases, we will like, use type sort of intervention to make sure that, like…to encourage the thing to be there basically."[547]

544 @aidachavez, Twitter, deleted.
545 @ezraklein, Twitter, February 26, 2020.
546 Project Veritas, "American Pravda, NYT Part I – Slanting the News & A Bizarre Comey Connection," October 10, 2017, YouTube video, 14:38.
547 Project Veritas, "American Pravda, NYT Part II – Exploiting Social Media & Manipulating the News," October 11, 2017, YouTube video, 11:37.

Dudich's admission of biases that affect news accessibility, of course, flies in the face of the *Times* ethics code, which states, "Journalists have no place on the fields of politics. Staff members…must do nothing that might raise questions about their professional neutrality or that of the *Times*."[548] So much for that.

Another *Times* employee, Desiree Shoe, a senior homepage editor, revealed her politically biased agenda in an "off the record" conversation. "It's hard to portray the President in an unbiased light," she said of Trump. As for Vice President Mike Pence, "He's extremely religious. Extremely religious…if we write about him, and how insanely crazy he is and how ludicrous his policies are, then maybe people will read it and be like, oh wow, we shouldn't vote for him."[549]

Shoe's home at the *Times* should not be a surprise. In December 2016, executive editor Dean Baquet admitted, "We don't get religion."[550] They obviously don't. For instance, after the Pulse Nightclub massacre in June 2016, a pair of *Times* "journalists" tried to shift the blame from Islamic terrorism to traditional Christianity by writing, "A Republican congressman read his colleagues a Bible verse from Romans that calls for the execution of gays."[551] The verse in question is Romans 1:18–32. It is worth the read to see what passes for news at the *New York Times*. The article remains on the paper's website uncorrected.

After the Project Veritas tapes were released, Baquet terminated one of the employees Project Veritas had reported on. *Times* spokeswoman Danielle Rhoades Ha said, "Based on what we've seen in the Project Veritas video, it appears that a recent hire in a junior position violated our ethical standards and misrepresented his role.[552] Shortly thereafter, the *Times* changed its social media guidelines. The new additions included, "Our journalists must not express partisan opinions, promote political views, endorse candidates, or make offensive comments."[553]

---

548 "Ethical Journalism: A Handbook of Values and Practices for the News and Editorial Departments," Section 62, *New York Times*, July 28, 2004.

549 Project Veritas, "American Pravda, NYT Part III – Senior Homepage Editor Reveals Biased Political Agenda at NYT," October 17, 2017, YouTube video, 13:17.

550 Bre Payton, "Top NYT Editor Confesses: We Don't Understand Religion At All," *The Federalist*, December 12, 2016.

551 Jeremy W. Peters and Lizette Alvarez, "After Orlando, a Political Divide on Gay Rights Still Stands," *New York Times*, June 15, 2016.

552 "The Times Responds to Project Veritas Video," *New York Times*, October 10, 2017.

553 "Social Media Guidelines for the Newsroom," *New York Times*, updated November 3, 2020.

## *"IF WE WRITE ABOUT HIM, AND HOW INSANELY CRAZY HE IS AND HOW LUDICROUS HIS POLICIES ARE, THEN MAYBE PEOPLE WILL READ IT AND BE LIKE, OH WOW, WE SHOULDN'T VOTE FOR HIM."*

———

Ignoring his own standards, Dean Baquet called the muckraker a "despicable person" at an event that aired on C-SPAN. Not fully averse to religious language, Baquet said that the muckraker had "sinned" and that he ran a "despicable organization." Baquet admitted that his employee, Nick Dudich, "said things he shouldn't have said. He said things that were damaging, and I will deal with that."[554] Odd, but he failed to thank Project Veritas for bringing this to his attention.

This sordid tale just begins with the big cheese's ad hominem attack on the muckraker. A Project Veritas reporter subsequently confronted Baquet and his deputy managing editor in the streets of New York. They ducked inside The Bagel Market in the Gowanus neighborhood of Brooklyn to evade him.[555] Baquet was walking with deputy managing editor Clifford Levy. Without the ability to deal in defamation, these elites were rendered mute. One year later, the muckraker saw Dean Baquet at an ivory tower event for journalism elites at Duquesne University in Pittsburgh.

At a dinner following the conference, the president of the university invited the muckraker to offer some remarks. To be sure, some of the people in attendance did not think that what Project Veritas does is journalism. The conference and dinner represented for this muckraker, quite literally, a "seat at the table." He felt proud to be in a room with all these distinguished journalists, and slightly ashamed for feeling proud given how Project Veritas had skewered so many of their sacred cows at one time or another.

Among those in attendance was Sreenath Sreenivasan, one of the deans of the Columbia Journalism School. The muckraker had confronted him with a microphone in 2011 as part of Project Veritas's "To Catch a Journalist" series. At the time, Sreenivasan stood up from his chair and started filming the muckraker. "It's the famous James O'Keefe!" said Sreenivasan, nervously falling backwards, fumbling with his iPhone, at-

---

554 Project Veritas, "O'Keefe Response: NYT Exec Editor Calls Him 'despicable,' Says Veritas Videos, 'damaging,'" October 13, 2017, YouTube video, 5:46.
555 Project Veritas, "Project Veritas Senior Journalist Christian Hartsock confronts NYT Executive Editor Dean Baquet," February 3, 2021, YouTube video, 1:33.

tempting a "reverse ambush." It wasn't a smart tactic. Not surprisingly, the well-trained journalism students greeted the episode with sneers and jeers, mocking the muckraker with delight and looking for an angle to protect their esteemed faculty.

This time, Sreenivasan smiled awkwardly when he saw the muckraker. Looking slightly uncomfortable, Sreenivasan gave him a wet noodle handshake. After a moment of awkward small talk, he pivoted to a man standing nearby. It was oil and water.

The muckraker, admittedly a little nervous, decided to approach Dean Baquet of the *Times* to say hello. He had expected Baquet to feign friendliness to a fellow member of "The Club," to be social and collegial, perhaps to lower his voice a note to remain gently adversarial. It was always possible, of course, that Baquet might say, "You got us good with that Nick Dudich story" and shake the muckraker's hand, maybe even offer a slight bit of praise notwithstanding his earlier criticisms. This was, after all, a conference celebrating the First Amendment.

However, when the muckraker approached, Baquet grimaced, made a slight whimpering gesture, and quickly turned his back without even spilling his chardonnay. He did not even want to acknowledge the muckraker's presence, let alone look at him directly. "Mr. Baquet," said the muckraker, his hand extended. Baquet murmured something unintelligible into the space between him and the glass wall overlooking the Pittsburgh skyline. The hand remained extended. The muckraker stood staring into the back of the turtleneck and blazer-clad elitist. He could smell the fear. The executive editor of the *New York Times* tells C-SPAN a man is despicable and now is too ashamed to acknowledge his existence; all of this against the ironic backdrop of a conference on the importance of keeping citizens informed.

In that moment, both parties were grappling with different but equally profound realizations. The muckraker had to come to grips with the fact that this supposed paragon of investigative journalism would *never* give him the time of day and may not have acknowledged his very humanity. That small part of him that still hungered for recognition and acceptance from the legitimate press—he once read the *New York Times* every morning—would never be satisfied. The self-pity passed in a flash.

Baquet meanwhile grappled with a problem that promised to only grow more intense. As big and powerful as his institution was, he was not used to others holding him, or it, accountable. There was no way for him to subdue his anxiety about a much smaller organization and its leader that embodied the First Amendment values he supposedly cherished and publicly espoused. He must have sensed his power ebbing.

## "THE MOMENT YOU STOP CARING WHAT PEOPLE THINK OF YOU, IS THE MOMENT YOU BECOME FREE."

If Baquet did adhere to at least some of his principles, he would have had nothing to fear. The unwillingness to engage was emblematic of the old guard's view of the new world. Integrity would have demanded Baquet at least acknowledge the muckraker's presence at the conference and discuss the merits of what caused him to "deal with" his own employee's conduct. Had it not been for Project Veritas, Baquet would have taken no disciplinary action against Nick Dudich. Given those actions, the merits of muckraking investigative journalism should have been self-evident to a man who does journalism for a living.

Faced with this ultimate irony and confronted by the leader of Project Veritas, quite literally standing next to him, Baquet could do nothing but wince like a scared puppy, desperately hoping the muckraker would go away. There was no camera capturing his insecurities; he didn't have to pretend as he did on the street in Greenwich Village. In that moment in Pittsburgh, he was no longer the head of the Old Gray Lady. He wasn't even, as the saying goes, a former hero who now became a competitor.

He was just a man in a restaurant.

The muckraker withdrew his extended hand. The 4 percent within him that sought Baquet's praise was reduced to zero in a Pittsburgh minute. And with that, his collar had come off completely. As Project Veritas attorney Paul Calli would later tell him, "The moment you stop caring what people think of you, is the moment you become free."

# CHAPTER 8
# POWER

## WORKS CITED

Boorstin, Daniel J. *The Image: A Guide to Pseudo-Events in America*. New York: Vintage, 2012.

Chambers, Whittaker. *Witness*. Washington: Regnery Publishing, 1969.

Ettema, James S. and Theodore L. Glasser. *Custodians of Conscience: Investigative Journalism and Public Virtue*. New York: Columbia University Press, 1998.

Harris, Leon A. *Upton Sinclair: American Rebel*. New York: Thomas Y. Crowell Company, 1975.

Hedges, Chris. *Wages of Rebellion*. New York: Perseus Books Group, 2016.

Herman, Edward S. and Noam Chomsky. *Manufacturing Consent: The Political Economy of the Mass Media*. New York: Knopf Doubleday Publishing Group, 2011.

Orwell, George. *1984*. New York: Signet Classics, 1950.

Wallraff, Gunter. *The Undesirable Journalist*. Woodstock: The Overlook Press, 1979.

## JOURNAL SOURCES

Lisheron, Mark. "Lying to Get the Truth." *American Journalism Review* (October/November, 2007).

Speier, Hans. "Nazi Propaganda and Its Decline." *Social Research* 10, no. 3 (September 1943): 358-377.

# CHAPTER 9

# PROPAGANDA

*A lie, frequently enough repeated, doesn't turn into the truth, but it survives, and after a while no one is really capable of telling true from the untrue.*[556]

-Leopold Tyrmand, Polish Anti-Communist

A s Noam Chomsky and Edward Herman observed more than thirty years ago, "Totalitarian states seize and maintain power overtly and by force, whereas democracy for special interest groups must be maintained covertly."[557] In a democratic republic, these groups control the flow of information, not through force, but through consent. They just do it under the radar.

## OVERT PROPAGANDA

In *1984*, Winston Smith's heart sinks as he writes in his forbidden diary a passage never meant to be read, "Freedom is the freedom to say that two plus two makes four. If that is granted, all else follows."[558] Winston knew what was true, but in Orwell's dystopian future, truth could not be acknowledged. The real-life Soviet Union differed little from Orwell's Oceania. Its propaganda was nearly as overt, so overt that, in time, people came to understand they were being lied to. Out of fear of retaliation, they pretended otherwise. Under the reign of Stalin, the citizenry participated in the lie publicly. Only in private did they tell jokes about those lies:

> A judge walks out of his chambers laughing his head off. A colleague approaches him and asks why he is laughing. "I just heard the funniest joke in the world!" "Well, go ahead, tell me!" says the other judge. "I can't – I just gave someone ten years for it!"

556 Leopold Tyrmand, "The Media Shangri-La," *The American Scholar* 45, no. 1 (Winter 1976).
557 Noam Chomsky, *Media Control: The Spectacular Achievements of Propaganda* (New York: Seven Stories Press, 2002).
558 George Orwell, *1984* (New York: Signet Classics, 1950), 103.

As the joke suggests, in totalitarian states, the truth was closely guarded. People had a legitimate fear that they would be betrayed and turned in to the State should they utter publicly some inconvenient truth. In *1984*, the tyrannical O'Brien eventually finds the secret diary in which is Winston's assertion that "freedom is the freedom to say two plus two makes four." The consequences were excruciating and brutal. Says Winston as he is attached to a torture device, "How can I help seeing what is in front of my eyes? Two and two are four." Replies O'Brien as he ratchets up the torture, "Sometimes, Winston. Sometimes they are five. Sometimes they are three. Sometimes they are all of them at once. You must try harder. It is not easy to become sane."[559]

Betrayal and lies were "a form of existence"[560] in the Soviet Union. As a matter of course, citizens feared being sold out by their own neighbors, even by their own families. Dissidents, even unwitting ones, were routinely sent to "gulags," forced labor camps in the hinterlands. While all but the willfully blind knew the truth, the incentive to betray friends and neighbors was often powerful enough to overcome the common bonds of humanity. As in the fictional case of Winston and girlfriend Julia, real-life totalitarians have not hesitated to lay human intimacy bare. Coerced into living by lies, surviving "only in a superficial, bodily sense,"[561] people grew callous and corrupt. Writes Solzhenitsyn:

> The permanent lie becomes the only safe form of existence, in the same way as betrayal…There is no man who has typed even one page…without lying. There is no man who has spoken into a microphone…without lying…If the children were still little, you had to decide what was the best way to bring them up, whether to start them off on lies instead of the truth (so that it would be easier for them to live) and then to lie forevermore in front of them too; or tell them the truth, with the risk that they might take a slip, that they might let it out, which mean that you had to instill into them from the start that the truth was murderous, that beyond the threshold of the house you had to lie, only lie, just like papa and mama. The choice was really such that one would rather not have any children.[562]

559 Orwell, *1984*, 316.
560 Aleksandr Solzhenitsyn, *The Gulag Archipelago*, vol. 2 (New York: Harper Perennial Modern Classics, 2007), 682.
561 Solzhenitsyn, *The Gulag Archipelago,* 688.
562 Solzhenitsyn, *The Gulag Archipelago,* 692.

## COVERT PROPAGANDA

Orwell feared tyranny and the heavy hand of censorship by brute force. A decade older than Orwell, British writer Aldous Huxley anticipated a dystopian future closer in spirit to the state of manufactured consent that characterizes the current media ecosystem, one "achieved under conditions of freedom."[563] Being largely free, the American media have been forced to act in a more sophisticated manner regarding their use of propaganda than the totalitarians. Instead of monotonously repeating the same lie, Big Media produces endlessly minor variations on a theme. Although not formally coordinated, the mainstream product gives the impression of a single hand arranging a slide carousel of pre-selected images.

### "PROPAGANDA IS TO A DEMOCRACY WHAT THE BLUDGEON IS TO A TOTALITARIAN STATE."

As media theorist Neil Postman describes the contrast between these two visions, "Orwell feared those who would deprive us of information. Huxley feared those who would give us so much that we would be reduced to passivity and egoism. Orwell feared the truth would be concealed from us. Huxley feared the truth would be drowned out in a sea of irrelevance."[564] Huxley's fear was that people would come to love their oppression and grow attached to the technologies that subverted their ability to think. To date, Huxley's has been the more accurate prediction. Independently, the media prey on the vanity of their audience. Collectively, they intimidate their audiences with their "humiliating and terrifying power." Writes Chomsky, "Propaganda is to a democracy what the bludgeon is to a totalitarian state."[565]

The main Soviet communications organ, *Pravda*, was backed by the power of the State. No dissent was permitted. By contrast, the *American Pravda*, the politically aligned coalition of Big Media and Big Tech, offers what Chomsky calls the "necessary illusions"[566] of freedom, but illusions they remain. Either in part or in whole, Americans have unwittingly embraced the covert propaganda thrust upon them by Hollywood, Silicon

563 Chomsky, *Media Control*, 37.
564 Neil Postman and Andrew Postman, *Amusing Ourselves to Death: Public Discourse in the Age of Show Business* (New York: Penguin, 2005).
565 Chomsky, *Media Control*, 20.
566 Noam Chomsky, *Necessary Illusions: Thought Control in Democratic Societies* (Brooklyn: South End Press, 1989).

Valley, the major news networks, and the educational establishment. The proof of how successful this endless stream of propaganda is, exists in the fact that people mistakenly believe there isn't any propaganda at all.[567] As the fictional uber-villain Keyser Söze reminds his prey, "The greatest trick the devil ever pulled was convincing the world he didn't exist."[568]

The American federal government officially entered the propaganda business in 1917 with the creation of the Committee on Public Information (CPI).[569] Democratic President Woodrow Wilson appointed George Creel to head the new US bureau. An investigative journalist by profession, Creel served as chairman alongside the secretaries of state, war, and navy. Formed a week after the US declared war on Germany, the Bureau had the immediate goal of shaping American public opinion about the war. Notwithstanding its original mission, any good the CPI may have done with regards to ending The Great War—not to be numbered until WWII twenty years later—was the first step down the slippery slope to Big Brotherhood in the United States.

Americans have PR campaigns shoved in their faces 24/7 on their televisions, their computers, their smart phones. Even before COVID-19, American adolescents were spending nearly eight hours a day in front of one screen or another. What they consume becomes their reality. It's as if Wilson's CPI multiplied a hundredfold. The ability to influence is everywhere. Every celebrity, journalist, and politician now has a public platform. The public has the ability to comment on all current events through these platforms in real time. The world has never been more connected—and never more separated.

For those who think critically, this inundation with content is a blessing. With the touch of an app, they can access information from all over the world. Unfortunately, not everyone thinks critically, and among those who don't are many people with huge public followings. The Babel of competing voices enables those who hope to control the information flow a way to creep in. Observes Chomsky, "The United States pioneered the public relations industry. Its commitment was 'to control the public mind,' as its leaders put it."[570] Even Chomsky could never have envisioned the reach of the multi-trillion-dollar *($1,000,000,000,000+)* tech industry.[571] For most people today, especially young people, tech and advertising are the primary sources of information.

---

567 Jason Stanley, *How Propaganda Works* (Princeton: Princeton University Press, 2015).
568 *The Usual Suspects*, directed by Bryan Singer, Bad Hat Harry Productions, 1985.
569 Michael Kazin, *The Populist Persuasion* (New York: Cornell University Press, 1995), 69.
570 Chomsky, *Media Control*, 22.
571 Aditi Ganguly, "Which 2 trillion Dollar Tech Giant Is a Better Buy: Apple or Microsoft?" *Stock-News.com*, July 8, 2021.

A generation ago, advertisers hoped to persuade you what to buy. Today, they hope to persuade you how to think. The messaging may change in the years to come, but national ads relentlessly spread scarcely concealed social justice propaganda. People are being marketed to constantly. These new and forever changing media are ripe for political action groups to insert themselves consciously and subconsciously into the American psyche.

Edward Bernays, the author of the aptly titled *Propaganda*, was cited in his 1995 obituary as the "father of public relations." In defense of the profession, he made the following eye-opening observation:

> If all men had to study for themselves the abstruse economic, political, and ethical data involved in every question, they would find it impossible to come to a conclusion about anything. We have voluntarily agreed to let an invisible government sift the data and high spot the outstanding issue so that our field of choice shall be narrowed to practical proportions.[572]

"The investigative journalist," confessed Bernays, "is the propagandist's natural enemy, as the former serves the public interest, while the latter tends to work against it."[573] The very thing Chomsky railed against, Bernays endorsed, arguing that the essence of democracy was "engineering the public's consent."[574] Journalism legend Walter Lippmann sided with Bernays. In fact, it was Lippmann who coined the term "the manufacture of consent,"[575] which he thought a good and necessary thing for a cohesive society. Like Bernays, Lippmann viewed the general population as "spectators." His contempt for the common man was in plain view when he argued that the "specialized class" needed to create "stereotypes"—a phrase that Lippmann introduced into common parlance—to fit complicated data into neat little models. These information packets could help the specialized class tame the "bewildered herd."[576]

"The investigative journalist," confessed Bernays, "is the propagandist's natural enemy, as the former serves the public interest, while the latter tends to work against it."

---

572 Edward Bernays, *Propaganda* (New York: Ig Publishing, 2004), 38.
573 Bernays, *Propaganda*, 26.
574 Bernays, *Propaganda*, 26.
575 Quoted in Chomsky, *Media Control*, 15.
576 Walter Lippmann, *Public Opinion* (CreateSpace Independent Publishing Platform, 2013).

Reinhold Niebuhr, an influential American intellectual known as "the theologian of the establishment," argued this same point. Niebuhr writes that due to the "stupidity of the average man," there is a need for "necessary illusions" and "oversimplifications" to "keep the ordinary person on course." Adds Niebuhr, "Rationality is a very narrowly restricted skill."[577] (Not surprisingly perhaps, Niebuhr was one of former FBI Director James Comey's heroes.) One could hear echoes of Niebuhr's thinking in the words of Obamacare architect Jonathan Gruber. Said Gruber of the Affordable Care Act in 2013, "Lack of transparency is a huge political advantage. And basically, call it the stupidity of the American voter or whatever, but basically that was really, really critical for the thing to pass."[578]

By contrast, a truly free press—the muckraker's domain—empowers people to make decisions for themselves. The undercover video of Project Veritas, for instance, offers up raw data that would have otherwise been unacceptable or inaccessible. By releasing these visuals directly to the audience, the muckraker has the power to shatter the Bernays doctrine "stereotypes" and upend "necessary illusions." The source of the information becomes less relevant than the information itself. Again, as Snowden reminds us, "The source of a given piece of information is a hell of a lot less important than if that information is true."[579]

*"THE INVESTIGATIVE JOURNALIST," CONFESSED BERNAYS, "IS THE PROPAGANDIST'S NATURAL ENEMY, AS THE FORMER SERVES THE PUBLIC INTEREST, WHILE THE LATTER TENDS TO WORK AGAINST IT."*

## BIG TECH

The American media are, in the final analysis, more powerful than all three branches of government. When you pull back the curtain on the relationships Big Media has with Big Tech, the truth of the above becomes evident. Either working together or independently, journalistic institutions only masquerade as news organizations.

Their sustainability directly relies upon their interdependency. The politically motivated media elites, in coordination with Big Tech oligarchs

577 As quoted in Chomsky, *Media Control.*
578 Patrick Howley, "Obamacare Architect: Lack of Transparency Was Key Because 'Stupidity Of The American Voter' Would Have Killed Obamacare," *Daily Caller,* November 9, 2014.
579 @Snowden, Twitter, December 16, 2020.

and an army of self-proclaimed objective "fact-checkers," have created a vertically integrated propaganda vortex. It systemically corrupts the way the public accesses information. The symbiotic nature of this cabal is disastrous for the truth and a danger to America's future.

The Big Tech nabobs have adopted the frightening and increasingly common practice of "playing selective God." So stated Google program manager Ritesh Lakhkar to a Project Veritas undercover journalist in summer 2020.[580] This coordinated effort to inject algorithmic control at the behest of the biased and corrupted media organizations that they themselves have deemed "credible" has deformed the public's ability to obtain information. Information that deviates from the accepted orthodox narrative has become increasingly inaccessible. With terrifying effortlessness, the social media giants have developed an ability to "shadow ban," "de-boost," render "algorithmically fair," and/or outright censor information in whichever way they see fit. They allow their audiences to see what they want them to see and little more of consequence.

As an example of Big Tech's increasing brazenness, one has to look no further than the Hunter Biden laptop scandal. Less than three weeks prior to the most anticipated election in recent American history, *New York Post* journalists Emma-Jo Morris and Gabrielle Fonrouge "slipped the DISC," as Eric Weinstein would say. They published an explosive story on October 14, 2020: "Smoking-gun email reveals how Hunter Biden introduced Ukrainian businessman to VP dad."[581] The article was substantiated by documents, images, and emails recovered from what the reporters had verified to be Hunter Biden's hard drive. The evidence was both as overwhelming and extremely damning as the story itself. Considering that the last-minute revelation of a decades-old DUI almost flipped the 2000 election in Al Gore's favor, this information was a pure game changer.

Tech overlord and chief activism officer at Twitter, Jack Dorsey, understood the story's potential impact and promptly flexed his company's political muscle in response. Within an hour of the article going live, Twitter stopped it dead in its tracks, issuing a statement that said:

> *The Post*'s stories violated policies against posting material that contained personal information and was obtained by hacking.[582]

580 Project Veritas, "Google Program Manager: Google 'Trying to Play God' via 'Drivers of Algorithms' in 2020 Election," October 19, 2020, YouTube video, 8:43.
581 Emma-Jo Morris and Gabrielle Fonrouge, "Smoking-gun email reveals how Hunter Biden introduced Ukrainian businessman to VP dad," *New York Post*, October 14, 2020.
582 Robert McMillan, "Twitter Unlocks New York Post Account After Two-Week Standoff," *The Wall Street Journal*, October 30, 2020.

Not only were Twitter users unable to retweet the original post, but they were also forbidden from linking to the story. Twitter then went further, locking the *Post* out of its main account. Dorsey and his cohorts at Twitter knew they had the power to drastically slow the spread of this informational virus, and in doing so, they could protect Joe Biden and the Democratic Party. To be effective, they had to send the story spiraling down an inaccessible black hole lest it spread to the left half of the blogosphere.

Dorsey himself was called in to a congressional hearing about partisan censorship as the evidence of his machinations began to pile up, but to little avail. After nearly two weeks, the Post was finally able to get access to its account, but the damage had been done. Twitter effectively executed the mission that Dorsey no doubt ordered. His people stopped the spread of the story to the public and reinforced their partisan media partners, proclaiming a narrative that the laptop was likely a fraud and possibly a Russian plant.[583]

Project Veritas sent shockwaves through the cyber landscape in December 2020 when its undercover video confirmed the Big Media collusion with Big Tech. By the grace of God and the help of a courageous insider, Project Veritas had been secretly recording CNN president Jeff Zucker's editorial phone calls with his senior staff every morning for months. In the days following the release of the *Post*'s story into Hunter and Joe Biden's business dealings with Ukraine and China, CNN's political director, David Chalian, was heard boasting:

> Obviously, we're not going with the New York Post story right
> now on Hunter Biden…[584]

The word "obviously" gives the game away. At CNN, the decision to spike the Hunter Biden story was the *obvious* one. Who would think to do so otherwise? To run the story would, of course, have been detrimental to the one cause Chalian and the rest of the leadership at the network had so aggressively supported for the past four years—removing sitting president Donald Trump from office.

---

583 Zack Budryk, "50 former intelligence officials warn NY Post story sounds like Russian disinformation," *The Hill*, October 20, 2020.
584 The Rubin Report, "Leaked CNN Tapes Revealed: Project Veritas Exposes Media's Agenda," December 2, 2020, YouTube video, 37:00.

## THEY HAD TO SEND THE STORY SPIRALING DOWN AN INACCESSIBLE BLACK HOLE LEST IT SPREAD TO THE LEFT HALF OF THE BLOGOSPHERE.

────────────

## MINNESOTA: PROPAGANDA AT WORK

In relatively free societies, propagandists work either by committing false-hoods or omitting truths. As Project Veritas can attest, sometimes they do both. Toward the end of September 2020, a month or so before the November elections, Project Veritas released an explosive voter fraud bomb-shell. The story involved a massive ballot harvesting scheme taking place in Minnesota. For those who may not know, ballot harvesting is the practice of rounding up ballots for a preferred candidate. In the past, operatives would canvass a district and identify their supporters. Then, on Election Day, they would put their touch on those supporters and make sure they got to the polls. Urban political machines were notorious for sending buses to senior citizen homes, public housing units, or even skid row to get their voters to the polling stations.[585]

In recent years, the harvesters made sure absentee ballots were sent to senior citizen communities, nursing homes, and residences for the developmentally disabled. They would then collect those ballots, often threatening negative consequences for those tempted to vote the wrong way. This strategy expanded in 2018 and 2020 when states, including Minnesota, loosened the rules for handling ballots. Now all voters could request a ballot in the mail and then either turn it in themselves or have operatives, the so-called "ballot harvesters," come by to collect them.[586]

The Project Veritas team had become quite familiar with Minnesota, having stayed there for several months leading up to the 2020 election investigating fraud. A few undercover journalists were deeply embedded within the Somali community of Minneapolis. Centered in the city's Ward 6, this community was the site of the most egregious practices of illegal ballot harvesting in the state.

The investigation grew from one lead to many leads, from one source to many sources. The muckrakers mapped out an entire ecosystem of elec-

─────────────

585 PBS NewsHour, "What we know and don't know about these videos alleging illicit strategies by Democrats," October 19, 2016, YouTube video, 3:35.
586 Chelsea Davidson, Michael Jacobs, Carlos Martinez, Spencer McManus, Yegina Whang, "The 2020 Minnesota Primary in the Wake of the Coronavirus," The Lawfare blog, entry posted September 15, 2020.

tion fraud. The deeper they delved, the more they realized that this community's unique history insulated it from the rest of the state. More than one hundred thousand Minnesotans were born in Somalia. Many members of the Somali-American community were recent arrivals from their war-torn land, and they brought with them tribal loyalties as well as the coping mechanisms one develops in political dealings with warlords. As a result, this corrupt electoral ecosystem was hidden from view behind a curtain of language and culture. The safety of the Project Veritas team members conducting this investigation was a constant concern.

Project Veritas kept going because the people helping its efforts were themselves members of the Somali-American community. The America they were experiencing did not seem to them the America they were promised. They were relying on Project Veritas to expose the corruption that the local authorities and media either ignored or enabled. One of the community sources helped Project Veritas record a live exchange of cash for a voter registration form in the middle of the street in Minneapolis. No one had ever seen anything like it. The exchange was brazen.

> **Harvester:** This is how you fill it out. Put your first name, last name, address, telephone number, ID number, or the last four digits of your Social Security number. After that, you will sign it. That's all.

> **Voter:** Yes, tonight we will close the deal, okay?

> **Harvester:** Yes, yes. Now take this [cash] for your pocket change.

> **Voter:** Okay. When I fill it out I will bring it to you.

> **Harvester:** That's clear. That's clear.[587]

On a recorded video, ballot harvester Osman Ali Dahquane showed not only an indifference to the law, but also an awareness of the risks he and his colleagues were running: "We don't mind illegal. If this [scheme] continues this direction, many people will go to prison, or no one will vote in the city of Minneapolis. It is very, very corrupt. We are in trouble if they come after us. We are in big trouble if they come after us."

---

587 Project Veritas, "Omar Connected Harvester SEEN Exchanging $200 for General Election Ballot. 'We don't care illegal,'" September 28, 2020, YouTube video, 13:49.

The most flagrant of the ballot harvesters Project Veritas exposed was Somali-American political operative Liban Mohamed, also known as Liban Osman. Liban is the brother of Jamal Osman, the winner of the Ward 6 City Council seat in the August 2020 special election. The election was critical to the Project Veritas investigation because it took place the day of the congressional primary, which offered team members the opportunity to observe House Representative Ilhan Omar's campaign practices, as well as those of her political operatives.

Although he resembled an old-school urban villain of the Boss Tweed mold, Liban was a new breed narcissist with all the new toys. He did not just brag about his crimes. He shot videos of himself on Snapchat committing them. One video showed him flipping through a stack of ballots, as if he were playing cards, while singing in accompaniment: "Two in the morning, still hustling."[588]

*"WE DON'T MIND ILLEGAL. IF THIS [SCHEME] CONTINUES THIS DIRECTION, MANY PEOPLE WILL GO TO PRISON, OR NO ONE WILL VOTE IN THE CITY OF MINNEAPOLIS. IT IS VERY, VERY CORRUPT. WE ARE IN TROUBLE IF THEY COME AFTER US. WE ARE IN BIG TROUBLE IF THEY COME AFTER US."*

There was not just one video. There were many in which Liban bragged in English and Somali about his exploits harvesting ballots for his brother's campaign. He had absolutely no shame. In fact, he seemed to think of the whole election as a joke. Take a look at just a few of the statements Liban made in one video we published:

> Numbers don't lie. Numbers don't lie. You can see my car is full. All these here are absentees' ballots. Can't you see? Look at all these. My car is full. All these are for Jamal Osman. We got three hundred [ballots] today for Jamal Osman only.

> Money is everything. Money is the king in this world. If you got no money, you should not be here, period. You know what I'm saying?

588 Project Veritas, "Ilhan Omar connected Ballot Harvester in cash-for-ballots scheme: 'Car is full' of absentee ballots," September 27, 2020, YouTube video, 16:42.

> Money is everything, and a campaign is managed by money. You cannot campaign with two hundred dollars or one hundred dollars you got from your grandmother or grandfather. You cannot campaign with that. You got to have an investment to campaign. You got to have fundraisers.[589]

Liban mocked the law. He was so certain he would get away with his actions that he had the audacity to post these videos on his own Snapchat page. Little did he know that Project Veritas had a source following his Snapchat account, @KingLiban1, who captured his Snapchat video. When he took it down, it was already too late.

The Project Veritas video documenting Liban's adventures would net in aggregate tens of millions of views across various social media platforms. The *New York Post* ran a front-page story about the video.[590] President Donald Trump, in addition to tweeting the video, mentioned the story at his rallies.[591] It was surreal for team members to observe how engaged the public was with the content. Those who watched the video had no doubt that serious illegalities were taking place in Minnesota. Unless, of course, those viewers were on Team Biden, a team that includes just about every mainstream journalist.

In no Project Veritas investigation has a malefactor so boldly taped himself bragging about his crimes as Liban. *Project Veritas* did not say that Liban had one hundred times the legal limit of ballots in his car. *Liban* said it himself on his Snapchat profile. He didn't just say it; he bragged about it and showed the evidence of his crime. At the time, it seemed certain that Liban's own videos were irrefutable proof of his malfeasance, but that just proved how naïve the muckraker still was about the depth of Big Media's depravity.

First, "credible journalists" claimed Project Veritas was wrong about the law and that there were no limits on ballot harvesting in Minnesota. Not surprisingly, they either chose to remain willfully ignorant of Minnesota state law or decided to deliberately misreport provisions of the law. Yes, there was a court challenge to the three-ballot limit. Yes, a state judge suspended *enforcement* of the law pending the challenge, but

---

589 Project Veritas, "Ilhan Omar connected Ballot Harvester."

590 Miranda Devine, "Project Veritas uncovers 'ballot harvesting fraud' in Minnesota," *New York Post*, September 27, 2020.

591 Ariel Zilber, "Donald Trump demands US attorneys launch an investigation into Ilhan Omar following report her supporters 'illegally harvested ballots in Minnesota,'" *Daily Mail*, September 28, 2020.

the *law* was never suspended. Ballot harvesters exceeded the three-ballot limit at their own risk, and they knew it. After the state's high court ruled that the law was valid, everything that Liban showed himself doing was confirmed as illegal. It was not, in fact, Project Veritas who said having more than three ballots was illegal. The Minnesota Supreme Court said it.[592] Big Media? Silence.

Three reporters who missed the point were rewarded for their incompetence with honored spots on our Wall of Shame: *ThinkProgress* founder Judd Legum, now with *Popular Information*; Darragh Roche of *Newsweek*; and Bethania Palma of Snopes. All three ignored Project Veritas requests insisting they make corrections and tell the truth. They remained silent, at least until the Project Veritas legal team notified their legal departments. As you might expect, the retractions soon followed. Each of the three "credible journalists" earned his or her Retracto award, but the Retracto Project Veritas relished most was the one given to Snopes's Palma.

### WHO WATCHES THE WATCHMEN? TODAY, THE QUESTION MIGHT BEST BE PHRASED: WHO FACT-CHECKS THE FACT-CHECKER?

Snopes calls itself, "The definitive Internet reference source for researching urban legends, folklore, myths, rumors, and misinformation."[593] In reality, Snopes is a left-leaning disinformation machine. Snopes's power derives from major social media platforms, like Facebook, that use Snopes as a "fact-checker" to justify shutting down profile pages and censoring content.

Centuries ago, the Roman poet Juvenal asked a question more relevant now than ever: *Quis custodiet ipsos custodies?*[594] Who watches the watchmen? Today, the question might best be phrased: Who fact-checks the fact-checker? When those fact-checkers give others the power to boot people off their social media platforms, just on their say-so, someone has to step up and counter that power. Years ago, Project Veritas accepted the challenge and has no intention of shirking that responsibility.

592 DSCC, et al. v. Simon, et al., Minnesota Supreme Court Case No. A20-1017 (September 4, 2020).
593 Heather Murphy, "Snopes Retracts 60 Articles Plagiarized by Co-Founder: Our Staff Are Gutted," *New York Times*, August 13, 2021.
594 Juvenal, *Satire 6*, ed. Lindsay Watson and Patricia Watson (Cambridge: Cambridge University Press, 2014), lines 347–348.

Project Veritas released the first Minnesota ballot harvesting story, the one featuring Liban, on September 27, 2020.[595] Palma sent an email on September 28 at 4:27 p.m. demanding answers by her "close of business" deadline. So sure Ms. Palma was of which fact she got wrong, she didn't even ask about the law. Ignorance, or an indifference to the truth, allowed her and her fellow hacks to take the evidence before their very eyes and twist it just enough to claim it was not real.

After many long days of work overseeing the Minnesota investigation, the muckraker traveled to Arizona for a speaking engagement. While he was on the flight, he received a message from a member of our communications department saying the *New York Times* had written an article about the Minneapolis story. The article was awkwardly headlined: "Project Veritas Video Was a 'Coordinated Disinformation Campaign,' Researchers Say."[596] The headline suggested that this was going to be really bad news. The article kicked off with the following allegation:

> A deceptive video released on Sunday by the conservative activist James O'Keefe, which claimed through unidentified sources and with no verifiable evidence that Representative Ilhan Omar's campaign had collected ballots illegally, was probably part of a coordinated disinformation effort, according to researchers at Stanford University and the University of Washington.[597]

Given the source, the muckraker was sure the *Times* article would cause the propaganda vortex to explode. With no evidence, *Times* reporter Maggie Astor claimed that the videos were deceptive. As mentioned earlier, but which cannot be repeated enough, even before the muckraker founded Project Veritas, he grounded all his investigations in video. Unlike traditional reporters who write their stories from their hastily taken notes, Veritas journalists rely on video. Video allows the viewer to see the subject's mouth move and hear his or her words spoken. This is the essential beauty of video as a direct medium—cinéma vérité. In Minnesota, video took viewers to places print never could.

The alignment of words and mouth movement is critical. In the age of COVID, masks hid all the non-verbal facial cues. White House chief of staff Mark Meadows understood this. When Meadows was ready to speak

595 Project Veritas, "Ilhan Omar connected Ballot Harvester."
596 Maggie Astor, "Project Veritas Video Was a 'Coordinated Disinformation Campaign,' Researchers Say," *New York Times*, September 29, 2020.
597 Astor, "Project Veritas Video Was a 'Coordinated Disinformation Campaign.'"

to a gaggle of Capitol Hill reporters, he took his mask off. The reporters protested his recklessness, but, as he explained, he would not give an interview with a mask covering his mouth. The mask gave the reporters too much opportunity to misquote him or even edit what he said.[598]

There was no possibility of misquoting Liban. The most incriminating videos were recorded by Liban himself and posted on Snapchat. Astor, however, alleged that Project Veritas used "unidentified sources" without any "verifiable evidence" of the ballot harvesting scheme. Clearly, she must have missed the sections in the video in which Liban, Osman Ali Dahquane, and other ballot harvesters were clearly identified committing their crimes and discussing them.

Most troubling of all was Astor's claim that the Project Veritas investigation was "probably part of a coordinated disinformation effort, according to researchers at Stanford University and the University of Washington."[599] Ladies and gentlemen, this is what journalism has been reduced to: journalists leading stories of major consequence with the word "probably." Astor was admitting from the get-go that she had absolutely no evidence to back her claims. She was writing this piece purely on her emotions and her projections.

The *Times* is notorious for its employment of the "to-be-clear" gambit. An example of the same was an October 15, 2020, article by technology columnist Kevin Roose, headlined, "Facebook and Twitter Dodge a 2016 Repeat, and Ignite a 2020 Firestorm."[600] In the column, Roose bangs on about Russians stealing emails from the Democratic National Committee and giving them to WikiLeaks, an allegation that has never been proven. Then, he makes the transition to Hunter Biden's laptop, praising Big Media and Big Tech for their foresight in suppressing stories about its contents. To cover his rear, Roose adds a "to-be-clear" caveat: "To be clear, there is no evidence tying the *Post*'s report to a foreign disinformation campaign."[601] Whoa! Basically, Roose conceded that his whole column was speculation and conjecture. A shaky premise about Hillary as victim of Russian disinformation led to a preposterous one about Hunter being the victim of the same. Roose continued, "Many questions remain about how the paper obtained the emails and whether they were authentic. Even so,

598 Rebecca Shabad, "Trump chief of staff Mark Meadows refuses to speak to reporters with mask on," ABC News, October 12, 2020.
599 Astor, "Project Veritas Video Was a 'Coordinated Disinformation Campaign.'"
600 Kevin Roose, "Facebook and Twitter Dodge a 2016 Repeat, and Ignite a 2020 Firestorm," *New York Times*, October 15, 2020.
601 Roose, "Facebook and Twitter Dodge a 2016 Repeat, and Ignite a 2020 Firestorm."

the social media companies were taking no chances."[602] Taking no chances? No, they were colluding to rig an election, and the *Times* was doing its best to facilitate them.

In her article, Astor did not even give Project Veritas a "to be clear" reprieve, and, unlike Roose's column, hers was a news article run in the news section in the boxed style of *New York Times* news stories. Astor's statement, "but the allegations come solely from unnamed people who speak with Project Veritas operatives in the video and whose faces are not shown," is ludicrous.[603] Viewers can clearly see the faces and hear the voices in the video. Astor's claim evokes the "final, most essential command" of the "Party" in Orwell's Oceania: "to reject the evidence of your eyes and ears."[604]

Astor's article made Orwell seem altogether too prophetic. "None of the material in the video actually proved voter fraud," she reported as a conclusion that was completely contrary to all the facts. "The power to make a reportable event is thus the power to make experience,"[605] wrote Daniel Boorstin more than fifty years ago, as though he had Astor in mind. For her to write, "None of the material...proved voter fraud," creates an experience for her readers that, although "reportable," defies all evidence.

Rather than reporting the news, Astor colluded with Stanford University and the University of Washington to invent a patently false narrative. This is what Boorstin would call a "pseudo-event." Using her "ability to manipulate," Astor created for her pre-conditioned readers images that were "more attractive, more impressive, and more persuasive than reality itself."[606] By claiming that Project Veritas videos involved "unidentified sources" with "no verifiable evidence," she crafted an article that was completely synthetic and almost criminally unscrupulous. Hers was an extreme form of psychological projection, a real-life recreation of Orwell's fiction.

Astor wasn't finished. Toward the bottom of her piece, she argued that Project Veritas's promotional posts promised the video would be released on Monday, but it was released on Sunday night "a few hours after the publication of the *Times's* investigation [into President Trump's tax returns]." Her brilliant academic researchers assured her that the timing was unlikely to be a coincidence given what they called "the huge marketing about a 9/28 release date."[607]

This was truly rich. Not only was she accusing Project Veritas of publishing "deceptive" videos, but she was also assuming that the video was

602 Roose, "Facebook and Twitter Dodge a 2016 Repeat, and Ignite a 2020 Firestorm."
603 Astor, "Project Veritas Video Was a 'Coordinated Disinformation Campaign.'"
604 Orwell, *1984*, 103.
605 Daniel J. Boorstin, *The Image: A Guide to Pseudo-Events in America* (New York: Vintage, 2012), 36.
606 Boorstin, *The Image*.
607 Astor, "Project Veritas Video Was a 'Coordinated Disinformation Campaign.'"

launched specifically to negate the impact of a *Times* story on President Trump's taxes. This was nuts. In fact, when the *Times* published its tax story, the Project Veritas team almost postponed the video launch out of fear that the tax story would limit the impact of the video exposé. If anything, Astor was guilty of projection: the antagonist accuses the protagonist of exactly what the antagonist is or intends on doing. It is just as likely that once Project Veritas revealed its intention to release a major voter fraud story, the *Times* "coincidentally" released its story on President Donald Trump's tax returns.

The moment was unforgettable. The muckraker would have shared it with Astor if she had bothered to call. He was at his desk staring at six large flat-screen monitors stacked like Marshall speakers at a 1970s KISS concert. Members of the Project Veritas communications, production, and legal teams were arrayed around the desk. Other staffers were sitting around the room, all ready to pounce on a tweet or respond to a call with a reporter or social media heavy hitter. No one was expecting the *Times* tax story.

Project Veritas had just developed a new tactic for releasing stories. Previously, stories were released on a weekday at or around 9 a.m. Staff would give preferred reporters and outlets the story in advance with an embargo that expired upon the video's release. This gave them a chance to have their story written and ready to post. This time, team members were set to post on all Project Veritas websites and social media platforms on a Sunday at 9 p.m. An advanced release had been sent only to a few social media "influencers" but not to any reporters or media outlets. By releasing at night, the staff thought they could catch the attention of the millions of people scouring social media for news, and give reporters and outlets enough time to write their articles for Monday's "flip," the time when sites change over their stories for the new day. Since the heart of the strategy was a push on social media, a few influencers were clued in early, but this strategy differed quite a bit from the media embargoes Project Veritas had run in the past.

Turns out the *Times* had a similar idea. Believing in the plan, the muckraker made the executive decision to stick with it even after the *Times*' earlier release. As it happened, the Project Veritas story blew the *Times* story out of the water. In fact, the plan worked out so well that the *Times* felt the need to recruit some random academics to study our release as though it were a scientific phenomenon.

By the way, the much-ballyhooed tax story, "Long-concealed Records Show Trump's Chronic Losses and Years of Tax Avoidance,"[608] was

---

608 Russ Buettner, Susanne Craig, **and** Mike McIntire, "Long-Concealed Records Show Trump's Chronic Losses and Years of Tax Avoidance," *New York Times*, September 27, 2020.

written with no on-the-record sources, nor any supporting documents. That said, Astor still felt she was in a position to lecture Project Veritas on how to do proper investigative journalism. The satisfaction ran deep throughout Project Veritas for having caused Astor to think the impact of the *Times* story had been neutralized by one of their muckraking videos. When you're catching flak, they say, it means you are over the target.

Gratifying or not, there is no denying the *Times* has a little bit more clout than Project Veritas. After reading through Astor's article and understanding the widespread fake news it would generate, the muckraker decided it was time to fight back. If its editors would not retract the story, Project Veritas was going to sue the *Times*. In a way, they thought a lawsuit could save what was left of the Old Gray Lady. Yes, the *Times* has long been the voice of the posh Left, but despite that bias, it had historically lived up to its reputation as "the paper of record."

### *THE TRADITIONAL NEWSROOM HAS BEEN SUBVERTED BY HALF-TRUTHS, INNUENDO, AND IDEOLOGY; MANUFACTURED BY EACH REPORTER'S OPINION ON PEOPLE AND EVENTS.*

The paper's credibility did not collapse all at once. The decline started in the late 1990s when, in response to a number of factors starting to affect print journalism and its profitability, the *Times* pushed its journalists to embrace *explaining*, and not *reporting*, the news. Now, nearly thirty years later, readers are no longer receiving quality factual journalism. The traditional newsroom has been subverted by half-truths, innuendo, and ideology; manufactured by each reporter's opinion on people and events. In July 2020, *Times* op-ed writer and editor Bari Weiss made this clear in her open resignation letter.[609] Wrote Weiss: "A new consensus has emerged in the press, but perhaps especially at this paper: that truth isn't a process of collective discovery, but an orthodoxy already known to an enlightened few whose job is to inform everyone else."[610] The *Times*'s product, however, is still packaged and sold as news just as it traditionally was.

609 Edmund Lee, "Bari Weiss Resigns From New York Times Opinion Post: In a letter posted online Tuesday, she cites 'bullying by colleagues' and an 'illiberal environment,'" *New York Times*, July 14, 2020.
610 Bari Weiss, "Resignation Letter," bariweiss.com, July 14, 2020.

Project Veritas Legal was of the opinion that one of the best defamation lawyers in the country was a woman by the name of Libby Locke. She had successfully sued the *New York Times* in the past, and, if need be, she was ready to do it again. Ms. Locke is a great attorney. What was most impressive about her was that she was not eager to sue. She was convinced that the paper had acted with malice and had treated Project Veritas unfairly, and she preferred to reach out to its executives privately to avoid a drawn-out lawsuit. Libby asked if she could first try, at least, to reason with them. She knew them, and they knew her. They knew she only took on solid cases. Project Veritas Legal agreed. Besides, if the *Times'* legal and editorial leadership did not behave reasonably, that would be further evidence of malice. On October 16, 2020, Ms. Locke made the following statement in a letter to the *New York Times'* senior vice president and deputy general counsel, David McCraw:

> We were very disappointed to hear that the *New York Times* is continuing to stand behind these false and defamatory articles, characterizing them as "a fairly plain-vanilla account of research"…There is not a single sentence within these articles that even attempts to consider Project Veritas' perspective - much less disclose to the *Times'* readers that these 'researchers' were engaging in rank 'speculation' or that - as we conclusively demonstrate with the *Times'* and Election Integrity Project's websites own metadata - the *New York Times* and the Election Integrity Project were engaged in their very own "coordinated disinformation campaign."

Toward the end of her letter, Libby concluded her argument by pointing out the blatant hypocrisy of the *Times* actions against Project Veritas:

> At bottom, it is clear that the *New York Times* and Stanford and the University of Washington were engaging in precisely the same nefarious conduct this 'research' and these articles accused Project Veritas of. Their coordinated effort furthers both the *Times'* and the researchers' bias-driven desires to undermine journalism that reflected poorly on a prominent Democratic politician, as well as the *Times'* vindictiveness about the Project Veritas report upstaging the *Times'* story about Donald Trump's taxes. In short, and quite ironically, this *Times* story was itself the product of a 'coordinated disinformation campaign' - a collaboration between the *Times* and left-leaning academics who shared the goal of discrediting Project Veritas and its groundbreaking report, as quickly and thoroughly as possible.

The message to the *Times* was clear: either retract the lies or get sued. Within a few weeks, it became clear the *Times* executives would not budge, certainly not before the November election. Their heels were dug in, and they showed no sign of retracting. On October 30, 2020, Project Veritas filed a lawsuit against the *Times* in the Supreme Court of the State of New York.[611] The muckraker truly hopes its shareholders are aware that Project Veritas is undefeated in litigation. Project Veritas will win this lawsuit as well. More on this in the next chapter.

Of course, once the mothership had given the cue to attack Project Veritas, the lesser, satellite media began to fire away. Project Veritas had taken many defamatory hits over the years, but few have been as outrageous as that of KMSP-TV, Fox 9 Minneapolis-St. Paul. The outlet's "investigative" reporter, Tom Lyden, aired an interview with Liban tellingly headlined, "Subject of Project Veritas voter fraud story says he was offered bribe."[612] Of course, the story linked to the *Times* hit piece by Maggie Astor. Fox 9 also published a pre-release picture of the muckraker with one of Project Veritas' influencers, MyPillow CEO Mike Lindell. The photo was intended to prove that Project Veritas was "coordinating" some sort of disinformation campaign. It is almost as if these media hacks have never heard of the term "embargoing."

In his interview with Lyden, Liban made accusations against Project Veritas so transparently false only a "credible journalist" could believe them. The truth is Lyden and Fox 9 had no intention of investigating what Project Veritas had uncovered. They were quite literally in cover-up mode. What follows are some of the more delusional remarks made by Liban that Fox 9 echoed without challenging:

> In his first interview, Liban Osman tells the FOX 9 Investigators he was offered $10,000 by community activist Omar Jamal to say he was collecting ballots for Congresswoman Ilhan Omar…Omar Jamal, who he had not met previously, told him Project Veritas would pay him $10,000 to say he was harvesting ballots for Congresswoman Ilhan Omar.[613]

---

611 Adam Klasfeld, "Project Veritas Sues *New York Times* for Calling Group 'Deceptive,'" Law & Crime, October 30, 2020.

612 Tom Lyden, "Subject of Project Veritas voter fraud story says he was offered bribe," Fox 9 KMSP, October 6, 2020.

613 Lyden, "Subject of Project Veritas voter fraud story says he was offered bribe."

...during the encounter outside Cedar Riverside Apartments, it is Jamal who is handing the man $200 which was intended for the family of a sick relative in Somalia.[614]

As jaded as the muckraker had become, he still had a hard time believing what he was seeing. In a spirited response, he pointed out just how pathetically unprofessional was Fox 9's report.[615] The response video went viral. Mr. Lyden has not heard the last of Project Veritas. Project Veritas never has and never will offer anyone a bribe for content. It was shameful for Fox 9 to allow Liban to make these claims and get away with it.

This muckraker was bewildered at how Lyden could have been so gullible as to believe the claim that the $200 cash exchange was not for a ballot, as it appeared, but for a "sick kid in Somalia."[616] Was it a common practice for Fox 9 to invite guests on their program and allow them to make up improbable stories without a shred of evidence? Historically, a journalist's job was to challenge apparent criminals and scrutinize their stories, but that was not the case at Fox 9. On the bright side, most viewers, at least beyond the Fox 9 newsroom, had enough common sense to reject the sappy "sick kid in Somalia" alibi and see the exchange for the voter fraud it clearly was.

If the *New York Times* and Fox 9 attacks were straightforward smears, *USA Today*'s Camille Caldera came at Project Veritas sideways. Headlined "Fact check: No proof of alleged voter fraud scheme or connection to Rep. Ilhan Omar,"[617] Caldera's article relied on everything but facts.

*THIS MUCKRAKER WAS BEWILDERED AT HOW LYDEN COULD HAVE BEEN SO GULLIBLE AS TO BELIEVE THE CLAIM THAT THE $200 CASH EXCHANGE WAS NOT FOR A BALLOT, AS IT APPEARED, BUT FOR A "SICK KID IN SOMALIA."*

614 Lyden, "Subject of Project Veritas voter fraud story says he was offered bribe."
615 Project Veritas, "James O'Keefe goes NUCLEAR in debunking bogus Fox 9 report that defends illegal ballot harvesting," October 6, 2020, YouTube video, 9:07.
616 Project Veritas, "Omar Connected Harvester SEEN Exchanging $200."
617 Camille Caldera, "Fact check: No proof of alleged voter fraud scheme or connection to Rep. Ilhan Omar," *USA Today*, October 16, 2020.

For starters, any reporter who begins an article claiming "Project Veritas, a right-wing organization" has already shown her hand. Hers was yet another baseless hit piece from an emotional reporter who apparently had been triggered by Project Veritas's Minnesota investigation and discoveries. Filled with lies and deception, the article is so profoundly misguided that it insults the paper's readers. Consider the following excerpt and judge for yourself:

> ...Mohamed's Snapchats, may have been taken out of context. For example, those clips - some of which appear to depict him handling absentee ballots - do not include a date stamp, meaning they may have been taken within the weeks this summer that it was legal to collect an unlimited number of absentee ballots in Minnesota.[618]

Nothing was "taken out of context" in the video evidence. Caldera could not name a single deceptive edit because there was none. Project Veritas posted the entirety of Mohammed's Snapchat. Additionally, the investigation clearly showed one of Liban's Snapchat videos dated July 2, 2020. Liban dated the video himself using Snapchat's filter, not Project Veritas. Another bit of slander:

> On July 28, a district court struck down Minnesota's three-ballot limit. Another court reinstated the state's limit on Sept. 4. If the activities Mohamed shared on Snapchat occurred between the rulings, they may have been legal.[619]

The claim that "a district court struck down Minnesota's three-ballot limit" on July 28 is completely false. The court simply suspended the *enforcement* of this law from July 28 through Sept. 4, but it was always illegal for Minnesota citizens to have more than three ballots in their possession. Plus, on July 2, when Liban made his video, the law *was* enforceable. Here is *USA Today*'s final assault on common sense:

> Our rating: False

> ...the claim that Project Veritas discovered a voter fraud scheme connected to Rep. Ilhan Omar is FALSE...given the use of unnamed sources and unverifiable translations... There's no link between Omar and the alleged fraud...Re-

---

618 Caldera, "Fact check: No proof of alleged voter fraud scheme."
619 Caldera, "Fact check: No proof of alleged voter fraud scheme."

searchers have also termed the videos part of a "coordinated disinformation campaign."[620]

*USA Today*'s "rating" decision was an insult to the institution of journalism. The Project Veritas investigation was very easy to corroborate since it was all on video. Representative Ilhan Omar was cited numerous times in the video as a beneficiary of the illegal ballot harvesting scheme. If Caldera had any doubts about the translation from Somali, she should have checked the translations herself. Furthermore, citing the *Times'* allegation of a "coordinated disinformation campaign" merely highlights the ability of the *Times* to spawn a "coordinated disinformation campaign" of its own.

*USA Today* is one of Facebook's preferred fact-checking partners. Its "fact check" allowed Facebook to mark the entire Minnesota investigation as "false information."[621] The same day the *USA Today* article was published, October 16th, Project Veritas started receiving text messages from all over the country about Facebook's censorship of its videos as a result of that article. Everyone who saw or shared the video on Facebook was being told, in essence, that Project Veritas was little more than a political dirty trick shop running another scam.

The Big Tech oligarchs in Silicon Valley had been aching to take action against Project Veritas. After all, the muckrakers had exposed their lies and deceptive practices many times over the past several years. In this case, Facebook went on the offensive and did what they could to stop people from seeing the Minnesota investigation video reports. Despite knowing better himself, even this muckraker was shocked that Facebook's *thought police* stooped to the point of declaring the Project Veritas videos *false*.[622]

**EVERYONE WHO SAW OR SHARED THE VIDEO ON FACEBOOK WAS BEING TOLD, IN ESSENCE, THAT PROJECT VERITAS WAS LITTLE MORE THAN A POLITICAL DIRTY TRICK SHOP RUNNING ANOTHER SCAM.**

---

620 Caldera, "Fact check: No proof of alleged voter fraud scheme."
621 Project Veritas, "LEGAL UPDATE: NYT FORCED by court to ANSWER Veritas's defamation allegations, STUNNING Admissions," April 28, 2021, YouTube video, 9:44.
622 Project Veritas, "NYT FORCED by court to ANSWER Veritas's defamation allegations."

In Minneapolis, Project Veritas had mapped out a small-scale ecosystem of election fraud. The overall response to the Minneapolis video revealed a frighteningly large-scale and multidimensional digital complex of election rigging with the *New York Times* at its center. The collusion between Big Media and Big Tech was breathtaking. The *Times* recklessly generated the false information, *USA Today* endorsed the false information, and Facebook used *USA Today*'s endorsement to disqualify substantiated video evidence of malfeasance and wrongdoing on one of the world's largest media platforms. If this isn't election rigging, what is? Does this mean evidence no longer matters in their newsmaking? If so, Orwell takes this round.

## THE DESIRE TO BE LOVED AND THE FEAR OF BEING DISLIKED

Project Veritas launched an investigation to determine potential political bias at Google, whose executive Jen Gennai was secretly recorded explaining why the tech giant shouldn't be broken up through antitrust legislation: "Smaller companies don't have the resources," she reasoned, to "prevent the next Trump situation."[623] This is not something a Google executive would ever share willingly with the media, but once caught, Gennai did admit on a *Medium* post that she had, in fact, said these things. "I was having a casual chat with someone at a restaurant and used some imprecise language," she wrote. "Project Veritas got me. Well done."[624] That wasn't all. In the secret recording, Gennai admitted to some planned technical refinements that the Stasi would have envied:

> We all got screwed over in 2016, again it wasn't just us, it was, the people got screwed over, the news media got screwed over, like, everybody got screwed over so we've rapidly been like, what happened there and how do we prevent it from happening again….We're also training our algorithms, like, if 2016 happened again, would we have, would the outcome be different?[625]

By "screwed," Gennai meant a failure to control the election outcome, a situation Google planned to not see repeated. Insider documents revealed Google's "Machine Learning Fairness" algorithm in action. One

623 Project Veritas, "Veritas Re-Uploads Google Expose Taken Down By YouTube Ahead of White House Social Media Summit," July 11, 2019, YouTube video, 25:10.
624 Jen Gennai, "This is not how I expected Monday to go!" *Medium* blog, entry posted June 24, 2019.
625 Gennai, "This is not how I expected Monday to go!"

confidential document forwarded to Project Veritas from then-employee Zach Vorhies was titled, "The Definition of Algorithmic Unfairness" and contained the following:

> "Algorithmic unfairness" means unjust or prejudicial treatment of people that is related to sensitive characteristics such as race, income, sexual orientation, or gender, through algorithmic systems or algorithmically aided decision-making.[626]

Another confidential Google document contained this question as a subhead: "If a representation is factually accurate, can it still be algorithmic unfairness?" Congresswoman Debbie Lesko admittedly learned the official Google answer by watching a Project Veritas video. She read it out loud during a Congressional hearing:

> Imagine that a Google image query for CEOs show predominantly men. Even if it were a factually accurate representation of the world, it would be algorithmic unfairness. In some cases, it may be appropriate to take no action if the system accurately affects current reality, while in other cases it may be desirable to consider how we might help society reach a more fair and equitable state, via either product intervention...[627]

When finished reading, Lesko asked the Google lobbyist in attendance, "What does that mean, Mr. Slater?" Project Veritas had already received the answer to Congresswoman Lesko's question: Jen Gennai confirmed the substance of the document in her conversation with undercover reporters:

> The reason we launched our A.I. principles is because people were not putting that line in the sand, that they were not saying what's fair and what's equitable so we're like, well we are a big company, we're going to say it.[628]

Google insider Zach Vorhies added, "[Google execs] are going to define a reality based on what they think is fair and based upon what they want, and what is part of their agenda."[629] In this case, the evidence was

---

626 Project Veritas, "Google 'Machine Learning Fairness' Whistleblower Goes Public, says: 'burden lifted off of my soul,'" August 14, 2019, YouTube video, 19:34.
627 "Social Media and Content Monitoring: Executives from Facebook, Twitter and Google testified on Capitol Hill about efforts to counter online terror content, hate speech, and misinformation on their platforms," C-SPAN, June 26, 2019.
628 Project Veritas, "Google 'Machine Learning Fairness' Whistleblower Goes Public."
629 Project Veritas, "Google 'Machine Learning Fairness' Whistleblower Goes Public."

abundant. There was a current Google employee on the record, testimony from a high-ranking Google executive on the hidden camera, *and* a document. The *New York Times*, however, could not figure out where the story was. Despite the fact that Google had assigned itself the task of "preventing the next Trump situation," the *Times* seemed unable to detect any bias. *Times* reporter Charlie Warzel disingenuously tweeted his confusion:

> so it seems to me that this 'investigation' about Google's bias is really just a bunch of non-technical ppl mixing up algorithmic bias w/ political bias. am i wrong? could one of you smart technologists who follow me explain?[630]

That afternoon, Warzel continued sharing his stream-of-consciousness:

> I mean obviously the video snippets from their 'whistleblower' are all completely contextless and thus not to be taken seriously. but the part about fairness and algos. That's just them seeing the word bias and not understanding what it means, right?[631]

Wetzel's tweet was quickly "ratioed," meaning there were far more replies than retweets. This is often an indicator that the audience rejected his arguments or at least chose not to endorse them. The muckraker tweeted back to Charlie:

> You guys at the NYT make your entire bread and butter off of quoting people anonymously where we can't see or hear their voices, or any context at all. Now you're calling an interview with a whistleblower risking his career "contextless?"[632]

Warzel did not mention the muckraker by name in characterizing his series of arguments as "bad faith." Tweeted Warzel in return:

> I realize I look like a total boob here because i'm attempting to engage or even spend time responding to ppl who seem to operate exclusively in bad faith. i get that. i also see that this is a huge story on half the internet and i still struggle w/ how to address that if at all.[633]

---

630 @cwarzel, Twitter, June 24, 2019.
631 @cwarzel, Twitter, June 24, 2019.
632 @jamesokeefeiii, Twitter, June 24, 2019. Accessed before permanent suspension.
633 @cwarzel, Twitter, June 24, 2019.

As of this writing, no responses to the thread exist on Twitter except for those from verified media people, CNN's Brian Stelter, and independent commentator, Tim Pool. Said Brian Stelter:

> watching fox, seeing the talk shows promote project veritas,
> I *googled* for a reliable news account about what's going on…
> and…can't really find one.[634]

## STELTER CAN BE SEEN YIELDING TO "A SYMBIOTIC RELATIONSHIP WITH POWERFUL SOURCES OF INFORMATION BY ECONOMIC NECESSITY AND RECIPROCITY OF INTEREST."

Stelter's lack of self-awareness is impressive. He was reporting the difficulty he had finding damning material about Google *on Google's platform* without seeing the irony of the search. So outrageous was the oversight that it created one of the largest ratios on Twitter possible. Fifty-three people retweeted and more than four thousand commented just on Stelter's reply to Warzel.[635] Said one commenter, "You Googled Google for reliable news about Google suppressing Google results Google doesn't like? This is Inception level stupid."[636]

A later interview between Stelter and Susan Wojcicki, the CEO of YouTube, which is owned by Google, appears to show a deeper and darker reason why Stelter succumbed to a seemingly awkward bit of cognitive Google dissonance. As viewed through the "Manufacturing Consent" prism of Noam Chomsky and Edward Herman, Stelter can be seen yielding to "a symbiotic relationship with powerful sources of information by economic necessity and reciprocity of interest."[637]

Apparently, Stelter has an ongoing relationship with Wojcicki and YouTube, having interviewed Wojcicki in April 2020 on CNN.[638] The discussion centered around YouTube's decision to remove "medically unsubstantiated" information about the COVID outbreak from its platform.

---

634 @brianstelter, Twitter, June 24, 2019.
635 @leninsidious, Twitter, June 26, 2019.
636 @navymig, Twitter, June 26, 2019.
637 Edward S. Herman and Noam Chomsky, *Manufacturing Consent: The Political Economy of the Mass Media* (New York: Knopf Doubleday Publishing Group, 2011), 18.
638 Brian Stelter, "YouTube CEO says people are discovering different kinds of videos as the pandemic rages," CNN Business, April 24, 2020.

During the interview, the CNN chyron read, "How YouTube is Tackling Misinfo During the Pandemic."[639] Wojcicki spoke openly about "removing information which is problematic." Asked to quantify and define information deemed "problematic," Wojcicki clarified, "anything that would go against World Health Organization recommendations" and CDC guidelines. Specific examples Wojcicki included were those videos that encouraged people to take "Vitamin C and turmeric."[640]

Stelter did not challenge Wojcicki's argument and affirmed her trust in "authoritative sources." He asked her again if she was "taking the lie down," specifically the "lie" that vitamin C could help people. Here, Stelter and CNN were relying upon what Chomsky and Herman have called "information provided by government and experts funded and approved by these primary sources and agents of power."[641]

This reliance highlights the tension that exists in the cozy relationship CNN has with its high-level sources inside Google. By "requiring a maximum access to the actors" at YouTube, as Chomsky and Herman would say, Stelter has a "maximum dependency on these actors."[642] In making the conscious decision to "choose" Google/YouTube as a high-level source, Stelter put himself utterly at Google's mercy. Were CNN to offer some theory contrary to YouTube guidelines, YouTube could deny CNN access to its site, and CNN needs YouTube much more than YouTube needs CNN. "There is a pricetag on such extraordinary access."[643]

639 "Inside YouTube's 'numerous policy changes' during the pandemic," Reliable Sources, CNN, April 19, 2019.
640 "Inside YouTube's 'numerous policy changes' during the pandemic."
641 Herman and Chomsky, *Manufacturing Consent*.
642 Herman and Chomsky, *Manufacturing Consent*.
643 Herman and Chomsky, *Manufacturing Consent*.

# CHAPTER 9
# PROPAGANDA

## WORKS CITED

Bernays, Edward. *Propaganda*. New York: Ig Publishing, 2004.

Boorstin, Daniel J. *The Image: A Guide to Pseudo-Events in America*. New York: Vintage, 2012.

Chomsky, Noam. *Media Control: The Spectacular Achievements of Propaganda*. New York: Seven Stories Press, 2002.

Chomsky, Noam. *Necessary Illusions: Thought Control in Democratic Societies* (Brooklyn: South End Press, 1989).

Juvenal. *Satire 6*. Edited by Lindsay Watson and Patricia Watson (Cambridge: Cambridge University Press, 2014).

Kazin, Michael. *The Populist Persuasion* (New York: Cornell University Press, 1995).

Lippman, Walter. *Public Opinion* (CreateSpace Independent Publishing Platform, 2013).

Orwell, George. *1984*. New York: Signet Classics, 1950.

Postman, Neil and Andrew Postman. *Amusing Ourselves to Death: Public Discourse in the Age of Show Business* (New York: Penguin, 2005).

Solzhenitsyn, Aleksandr. *The Gulag Archipelago*, Volume 2. New York: Harper Perennial Modern Classics, 2007.

Stanley, Jason. *How Propaganda Works*. Princeton: Princeton University Press, 2015.

## JOURNAL ARTICLES

Tyrmand, Leopold. "The Media Shangri-La." *The American Scholar* 45, no.1 (Winter 1976).

## COURT CASES

DSCC, et al. v. Simon, et al., Minnesota Supreme Court Case No. A20-1017 (September 4, 2020).

# CHAPTER 10
# LITIGATION

*A nation that is afraid to let its people judge the truth and falsehood in an open market is a nation that is afraid of its people.*[644]

-John F. Kennedy, 1962

U nlike that of most businesses and even most nonprofits, the legal strategy of Project Veritas is guided by something other than commercial imperatives or monetary gain. Businesses settle lawsuits when their bottom lines begin to bleed. At that juncture, they complain there are no winners in litigation other than the lawyers and pay out some nuisance costs to make certain cases go away.

## REFUSING TO SETTLE

The opposition doesn't understand the Project Veritas model. Opponents tend to project their own mercenary values and fail to recognize that serious muckrakers are driven by mission, not by money. For Project Veritas, litigation is not a nuisance to be eliminated. It is an opportunity, offering, as it does, a further chance to expose corrupt media outlets. If profit-oriented corporations recoil from the expense of "discovery"—the process by which a party to a suit can force the opposing party to answer questions—Project Veritas welcomes discovery. The muckraker welcomes the inspection, the oversight, and the criticism. We are not afraid of discovery. For muckrakers, discovery *is* the point. Although Project Veritas has won every lawsuit ever filed against it, a "win" does not necessarily come in the form of a judgment. Victory is found in exposing the opposition for who they really are. A deposition legally compels a party to say the quiet part out loud, under oath. By initiating the discovery process, muckrakers turn their opponents into unwitting whistleblowers on themselves.

---

644 John F. Kennedy, "Address on the 20th Anniversary of the Voice of America," American Rhetoric Online Speech Bank, February 28, 1962.

## TWELVE JURORS ON THE SHOULDER AT EVERY STAGE

These recorded conversations under oath are damning for the cartel of detractors working against Project Veritas. Media scholar Paul S. Voakes argues that journalists "should do investigative reporting as if we were in a goldfish bowl, or as if there were 12 jurors looking over my shoulder at every stage."[645] For years, Big Media has ignored the "twelve jurors" rule. Discovery, however, exposes its vulnerabilities: sloppy reporting, glaring errors, unscrupulous actions, and even "malice."

The muckraker believes in transparency. Nothing revealed about Project Veritas through litigation has ever been damaging. For opponents, however, post-facto scrutiny remains an existential threat. It shouldn't be—Big Media would have no fear of transparency if they acted in private as they proclaim in public. Instead, forced transparency means a loss of total control over internal communications that could potentially ruin a media outlet's public posture. It's "propaganda," said CNN technical director Charlie Chester of his network's news product. He even boasted to a Veritas undercover journalist that CNN "got Trump out."[646]

*BY INITIATING THE DISCOVERY PROCESS, MUCKRAKERS TURN THEIR OPPONENTS INTO UNWITTING WHISTLEBLOWERS ON THEMSELVES.*

"We were creating a story there that we didn't know anything about. I think that's propaganda," Chester confessed. He said the quiet part out loud, albeit at a restaurant table and not on the witness stand; the media are merely an extension of the systems of power they are alleged to be holding to account. The aim of undercover investigation is to engage in the witness stand of life. The goal of which is to reveal a truth that could only otherwise be acquired in a sworn deposition.

---

645 Paul S. Voakes, "What Were You Thinking? A Survey of Journalists Who Were Sued for Invasion of Privacy," *Journalism and Mass Communication Quarterly* 75, no. 2 (Summer, 1998): 378-393.
646 Project Veritas, "PART 1: CNN Director ADMITS Network Engaged in 'Propaganda' to Remove Trump from Presidency," April 13, 2021, YouTube video, 8:58.

## DEFEATING THE *NEW YORK TIMES* MOTION TO DISMISS

Discovery opens the liar's notebook. It shows the collusion. Maggie Astor of the *New York Times*, supposedly reporting on what academic researchers had said about Project Veritas, wrote that the Minnesota ballot harvesting video was "probably" part of a "coordinated disinformation campaign." She wrote this because Project Veritas embargoed a copy of the video with reporters and influencers before it was released. This was rich. Just two years prior, the *Times* had published an article titled, "Ready, Set, Embargo." Wrote reporter Melina Delkic:

> Embargoes, set by government agencies, medical journals, theater groups, publishing houses and countless other sources are a common practice in journalism. They entail an agreement between a source and a reporter, or the reporter's publication, that the story will not be published before a given date and time.[647]

So why did the *Times* feel compelled to shine a floodlight on Project Veritas's everyday use of the same technique? The answer is simple: Project Veritas represents a threat. The Big Media cartel is losing the ability to control the dissemination of information. On the *Times*' "Journalism" website, the Gray Lady paints a rosy picture of its own stellar place in the media universe. The self-congratulatory accolades abound with flowering praise of its journalists, who "provide the context and analysis that readers need to better understand what's happening around them."[648] Its "news coverage," the *Times* proclaims, "helps people understand the world."[649] This fulsome language invites the reader to conjure a world in which the *Times* does not exist, a world in which people would be lost and adrift, meandering around in ignorance waiting for the *Times* with its "trusted guidance" to lead them home.

The *Times*' "Opinion Report" would seem even more important than the news. A *Times* op-ed, the reader is told, transcends the mission of understanding the world as it is and instead "helps people imagine the world as it could be through rich discussion and intelligent debate."[650] The *Times*' "opinion journalists are experts in their fields," the reader is assured, "who offer informed viewpoints on significant issues."[651] If only the *Times* editors

---

647 Melina Delkic, "Ready, Set, Embargo," *New York Times*, August 11, 2018.
648 "Journalism," The New York Times Company.
649 "Journalism."
650 "Journalism."
651 "Journalism."

had control of every system on earth, Utopia would surely be within their grasp. Intolerant of active dissent, they sought to shut down Project Veritas's reporting in Minnesota. This muckraker sued. The *Times* editors finally admitted that the very article in which they lambasted our routine news embargo as a "coordinated disinformation campaign" was itself a coordinated disinformation campaign.[652] The researchers who were mentioned in Astor's reporting gave her a copy of their blog post before it was published, and she waited until the embargo was lifted before submitting for publication.[653]

Astor, of course, didn't disclose this. This is only known because Project Veritas went to court and thwarted the *Times*' attempt to get the case dismissed. Very few get this far in our American legal system against the *New York Times*. Not many sue at all. Since the seminal 1964 Supreme Court case of *New York Times v. Sullivan*, only a handful of cases have survived the *Times*' motion to dismiss. Constitutional law professor Jonathan Turley described the victory by Project Veritas as "major." As Turley notes, this might explain why "it has received little coverage in the mainstream media."[654]

By defeating the *Times*' motion to dismiss, Project Veritas opened up discovery into the "Paper of Record." Turley noted that discovery "can be extremely difficult for a news organization." Big Media is fearful of transparency because it reveals their journalism to be subjective, biased, and rooted in untruths. Turley called this "advocacy journalism," which he noted, "has led to polls showing record lows in terms of trust for the media."[655] Gallup recently found that only 36 percent of independents trust the media to report the news "fully, accurately, and fairly."[656] In 2018, the *Times* executive editor blamed this loss of trust on Trump, saying the president "has hurt [the *Times*] credibility, and we don't deserve it."[657] Of course. It's always someone else's fault. The *Times* ignores the public's loss of confidence in the media to accurately report the news. The public trust had been on a steady decline, some would say plummeting, among people of all political persuasions long before Trump took office. A majority of self-identifying independent voters trusted the media in 2002. By 2016, Independents' trust in the media had cratered. In 2005, 70 percent of Democrats trusted

652 Project Veritas, "LEGAL UPDATE: NYT FORCED by court to ANSWER Veritas's defamation allegations," April 18, 2021, YouTube video, 9:44.
653 Project Veritas, LEGAL UPDATE."
654 Jonathan Turley, "Project Veritas Wins Victory against *New York Times* in Defamation Action," The Jonathan Turley blog, entry posted March 21, 2021.
655 Turley, "Project Veritas Wins Victory."
656 Megan Brenan, "Americans Remain Distrustful of Mass Media," Gallup, September 30, 2020.
657 Dean Baquet interview with Christiane Amanpour, "NY Times editor: Trump has damaged the press," Amanpour on CNN, January 12, 2018.

the media.[658] By the time Trump took office, that confidence plummeted nineteen percentage points, only recovering when the media declared war on the former president. Big Media loved Trump because he was their scapegoat. By blaming him for their decline, they would not have to focus on their own wrongdoing.

The reality is that the media hurt their own credibility. In the *Times* case, Maggie Astor, a news reporter, wrote—in the news section—that the Project Veritas Minnesota ballot harvesting video investigation was "deceptive." Once sued, the *Times* claimed Astor's description was just her "unverifiable expression of opinion."[659] This is important. Under existing law, an "opinion" cannot be proven true or false. By extension, it cannot be considered factual. The *Times* defense of its news article was, in effect, to argue that it was not based on fact. It clearly wasn't. In its response to the lawsuit, the *Times* had to admit that Astor had not bothered to contact any of Project Veritas' named sources or to familiarize herself with Minnesota law.

> ### ONCE SUED, THE TIMES CLAIMED ASTOR'S DE-SCRIPTION WAS JUST HER "UNVERIFIABLE EXPRESSION OF OPINION."

In sum, the *Times* did not disclose to its readers that the "news" they were reading as "fact" was, according to the *Times*, an "expression of opinion." Justice Charles Wood of the New York State Supreme Court explained that readers read news "expecting facts, not opinion." Wood continued:

> The Articles that are the subject of this action called Video "deceptive," but the dictionary definitions of "disinformation" and "deceptive" provided by the [*New York Times'*] defendants' counsel certainly apply to [*Times* reporters Maggie] Astor's and [Tiffany] Hsu's failure to note that they injected their opinions in news articles, as they now claim.[660]

The *Times*, apparently disappointed it could no longer defend its nonfactual news articles as opinion without disclosing it to their readers, appealed the court's decision. Yet, its executives continue to wonder why the

658 Megan Brenan, "Americans Remain Distrustful of Mass Media."
659 Project Veritas, "LEGAL UPDATE."
660 Project Veritas v. The New York Times Company, Maggie Astor, Tiffany Hsu, and John Does 1-5, No. 63921 Sup. Ct. NY (2020).

public has lost faith in them. The State Supreme Court's undressing of the *Times'* factual façade "could prove a critical shot across the bow for many in the media that the blurring of opinion and fact could come at a high price," wrote Turley. That price would be not only "the loss of core trust," but also "of core legal protections."[661]

The *New York Times* argued, as any so-called "credible" newspaper would do, that it can print whatever it likes regardless of whether it is true or false for the simple reason that other people said bad things about Project Veritas first. Project Veritas, the *Times* argued, was essentially "libel-proof."[662]

This was a bold claim coming from an outlet that cited Wikipedia among its sources to prove that Project Veritas has "a reputation" for being "'partisan zealots,' with 'a history of distorting facts or context,' 'running cons,' 'misleadingly editing video,' and being known for 'deceptively edited videos.'"[663] Attorney David Freiheit described the defense as a "vicious circle." The *Times* argued, in effect, "Project Veritas cannot sue us because they are libel-proof because we said so many bad things about them that they have to be bad, and they cannot sue us because we said bad things about them."[664] Jonathan Turley called this argument a "Hail Mary" defense that "likely lost credibility with the court and highlighted the alleged bias" of the *Times.*[665]

It's not that the *Times* dislikes investigative journalism—Dean Baquet recently agreed it is the journalist's job to "do the kind of deep reporting we all grew up doing"—but rather that the *Times* dislikes Project Veritas doing real reporting while its reporters sit idly by watching journalism at work. This elitist mindset, rooted in jealousy, presupposes that only the *Times* can have anonymous sources, go undercover, or release groundbreaking stories. Dissenting voices challenge the self-important mission of *Times* editors to shape the world as they want it to be shaped at their peril. A defamatory-prone echo chamber stands ready to help the *Times* quash dissent, one media ally after another, citing the supposed *opinion* of *Times'* reporters as *news*, indifferent even to its truth.

The *Times* dared argue that previous negative coverage on the part of the major media would support its claim of Project Veritas's alleged deception. Justice Wood was having none of that. "Polling does not decide truth,

---

661 Turley, "Project Veritas Wins Victory."

662 Project Veritas, "New York Supreme Court Judge DENIES NYT 'Motion To Dismiss' In Veritas Defamation Lawsuit," April 5, 2021, YouTube video, 18:03.

663 Project Veritas v. The New York Times Company et al.

664 Byron York, "The *New York Times*'s embarrassing defense in the Project Veritas case," *Washington Examiner*, March 24, 2021.

665 Turley, "Project Veritas Wins Victory."

nor speak to evidence," Wood wrote in rejecting the *Times*' self-aggrandizing argument, "and Defendants have not met their burden to prove that the reporting by Veritas in the Video is deceptive."[666]

Accomplishing anything through litigation, however, is difficult. Writes Mark Hertsgaard in *Bravehearts: Whistle-Blowing in the Age of Snowden*: "Litigation needs to go to court, which is the turf of the status quo."[667] That conceded, Project Veritas is not alone in its quest for justice inside the court system. Others have stepped forward and sought their remedy through litigation, among them former vice presidential candidate Sarah Palin.

## *"POLLING DOES NOT DECIDE TRUTH, NOR SPEAK TO EVIDENCE."*

In 2017, the *New York Times* published an opinion piece attempting to link the tragic 2011 shooting of Arizona representative Gabby Giffords to a political map published by Sarah Palin's PAC targeting vulnerable opponents in an upcoming election. Bizarrely, the editorial hyperlinked to an ABC News article, expressly stating there was no connection between Palin's map and the shooting of Giffords by a deranged apolitical gunman.[668] The authors taking credit for the hit piece on Palin were editorial page editor James Bennet and de facto Bernays-style propagandists in chief of the holiest-of-holy bastions of opinion journalism, the *New York Times* Editorial Board. Bennet admitted under oath that he hadn't even been aware of any facts actually showing a connection between Palin and the 2011 shooting. He took it upon himself to reach journalistic conclusions unsubstantiated by clear fact. What he wrote was patently false and disproven time and time again, including by his own newspaper. In fact, the same day Bennet's editorial was published, the *Times* published yet another article confirming "no connection" between the Sarah PAC map and the crime.[669] Fact-checker PolitiFact rated Mr. Bennet's editorial "False," and it was.[670]

---

666 Project Veritas v. The New York Times Company et al.
667 Mark Hertsgaard, *Bravehearts: Whistle-Blowing in the Age of Snowden* (New York: Hot Books, 2016), 65.
668 Josh Gerstein, "Appeals court revives Palin libel suit against *New York Times*," Politico, August 6, 2019.
669 Alexander Burns, "Shooting Is Latest Eruption in a Grim Ritual of Rage and Blame," *New York Times*, June 14, 2017.
670 John Kruzel, "No evidence Sarah Palin's PAC incited shooting of Rep. Gabby Giffords," PolitiFact.com, June 15, 2017.

Though the case is now headed for trial, thanks to an appeal, a lower court initially dismissed the case, and Bennet kept his job. Years later, Bennet was finally forced to resign, but not for writing a blatantly false article. He was forced to resign for permitting a Republican, Arkansas senator Tom Cotton, to publish an opinion piece in the *Times*.[671] False articles were acceptable. Dissenting voices were not.

Ida Tarbell, while investigating Standard Oil, went to the courts to fight for her investigative stories. Observed Stephanie Gorton in a recent retrospective on Tarbell's work, "It was these private lawsuits that yielded the stories never previously reported by journalists."[672] The libel suit was historically considered an "entering wedge." Elaborated veteran journalist Daniel Schorr, "All you have to do now is just file a libel suit…just to get that discovery process and get people to sit down and have to answer all those questions you want to ask them."[673]

For the most part today, the media do not report the news as though there were a jury looking over their shoulders. In fact, many of them tend to do the opposite and will only fully scrutinize their work when forced to do so by legal action, the possibility of termination, or public ridicule. When the press fails to do its duty, ordinary people are caught in the crossfire and can be destroyed in the time it takes to post a tweet.

### *IN AN AGE OF UNAPOLOGETIC LIES AND UNIVERSAL DECEIT, THE NEED FOR A COMMON FINANCIAL COFFER FOR THOSE UNFAIRLY PERSECUTED BY THE PRESS IS BECOMING MORE AND MORE EVIDENT.*

In a February 2020 podcast, Tim Pool noted, "The issue is there are a lot of people now who are finding themselves in the public sphere who have small careers as pundits and journalists. They can't go up against the *New York Times*…. They can't afford to sue."[674] Pool is correct, and the *Times*, along with its media cohorts, count on this imbalance. They presume they can launch a war of attrition that their opponents cannot afford to endure.

671 Rishika Dugyala, "NYT opinion editor resigns after outrage over Tom Cotton op-ed," Politico, June 7, 2020.

672 Stephanie Gorton, "Ida Tarbell: Reporting the Oil Region," Belt, March 3, 2020.

673 CUNY TV, "Television in America: An Autobiography – Daniel Schorr," taped January 1, 2003, YouTube video, 55:53.

674 Timcast IRL, "Project Veritas Scores EPIC Win Against New York Times, Making The NYT Look Like LOSERS," April 29, 2021, YouTube video, 15:21.

Few dare take the *Times* further than a complaint. Project Veritas does and will continue to do so, while helping others do the same.

In an age of unapologetic lies and universal deceit, the need for a common financial coffer for those unfairly persecuted by the press is becoming more and more evident. Pool called it "The People's Defamation Defense Fund."

We call it Project Veritas Legal.

It is clear that as information continues to move toward centralized control under the thumbs of like-minded editors and producers, someone has to step forward to find alternative ways of protecting those who've had their names trashed and their reputations sullied, but who lack the monetary means necessary to fight these massive media outlets. There have been too many cases like those of Nick Sandmann, from Covington High School, whose only crime was being in the wrong place, at the wrong time, while the cartel of cameras were rolling and the false narratives were forming.

Project Veritas Legal, a law firm for the defamed, exists to defend citizens and journalists alike—for free—from unfair treatment by the press that causes unnecessary harm. Project Veritas Legal gives those citizens and journalists the resources and litigation power to fight back against the likes of the *New York Times*, CNN, and Twitter like we have done. Litigation is an unfortunate but necessary reality. The game has changed from checkers to chess. To do nothing is to lose, and to lose is to be silenced, subdued, and withdraw from participation in our democracy. To cede control of the information citizens need to self-govern is to allow Big Tech and Big Media to shape the future. There will be those who decry litigation as a departure from, or attack on, the First Amendment. They are wrong: holding to account those who abuse the First Amendment is a defense of the Constitution.

"The freedom that the First Amendment protects," writes free speech advocate Alexander Meiklejohn, "is the presence of self-government."[675] As Meiklejohn understood, self-government depended on having an informed citizenry:

> Public discussions of public issues, together with the spreading of information and opinion bearing on those issues must have a freedom unabridged by our agents. Though they govern us, we, in a deeper sense, govern them. Over our governing, they have no power. Over their governing, we have sovereign power.[676]

675 Alexander Meiklejohn, "The First Amendment is an Absolute," *The Supreme Court Review* 1961 (1961): 245-66.
676 Meiklejohn, "The First Amendment."

Decades of case law made it clear that public officials lack authority to censor dissenting voices in America for this very reason. So, in 1996, the Communications Decency Act was passed, by which those frustrated public officials, unable to censor the citizenry themselves, decreed blanket immunity on Big Tech and Big Media to censor private citizens—effectively ceding control of the public square to unaccountable private powers. Unrestrained by government, Big Tech and Big Media happily take up the torch of censorship, casually banning, de-boosting, and defaming those with whom they don't agree. Perhaps most egregiously, public officials now use the very system they created to accomplish that which the law says public officials could not do: censor private speech. Before the Communications Decency Act, the government used to simply remove speech they disagreed with, only to be told they could not.[677] Now, they remove speech they disagree with by demands,[678] thinly veiled threats to Big Tech,[679] and do so with apparent impunity with few judges other than Clarence Thomas willing to call foul.[680]

Shutting down discussion is antithetical to a free society. "As we try to create and enlarge freedom, such universal discussion is imperative," writes Meiklejohn.[681]

Since its creation, Project Veritas has been the "tip of the spear" in the battle for free speech. Project Veritas Legal is the tip of the spear in the legal battle for the right to participate in our democracy without fear of being defamed. The muckraker will not be silenced, and he will not stand by while those in power seek to silence others by defamation. Meiklejohn argues the "authority of citizens to decide what they shall write and, more fundamental, what they shall read and see, has not been delegated to any of the subordinate branches of government."[682] Neither has it been delegated to Twitter, CNN, or the *New York Times*.

Despite the obvious merit behind Project Veritas Legal in the Washington media circles, waging these lonely legal battles is hard to come by. Too many journalists refuse to rock the boat for fear that they one day will

---

677 Island Trees Union Free School District v. Pico by Pico, 457 US 853 (1982).
678 "Judicial Watch: Documents Show CA State Officials Coordinated with Big Tech to Censor Americans' Election Posts," Judicial Watch, April 27, 2021.
679 "Schiff Sends Letter to Google, Facebook Regarding Anti-Vaccine Misinformation" Adam Schiff, chiff.house.gov, February 14, 2019.
680 Betsy McCaughey, "Justice Thomas shows how we can end Big Tech censorship for good," *New York Post*, April 6, 2021.
681 Meiklejohn, "The First Amendment."
682 Meiklejohn, "The First Amendment."

not be allowed to climb back on board. The muckraker will rock the boat for them, unwavering in response to their biting criticism and false claims. With the formation of Project Veritas Legal, everyday Americans previously unable to fight back against career-destroying defamation by journalists have a warrior to go to battle with. With every defamation demand, we chip away at Big Media's belief that they will never be held accountable. With every lawsuit that proceeds to discovery, we peel back the curtain and expose Big Media for the biased commercial imperative hypocrites they are. The cries of desperation by which the silent majority ask, "What can I do?" can now be answered yet again.

Stand up and fight.

We've got your back.

# LITIGATION

## WORKS CITED

Hertsgaard, Mark. *Bravehearts: Whistle-Blowing in the Age of Snowden*. New York: Hot Books, 2016.

## JOURNAL ARTICLES

Meiklejohn, Alexander. "The First Amendment is an Absolute." *The Supreme Court Review* 1961 (1961).

## COURT CASES

Island Trees Union Free School District v. Pico by Pico. 457 U.S. 853 (1982).

Project Veritas v. The New York Times Company, Maggie Astor, Tiffany Hsu, and John Does 1-5. No. 63921 Supreme Court of New York (2020).

# CHAPTER 11
# VERITAS

*Turning and turning in the widening gyre,*
*The falcon cannot hear the falconer;*
*Things fall apart; the centre cannot hold;*
*Mere anarchy is loosed upon the world,*
*The blood-dimmed tide is loosed, and everywhere.*
*The ceremony of innocence is drowned;*
*The best lack all conviction, while the worst*
*Are full of passionate intensity.*[683]

-William Butler Yeats

January 6, 2021 was, to say the least, a memorable day. Among the messages received at Project Veritas on January 7, many were profoundly hopeless, others deeply cynical. Some examples:

"Nothing will come of exposing them."

"Nobody is ever arrested or held accountable."

"Your work is of no use."

"We have already exposed them, and nothing happens."

"You're naive, there is no more hope."

"The truth will set you free is pure bullshit because the other side has no morals."

---

683 William Butler Yeats, *The Collected Poems of W.B. Yeats: A New Edition.* ed. Richard J. Finneran, (Palgrave, 2003), 187.

"There is no law and order for the elites."

"You've uncovered many things, and it all gets ignored by the swamp republicans."

"I know you're saying don't quit, but most of us are mentally exhausted."

"Words, words, words, people have been hearing stuff like this for months and it keeps heading down the same rabbit hole to nowhere. But thanks for the words."

"It's hard to fight when the whole system is stacked against it all…seriously."

"What a useless message."

"So much evidence and even our own people didn't fight for us."

"Maybe fifty years from now something will start to change, but I doubt it."

"I've surrendered myself to death in some form or another because I see no point in fighting for this anymore. My only wish is that my enemies choke on my guts as they eviscerate me. Metaphorically of course."

Understandably, people today are worried about real political persecution—deplatformed media sites, targeted audits, possible arrests, and forced exiles to the gulags, metaphorical and perhaps even literal. This is nothing new. From the first days of the Republic, citizens have worried about political persecution, and with good cause. In 1798, President John Adams signed into the law the Sedition Act that outlawed, among other things, any "false, scandalous and malicious writing" against Congress or the president, and made it illegal to conspire "to oppose any measure or measures of the government."[684] In the three years the law was on the books, US federal courts prosecuted at least twenty-six citizens, many of them editors of Republican newspapers, and all of them opposed to the Adams administration.[685] Throughout American history, journalists have risen up against the abuse of power and pushed back, none more prominently than the "muckrakers," a term first used by President Theodore Roosevelt, as much of a caution as a commendation. Said Roosevelt, "The men with the muck rakes are often indispensable to the well-being of society; but only if they know when to stop raking the muck."[686] The *Encyclopedia Britannica* put a little meat on the definition:

> **Muckraker**, any of a group of American writers identified with pre-World War I reform and exposé literature. The muckrakers provided detailed, accurate journalistic accounts of the political and economic corruption and social hardships caused by the power of big business in a rapidly industrializing United States.[687]

## *"THE MEN WITH THE MUCK RAKES ARE OFTEN INDISPENSABLE TO THE WELL-BEING OF SOCIETY; BUT ONLY IF THEY KNOW WHEN TO STOP RAKING THE MUCK."*

Muckraking has never been easy. "They're going to ban you and jail you," is what the muckraker hears, and has always heard. As has happened in the past, many citizens are willing to throw in the towel and say, "I'm done. Now it's time for me to look after Number One." As one commenter said all too hopelessly on January 7, "Nothing matters." But things do matter. From the perspective of the American muckraker, the only thing we have to fear is hopelessness itself.

The people expressing their discontent—let's call them the *demoralized*—have a passion for justice in a world where they believe justice is being destroyed. Some think justice an apparition, a pipe dream, rarely attainable in the best of circumstances, utterly impossible in the worst. They come to doubt whether truth itself exists, and when something true is

---

684 "Transcript of Alien and Sedition Acts (1798)," ourdocuments.gov.
685 History.com Editors, "Alien and Sedition Acts," History.com, updated March 5, 2020.
686 Theodore Roosevelt, "The Man with the Muck Rake," American Experience, PBS, April 15, 1906.
687 Britannica, T. Editors of Encyclopaedia, "Muckraker," *Encyclopedia Britannica*, April 14, 2020.

reported in the media, they are understandably suspicious of it. As Hunter S. Thompson observed, "Absolute truth is a very rare and dangerous commodity in the context of professional journalism."[688]

### THE PENDULUM MAY SWING BACK IN THE IMMEDIATE YEARS AHEAD, BUT OVER TIME, AS THE RIGHT FIGHTS TO PRESERVE THE STATUS QUO, THE LEFT CONTINUES ITS LETHAL HUNDRED-YEAR MARCH FORWARD, AND THE CENTER CANNOT HOLD.

The "conservative movement" has failed the demoralized. It failed because once it achieved its limited goals, it focused on sustaining its own commercial imperative: buy my books, read our white paper, sponsor our conferences. Movement leaders refuse to realize these are no longer the most effective means of persuasion and influence. In reality, these are among the least effective. Fact-finding works only in a world where facts on a printed page matter, but the institutional right has been slow to get that message. Money and ratings have become the end goal of too many organizations, even philanthropic ones. As we've seen, not even the best of causes is immune to blue collar philosopher Eric Hoffer's dictate, "What starts out here as a mass movement ends up as a racket, a cult, or a corporation."[689]

Subversion and revolution, by contrast, demand the kind of long, slow march through society's institutions that Italian Communist Antonio Gramsci envisioned a century ago. The pendulum may swing back in the immediate years ahead, but over time, as the right fights to preserve the status quo, the left continues its lethal hundred-year march forward, and the center cannot hold.

To a certain extent, elections have failed almost everyone, at least everyone who believes in republican government. Representative democracy has become less meaningful as Congress abdicates its responsibility to a permanent, unelected, administrative state, and the White House gobbles up much of the remaining power through executive orders, often undone by the executive orders of a succeeding administration. Government has lapsed into a state of increasing sclerosis. For years now, the world's greatest deliberative body has been divided by the thinnest of margins with the result, as of this writing, that an otherwise obscure senator from West Virginia dictates the national agenda.

---

688 Hunter Thompson, *The Great Shark Hunt* (New York: Simon & Schuster, 2003), 71.
689 Eric Hoffer, *The Temper of Our Time* (New York: Harper & Row, 1969), 60.

As Dan Pfeiffer has acknowledged, "There is an amoral (and often immoral) nihilism to an approach that strives for political power for political power's sake."[690] And Pfeiffer should know. He was a White House operative. In yielding power to the nihilists, we have come to accept the world as it is, a world in which Congress doesn't pass laws to help society, but to seduce voters into extending the ruling party's power and pick winners and losers. Radical activist Saul Alinsky was nothing if not a realist. "In this world irrationality clings to man like his shadow so that the right things are done for the wrong reasons," Alinsky wrote more than a half century ago. "Afterwards, we dredge up the right reasons for justifications. It is a world not of angels but of angles, where men speak of moral principle but act on power principles."[691]

Unfortunately, as the pendulum swings back and forth, deficits rise, and our rights diminish. This regression evokes in the demoralized an increasing sense of pain and futility. Understandably, they project that pain onto the people who do take action as a way of rationalizing their own apathy and that of others like them. In the depths of this spiritual, moral, legal, and political malaise, the American muckraker sees things differently. So differently, in fact, he may seem to have gone completely mad.

"Every good investigative reporter has to be slightly mad," writes journalism scholar James Dygert. "Not only must he manifest the customary skills and characteristics of a journalist, he must do so to excess, and be ever ready to attempt the impossible." Success, Dygert argues, comes only through persistence, a persistence that borders on obsession. "When failure is inevitable and further work will be a waste of time, because the truth or the proof, to be realistic, is unattainable, the investigative reporter can't accept it. He argues, rants, and pleads against surrender." In sum, writes Dygert, "There's no such thing as defeat."[692]

A muckraker's obsession is made whole by a genuine sense of passion. Dostoevsky writes in his 1877 short story, "The Dream of a Ridiculous Man," of a hopeless fellow who has a great spiritual awakening after experiencing a transformative dream. When the man wakes again to the benighted world around him, he understands universal timeless truths that have awakened his spirit. He understands how important it is to love others as much as he loves

---

690 Dan Pfeiffer, *Un-Trumping America: A Plan to Make America a Democracy Again* (New York: Twelve, 2020), 10.
691 Saul D. Alinsky, *Rules for Radicals* (New York: Random House, 1971), 13.
692 James Dygert, *Investigative Journalist*, 117.

himself. Writes Dostoevsky, "Nothing else is required. That would settle everything. Yes, of course it's nothing but an old truth that has been repeated and reread millions of times - and it still hasn't taken root."[693]

Dostoevsky understood the alternative. In *The Brothers Karamazov*, he outlines what happens to a man in the absence of genuine passion:

> Not respecting anyone, he ceases to love, and having no love, he gives himself up to the passions and coarse pleasures, in order to occupy and amuse himself, and in his vices reaches complete bestiality, and it all comes from lying continually to others and to himself.[694]

Within forty years of Dostoevsky explaining this simple truth, Russia would embark on an experiment in government in which, writes Soviet dissident Aleksandr Solzhenitsyn, "The permanent lie becomes the only safe form of existence."[695]

Lest America, too, become a nation of feckless cowards, citizens must fight. For the American muckraker, the fight for the truth is so much bigger than this moment in time. Holding people's feet to the fire is an eternal calling. Shaming the corrupt by creating a frenzy of what the original muckrakers called "righteous indignation" never goes out of style. Demoralized friends and allies may want to be left alone, but in the memorable words of the enraged anchor Howard Beale in the film classic, *Network*, "I'm not going to leave you alone, I want you to get mad, I am a human being God damn it, my life has value…I'm mad as hell, I'm not going to take this anymore."[696]

Fighting for what is right and standing on principle matters. Exposure is the one thing the chronically dishonest fear. Citizens must make a conscious choice, as Solzhenitsyn did, to "live not by lies."[697] If they accept lies, they enable liars. If they yield to nihilism and futility, they invite corruption. If they look out for Number One, they may end up ratting out their brothers and sisters. This is not the kind of society any normal citizen wants. Citizens can choose, like Dostoevsky's passionless man, to say, "nothing matters," and narrow their vision of life to material pleasures and amoral political outcomes. But if they choose the path of integrity, regard-

693 Fyodor Dostoevsky, *Notes from Underground, White Nights, The Dream of a Ridiculous Man, and Selections from The House of the Dead* (New York: New American Library, 1961), 229.

694 Fyodor Dostoevsky, *The Brothers Karamazov* (New York: Farrar, Straus and Giroux, 2002), 44.

695 Aleksandr Solzhenitsyn, *The Gulag Archipelago*, vol. 2 (New York: Harper Perennial Modern Classics, 2007), 692.

696 *Network*, directed by Sidney Lumet, Metro-Goldwyn-Mayer, 1976.

697 Solzhenitsyn, *The Gulag Archipelago*, 692.

less of where it leads, they ennoble their existence and give their life point and purpose. Why live it otherwise?

As for the concerns about political persecution, this much needs to be said: citizens must be willing to have their reputations shattered and their lives turned upside down. They must be ready to be falsely accused, to stand trial, even to go to prison.

The American muckraker has experienced some or even all of this. He knows the brutality of trials by the media and betrayals by his allies. He knows the hell that can rain on his loved ones. He may even know what the inside of a jail cell looks like. These attacks hurt, sometimes a lot, but they do not hurt nearly enough to kill a spirited movement.

The American muckraker understands that the path to truth includes suffering and sacrifice. Writes anti-Communist whistleblower Whittaker Chambers, who experienced his share of both: "You will know that life is pain, that each of us hangs always upon the cross of himself. And when you know that this is true of every man, woman and child on earth, you will be wiser."[698] But, as Chambers suggests, suffering brings wisdom.

The muckraker dreams of an army of truth-tellers, of people willing to fight, even to suffer, to expose the truth. His nightmare is that this dream does not come to fruition. An extended nightmare is a society without faith, a society in which humanity has little meaning and humans have lost their worth, a society in which Americans quench their unvoiced pain with alcohol, drugs, anti-anxiety medication, video games, Netflix, and power politics. Writes Chambers, "Human societies, like human beings, live by faith and die when faith dies."[699]

Aleksandr Solzhenitsyn spent more than fifty years in study, many of those as a prisoner in Soviet gulags. He consumed thousands of books and collected firsthand accounts of a revolution that killed upwards of sixty million people. After "clearing away the rubble," Solzhenitsyn comes to one inarguable conclusion: "Men have forgotten God. That's why all this has happened."[700]

Just imagine, if all stalwart citizens stood up together, took out their cameras, and exposed the deceivers in their midst. Imagine if people with real skin in the game—Big Tech insiders, Big Media journal-

---

698 Whittaker Chambers, *Witness* (Washington: Regnery Publishing, 1969), introduction, xlx.
699 Chambers, *Witness*, introduction, xxxiv.
700 Aleksandr Solzhenitsyn, "'Men Have Forgotten God': Aleksandr Solzhenitsyn's 1983 Templeton Address," *National Review*, December 11, 2018.

ists, Deep Staters of every variety—followed their consciences. What if Loretta Lynch recorded her secret meeting with Bill Clinton on that Phoenix tarmac? What if the counting rooms in Detroit and Philadelphia and Atlanta were livestreamed? What if all government officials lived their lives in fear of being recorded while abusing their power? If our leaders knew they were being surveilled, they would be far less inclined to surveil the rest of us.

Imagine infiltrating the bunker of an evil enemy regime and shining light in the darkness. That would change things, create consensus, inform the populace. It would be the end itself instead of a means to a political end. As sure as rock beats scissors, light defeats corruption. The American muckraker knows this light will shine, and he knows the only thing that can stop it from shining is, well, stopping. The only thing that can stop inspired citizens is themselves. We will prevail because good is stronger than evil and worth fighting for, always. Indeed, we cannot lose. We've already won. Things just have to play out. As the African proverb states, "If there is no enemy within, the enemy outside can do us no harm."[701] Abraham Lincoln may have been right when he said America cannot be destroyed from the outside, and, if it falters, it is because "a house divided cannot stand."[702]

### *JUST IMAGINE, IF ALL STALWART CITIZENS STOOD UP TOGETHER, TOOK OUT THEIR CAMERAS, AND EXPOSED THE DECEIVERS IN THEIR MIDST.*

When this muckraker was going through his darkest days on federal probation a decade ago, unable to travel and unable to work, with all hope seemingly lost, he was told by family members, "Even if there is one person who will listen, tell the truth." As Winston Churchill reminded his listeners, "No one can guarantee success in war, but only deserve it."[703] The American muckraker cannot give up or give in as long as there is oxygen in his lungs and brave allies willing to blow the whistle. These worthy souls are the fuel that gives the muckraker hope. They are what render corrupted political leadership impotent.

---

701 Anonymous.
702 Abraham Lincoln, "House Divided Speech, June 16, 1858," Abraham Lincoln Online, 2018.
703 Winston Churchill, *Their Finest Hour* (London: Cassell, 1947), 434.

## *"EVEN IF THERE IS ONE PERSON WHO WILL LISTEN, TELL THE TRUTH."*

━━━━━━━

Among the thousands of cynical tweets and emails posted after the seeming futility of that fateful day in January, there were glimmers of hope. More than a few brave souls were reborn. Every ten thousand people who complained could be offset, the muckraker understood, by one valiant warrior willing to leave the sidelines and make a personal sacrifice for his country.

In Washington, DC, that January 6, watching live as the Capitol building was overrun, one brave federal employee told the muckraker, "That's it. I'm going to record everything." The would-be whistleblower continued, "As long as it's not classified, people have a right to know. They must know about this corruption." When asked about fear of possible retribution, this person answered, "Let them come after me, I'm ready for that. As long as you don't stop, I won't stop." This whistleblower has a heartfelt belief in the concept of *veritas ad populum*, truth to the people, a cause that is bigger than any one individual.

The American muckraker's job is to expose the truth. Why does the truth matter? On a fundamental level, public sentiment "is everything," said Abraham Lincoln. Lincoln added, "With public sentiment, nothing can fail; without it nothing can succeed. Consequently he who moulds public sentiment, goes deeper than he who enacts statutes or pronounces decisions. He makes statutes and decisions possible or impossible to be executed."[704] Remember, too, there is joy to be had in the fight itself. Courage in the face of adversity is a virtue as old as adversity itself. No one has memorialized this virtue better than Mexican revolutionary Emiliano Zapata. Said he for the ages, *Prefiero morir de pie que vivir de rodillas*, "I'd rather die on my feet, than live on my knees."[705] Historian Thomas Babington Macaulay reminds us of the valiant defense of the Sublican Bridge by Horatius from the invading Etruscans in the heroic early days of the Roman Republic:

---

704 Abraham Lincoln, "First Debate: Ottawa, Illinois, Mr. Lincoln's Speech," Lincoln Home, nps.gov, August 21, 1858.
705 Gerald H. Anderson and Thomas F. Stransky, *Mission Trends: Liberation Theologies in North America and Europe* (Grand Rapids: Wm. B. Eerdmans Publishing Co., 1979), 281.

*Then out spake brave Horatius,*

*The Captain of the Gate:*

*To every man upon this earth*

*Death cometh soon or late.*

*And how can man die better*

*Than facing fearful odds,*

*For the ashes of his fathers,*

*And the temples of his Gods*[706]

Although often facing fearful odds, the muckraker is the tyrant's natural enemy. Tyrants fear, above all else, a free press. For far too long, however, salaried journalists have shied from the responsibilities of freedom, preferring instead, as Noam Chomsky and Edward Herman wrote, to uphold "a normative order of authorized knowers in our society."[707] For years, ordinary citizens have had little recourse but to complain about the media. Those days are over. Real journalism today is an act not of being, but of doing—of observing, of recording, of providing the content for an increasing number of platforms. If the muckraker is removed from one platform, he or she will be talked about on other platforms—collectively, in the words of the Supreme Court, "The Modern Public Square."[708] If his stories are strong enough, people will talk about them. Patriots will force the stories into mainstream circulation via distribution by proxy. This informal networking is what dissidents in the lethally oppressive Soviet Union called the *samizdat,* or "self-publishing."

Content, not platform, is king, always and everywhere. If the story is powerful enough, it will force its way into mainstream circulation. With Big Media comfortably serving as State propagandist, the muckraker must

---

706 Thomas Babington, "Macaulay," Representative Poetry Online, University of Toronto, 217-224.
707 Edward S. Herman and Noam Chomsky, *Manufacturing Consent: The Political Economy of the Mass Media* (New York: Knopf Doubleday Publishing Group, 2011), 19.
708 Barak Richman and Francis Fukuyama, "How to Quiet the Megaphones of Facebook, Google and Twitter," *Wall Street Journal,* updated February 12, 2021.

234 | AMERICAN MUCKRAKER

be the custodian of the public's conscience. It has been left to the muckraker to patrol the boundaries of the moral order and to summon righteous indignation among the citizenry. If crucified for his content, he knows a new breed of heroes will rise up, and in so doing, ultimately give hope to the hopeless.

*BE BRAVE.*

*DO SOMETHING.*

**"I'D RATHER DIE ON MY FEET, THAN LIVE ON MY KNEES."**

━━━━━━━━━━━━━

# CHAPTER 11
# VERITAS

## WORKS CITED

Alinsky, Saul D. *Rules for Radicals*. New York: Random House, 1971.

Anderson, Gerald H. and Thomas F. Stransky. *Mission Trends: Liberation Theologies in North America and Europe*. Grand Rapids: Wm. B. Eerdmans Publishing Co., 1979.

Chambers, Whittaker. *Witness*. Washington: Regnery Publishing, 1969.

Churchill, Winston. *Their Finest Hour*. London: Cassell, 1947.

Dostoevsky, Fyodor. *The Brothers Karamazov*. New York: Farrar, Strauss and Giroux, 2002.

Dygert, James H. *The Investigative Journalist: Folk Heroes of a New Era*. Hoboken: Prentice-Hall, 1976.

Herman, Edward S. and Noam Chomsky. *Manufacturing Consent: The Political Economy of the Mass Media*. New York: Knopf Doubleday Publishing Group, 2011.

Hoffer, Eric. *The Temper of Our Time*. New York: Harper & Row, 1969.

Pfeiffer, Dan. *Un-Trumping America: A Plan to Make America a Democracy Again*. New York: Twelve, 2020.

Solzhenitsyn, Aleksandr. *The Gulag Archipelago*, Volume 2. New York: Harper Perennial Modern Classics, 2007.

Thompson, Hunter S. *The Great Shark Hunt*. New York: Simon & Schuster, 2003.

Yeats, William Butler. *The Collected Poems of W.B. Yeats: A New Edition*. Edited by Richard J. Finneran, (Palgrave, 2003).

# APPENDIX
# MEDIA SOURCES BY CHAPTER

## PREFACE

Boburg, Shawn and Jacob Bogage. "Postal worker recanted allegations of ballot tampering, officials say." *The Washington Post*, November 10, 2020. Accessed August 30, 2021. https://www.washingtonpost.com/investigations/postal-worker-fabricated-ballot-pennsylvania/2020/11/10/99269 a7c-2364-11eb-8599-406466ad1b8e_story.html.

*The Very Best of Maria Callas*. "06 La Mamma Morta from Andrea Chenier." Composer Umberto Giordano. EMI Classics CD57230, 2002.

India, Maria. "My Generation Isn't Suffering Enough." The Quillette Blog, entry posted February 28, 2021. Accessed August 30, 2021. https://quillette.com/2021/02/28/my-generation-isnt-suffering-enough/.

*The Insider*, directed by Michael Mann, Touchstone Pictures, 1999.

@jamesokeefeiii. "The verdict in the David Daleiden case is a complete travesty of justice and a significant wound to the First Amendment." Twitter, November 16, 2019. Accessed before permanent suspension. https://twitter.com/jamesokeefeiii/status/1195461762302271489?lang=en:.

Meredith Digital Staff. "Report: Postal worker recants claim of ballot tampering." Fox10 News, November 11, 2020. Accessed August 30, 2021. https://www.wfsb.com/report-postal-worker-recants-claims-of-ballot-tampering/article_2e00bb48-18c4-566e-a4c6-3cc1df010d1a.html.

Tilove, Jonathan. "Activist says Landrieu plot was the uncover dodged phone calls." *The Times-Picayune*, June 25, 2010. Accessed August 30, 2021. https://www.nola.com/news/politics/article_e10872d7-7cb6-5c3c-aae4-633fc3e15333.html.

Patterico. "Exclusive: Judge Orders Potentially Exculpatory Evidence in O'Keefe Case to Be Destroyed." The Patterico Pontifications blog, entry posted May 5, 2020. Accessed August 30, 2021. http://patterico.com/2010/05/27/exclusive-judge-orders-potentially-exculpatory-evidence-in-okeefe-case-to-be-destroyed.

Project Veritas. "Project Veritas Features – Pinterest Insider Speaks Out: The tech companies can't fight us all." June 13, 2019. YouTube video, 19:33. Accessed August 30, 2021. https://www.youtube.com/watch?v=yuX-87JFzLFc.

Project Veritas. "USPS Whistleblower Richard Hopkins Gives New Interview Detailing Coercion Tactics Used By Fed Agents." November 11, 2020. YouTube video, 7:02. Accessed August 30, 2021. https://www.youtube.com/watch?v=gKhXBU_IgYo&t=195s.

Project Veritas Action. "O'Keefe Exposes DOJ Corruption in Louisiana US Attorney Office and DOJ Civil Rights Division." December 4, 2014. YouTube video, 7:54. Accessed August 30, 2021. https://www.youtube.com/watch?v=aIxEC0vLlGA.

WSDU News. "Mann, Perricone gave up licenses 'in lieu of disciplinary action.'" May 1, 2014. YouTube video, 2:24. Accessed August 30, 2021. https://www.youtube.com/watch?v=lcNHxlaUfmk.

Yahoo Finance. "Governor Cuomo holds press briefing (audio only)." March 12, 2021. YouTube video, 34:00. Accessed August 30, 2021. https://www.youtube.com/watch?v=B1aNkXYV9d8.

## CHAPTER 1

Barstow, David. "Donald Trump Tax Records Show He Could Have Avoided Taxes for Nearly Two Decades, The Times Found." *The New York Times*, October 2, 2016. Accessed August 31, 2021. https://www.nytimes.com/2016/10/02/us/politics/donald-trump-taxes.html.

Bezos, Jeff. "No thank you, Mr. Pecker." Jeff Bezos blog on *Medium*, entry posted February 7, 2019. Accessed August 31, 2021. https://medium.com/@jeffreypbezos/no-thank-you-mr-pecker-146e3922310f.

Boburg, Shawn and Jacob Bogage. "Postal worker recanted allegations of ballot tampering, officials say." *The Washington Post*, November 10, 2020. Accessed August 30, 2021. https://www.washingtonpost.com/investigations/postal-worker-fabricated-ballot-pennsylvania/2020/11/10/99269a7c-2364-11eb-8599-406466ad1b8e_story.html.

Bode, Karl. "The FBI Says Your TV Is Probably Spying on You." Techdirt, December 6, 2019. Accessed August 31, 2021. https://www.techdirt.com/articles/20191203/06384543493/fbi-says-your-tv-is-probably-spying-you.shtml.

Brenner, Marie. "The Man Who Knew Too Much." *Vanity Fair*, April 1, 2004. Accessed August 31, 2021. https://www.vanityfair.com/magazine/1996/05/wigand199605.

Brockwell, Gillian. "Deep Throat." *The Washington Post*, September 27, 2019. Accessed August 31, 2021. https://www.washingtonpost.com/history/2019/09/27/deep-throats-identity-was-mystery-decades-because-no-one-believed-this-woman/.

Caramanica, Jon. "The Young Men's Style Council of TikTok." *The New York Times*, July 8, 2021. Accessed August 31, 2021. https://www.nytimes.com/2021/07/08/style/the-young-mens-style-council-of-tiktok.html.

Dean, Brian. "Social Network Usage & Growth Statistics: How Many People Use Social Media in 2021?" Backlinko.com, August 10, 2021. Accessed August 31, 2021. https://backlinko.com/social-media-users.

Dunlap, David W. "Looking Back: 1896 'Without Fear or Favor.'" *The New York Times*, August 14, 2015. Accessed August 31, 2021. https://www.nytimes.com/2015/09/12/insider/1896-without-fear-or-favor.html.

The Editorial Board. "Fact-Checking Facebook's Fact Checkers." *Wall Street Journal*, March 16, 2021. Accessed August 31, 2021. https://www.wsj.com/articles/fact-checking-facebooks-fact-checkers-11614987375.

The Editoral Board. "Speech and Sedition in 2021: The progressive press decides that dissenters should be suppressed." *Wall Street Journal*, January 29, 2021. Accessed August 31, 2021. https://www.wsj.com/articles/speech-and-sedition-in-2021-11611962910.

Franzen, Jonathan. "Imperial Bedroom." *The New Yorker*, October 5, 1998. Accessed August 31, 2021. https://www.newyorker.com/magazine/1998/10/12/imperial-bedroom.

Friedersdorf, Conor. "Andrew Breitbart Talks Down Talk Radio." *The Atlantic*, June 17, 2011. Accessed August 31, 2021. https://www.theatlantic.com/politics/archive/2011/06/andrew-breitbart-talks-down-talk-radio/240604/.

Grynbaum, Michael M., Tiffany Hsu, Katie Robertson, and Keith Collins, "How Right-Wing Radio Stoked Anger Before the Capitol Siege," *The New York Times*, February 12, 2021. Accessed August 31, 2021. https://www.nytimes.com/2021/02/10/business/media/conservative-talk-radio-capitol-riots.html.

Janofsky, Michael. "On Cigarettes, Health and Lawyers." *The New York Times*, December 6, 1993. Accessed August 31, 2021. https://www.nytimes.com/1993/12/06/business/on-cigarettes-health-and-lawyers.html.

Jenkins, Jr., Holman W. "How to Have More Police Shootings." *Wall Street Journal*, April 23, 2021. Accessed August 31, 2021. https://www.wsj.com/articles/how-to-have-more-police-shootings-11619213893.

Lisheron, Mark. "Lying to Get the Truth." *American Journalism Review*, October/November 2007. Accessed August 31, 2021. https://ajrarchive.org/Article.asp?id=4403&id=4403.

Miller, D. Patrick. "Notes Toward a Journalism of Consciousness." *The Sun Magazine*, January 1990. Accessed August 31, 2021. https://www.thesunmagazine.org/issues/170/notes-toward-a-journalism-of-consciousness.

Mims, Christopher. "GameStop, Bitcoin and QAnon: How the Wisdom of Crowds Became the Anarchy of the Mob." *The Wall Street Journal*, January 29, 2021. Accessed August 31, 2021. https://www.wsj.com/articles/gamestop-bitcoin-and-qanon-how-the-wisdom-of-crowds-became-the-anarchy-of-the-mob-11611928823.

Mims, Christopher. "How Congress Might Upend Section 230, the Law Big Tech Is Built On." *The Wall Street Journal*, February 13, 2021. Accessed August 31, 2021. https://www.wsj.com/articles/how-congress-might-upend-section-230-the-internet-law-big-tech-is-built-on-11613172368.

Nicolau, Anna and James Fontanella-Khan. "The Fight for the Future of America's Local Newspapers." *Financial Times*, January 20, 2021. Accessed August 31, 2021. https://www.ft.com/content/5c22075c-f1af-431d-bf39-becf9c54758b.

NPR. "Final Words: Cronkite's Vietnam Commentary." All Things Considered hosted by Guy Raz. Broadcast on July 18, 2009. Accessed August 31, 2021. https://www.npr.org/templates/story/story.php?storyId=106775685.

NPR. "Fresh Air Remembers Mike Wallace of '60 Minutes.'" Fresh Air. Broadcast on April 9, 2012. Accessed August 31, 2021. https://www.npr.org/2012/04/09/150282652/fresh-air-remembers-mike-wallace-of-60-minutes.

Open the Books. "Every Dime. Online. In Real Time." Openthebooks.com, 2021. Accessed August 31, 2021. https://www.openthebooks.com/about-us/.

Project Veritas. "American Pravda: CNN Producer Says Russia Narrative "bullsh*t." June 27, 2017. YouTube video, 8:48. Accessed August 31, 2021. https://www.youtube.com/watch?v=jdP8TiKY8dE&t=225s.

Project Veritas. "Facebook Insider Leaks: Zuckerberg & Execs Admit Excessive Power." January 31, 2021. YouTube video, 2:15. Accessed August 31, 2021. https://www.youtube.com/watch?v=e2y4b83Je8s.

Project Veritas. "FB exec says Zuckerberg is too powerful." March 16, 2021. YouTube video, 2:01. Accessed August 31, 2021. https://www.youtube.com/watch?v=DRXeSJmeigc.

Project Veritas. "Part 3: CNN Field Manager: Zucker's 9am Calls 'BS;' "… Totally Left-Leaning…Don't Want to Admit it." October 17, 2019. YouTube video, 15:48. Accessed August 31, 2021. https://www.youtube.com/watch?v=qbQwAQ0tDTQ&t=171s.

Project Veritas. "'Socialist' ABC Reporter Admits Bosses Spike News Important to Voters, 'Don't Give Trump Credit.'" YouTube video, 7:31. Accessed August 31, 2021. https://www.youtube.com/watch?v=SZG1v5EcwUI&t=364s.

Richman, Barak and Francis Fukuyama. "How to Quiet the Megaphones of Facebook, Google and Twitter." *The Wall Street Journal*, February 12, 2021. Accessed August 31, 2021. https://www.wsj.com/articles/how-to-quiet-the-megaphones-of-facebook-google-and-twitter-11613068856.

Roose, Kevin. "In Pulling Trump's Megaphone, Twitter Shows Where Power Now Lies." *The New York Times*, January 11, 2021. Accessed August 31, 2021. https://www.nytimes.com/2021/01/09/technology/trump-twitter-ban.html.

Ross, Alex. "Encrypted: Translators confront the supreme enigma of Stephane Mallarme's poetry." *The New Yorker*, April 4, 2016. Accessed September 29, 2021. https://www.newyorker.com/magazine/2016/04/11/stephane-mallarme-prophet-of-modernism.

Russia Today, "The truth suffers: ABC employee in leaked tape by Project Veritas." February 27, 2020. YouTube video, 1:07. Accessed August 31, 2021. https://www.youtube.com/watch?v=nAHBiqaI_Cc.

Rutenberg, Jim. "Trump is Testing the Norms of Objectivity in Journalism." *The New York Times*, August 7, 2016. Accessed August 31, 2021. https://www.nytimes.com/2016/08/08/business/balance-fairness-and-a-proudly-provocative-presidential-candidate.html.

Shachtman, Noah. "How Andrew Breitbart Hacked the Media." *Wired*, March 11, 2010. Accessed August 31, 2021. https://www.wired.com/2010/03/ff-andrew-brietbart/.

Silverstein, Ken. "Lobby Shops for Turkmenistan: Will lie for money." *Harper's Magazine*, June 24, 2007. Accessed August 31, 2021. https://harpers.org/2007/06/lobby-shops-for-turkmenistan-will-lie-for-money/.

Solzhenitsyn Center. "Harvard Address." April 12, 2013. YouTube video, 1:02:29. Accessed August 31, 2021. https://www.youtube.com/watch?v=WuVG8SnxxCM.

Stein, Harry. "How '60 Minutes' Makes News." *The New York Times*, May 6, 1979. Accessed August 31, 2021. https://www.nytimes.com/1979/05/06/archives/how-60-minutes-makes-news-60-minutes.html.

Sullivan, Margaret, "The 'audacious lie' behind a hedge fund's promise to sustain local journalism." *The Washington Post*, February 17, 2021. Accessed August 31, 2021. https://www.washingtonpost.com/lifestyle/media/tribune-alden-sale-local-journalism/2021/02/17/04411fc2-712a-11eb-85fa-e0ccb3660358_story.html.

Swain, Barton. "Trump and the Failure of the Expert Class." *Wall Street Journal*, January 22, 2021. Accessed August 31, 2021. https://www.wsj.com/articles/trump-and-the-failure-of-the-expert-class-11611341116.

Taranto, James. "Finale." *Wall Street Journal*, January 3, 2017. Accessed August 31, 2021. https://www.wsj.com/articles/finale-1483467462.

Tracy, Marc. "How Marty Baron and Jeff Bezos Remade The Washington Post." *The New York Times*, February 27, 2021. Accessed August 31, 2021. https://www.nytimes.com/2021/02/27/business/marty-baron-jeff-bezos-washington-post.html.

Turley, Jonathan. "Project Veritas Wins Victory Against New York Times in Defamation Action." The Jonathan Turley blog, entry posted March 21, 2021. Accessed August 30, 2021. https://jonathanturley.org/2021/03/21/project-veritas-wins-victory-against-new-york-times-in-defamation-action/.

Wasserman, Edward. "The Insidious Corruption of Beats." Edward Wasserman blog archive of columns written while employed at the *Miami Herald*, January 8, 2007. Accessed August 31, 2021. https://ewasserman.com/2007/01/08/the-insidious-corruption-of-beats/.

Waters, Richard and Hannah Murphy. "Donald Trump, Twitter and the messy fight over free speech." *Financial Times*, January 15, 2021. Accessed August 31, 2021. https://www.ft.com/content/78a3ed8c-d930-4bf5-9f6e-1b6b4751090f.

Weaver, Paul H. "The new journalism and the old – thoughts after Watergate." *National Affairs*, Spring 1974. Accessed August 31, 2021. https://www.nationalaffairs.com/public_interest/detail/the-new-journalism-and-the-old-thoughts-after-watergate.

WGBH/Frontline. "Anatomy of a Decision: Facts and context in the '60 Minutes' decision not to air a tobacco industry expose." PBS, 1999. Accessed August 31, 2021. https://www.pbs.org/wgbh/pages/frontline/smoke/cron.html.

## CHAPTER 2

Adelson, Aaron. "69-year-old woman allegedly punched in face by Trump supporter outside NC rally." WLOS ABC-13, updated May 9, 2017. Accessed September 1, 2021. https://wlos.com/news/local/69-year-old-woman-punched-in-face-outside-rally-by-trump-supporter.

@EricRWeinstein, "But where do we start? As the Distributed Idea Suppression Complex, it isn't under central control. It is a loosely coupled emergent structure. But the most obvious sector is the one which has fallen the farthest because it once grew the quickest: the modern research university." Twitter, January 16, 2020. Accessed September 1, 2021. https://twitter.com/EricRWeinstein/status/1217886561829670912.

@EricRWeinstein. "Why is this person suspended?? Because he's a 'socialist'? Because he thinks Trump is a 'dick'? Because he discusses the 'dinosaur' broadcast channels? Because he is thinking about institutional bias? Dunno. I also have to admit: I hate this shitty hidden camera 'gotcha' crap." Twitter, February 26, 2020. Accessed September 1, 2021. https://twitter.com/EricRWeinstein/status/1232728006176604160?s=20.

BGH News. "Project Veritas Gets ABS Correspondent Suspended." February 28, 2020. Originally broadcast by PBS *Beat the Press*. YouTube video, 5:35. https://www.youtube.com/watch?v=x1JhN8eB1cI.

Goodman, Walter. "Beyond ABC v Food Lion." *The New York Times*, March 9, 1997. Accessed September 1, 2021. https://www.nytimes.com/1997/03/09/arts/beyond-abc-v-food-lion.html.

Holmes, Oliver Wendell. "The Stereoscope and the Stereograph." *The Atlantic*, June 1859. Accessed September 1, 2021. https://www.theatlantic.com/magazine/archive/1859/06/the-stereoscope-and-the-stereograph/303361/.

@jamesokeefeiii, "You hate 'this shitty hidden camera gotcha crap?' Wright was in a public space speaking freely among his peers. In newspapers, that's called 'reporting.' Your prejudice against the method doesn't make any sense. You prefer I report this without the audio 'anonymously sourced?,'" Twitter, February 26, 2020. Accessed before permanent suspension. https://twitter.com/JamesOKeefeIII/status/1232729139829972995.

Junior, Brit. "The Man from Atlanta." August 24, 2014. Originally broadcast by BBC, August 23, 1982. YouTube video, 39:35. Accessed September 1, 2021. https://www.youtube.com/watch?v=q-uGoKQ7phs.

Kurtz, Howard. "NPR's Polarizing Shake-Up: Vivian Scholler Resigns Over O'Keefe Video." *Daily Beast*, July 13, 2017. Accessed September 1, 2021. https://www.thedailybeast.com/nprs-polarizing-shake-up-vivian-schiller-resigns-over-okeefe-video?ref=scroll.

Project Veritas. "Project Veritas Action – Patrick Davis Manager of Field Ops at CNN." January 16, 2020. YouTube video, 0:39. Accessed September 1, 2021. https://www.youtube.com/watch?v=GwT1rloqpOE.

Ross, Jamie. "ABC News Suspends Correspondent David Wright Over Secret Video Footage: Report." *Daily Beast*, February 26, 2020. Accessed September 1, 2021. https://www.thedailybeast.com/david-wright-suspended-by-abc-news-over-mysterious-footage-says-report.

Ryan, Melissa. "Why James O'Keefe Still Has Power." Melissa Ryan blog on *Medium*, entry posted March 1, 2020. Accessed September 1, 2021. https://melissaryan.medium.com/why-james-okeefe-still-has-power-cf309926534d.

Shachtman, Noah. "How Andrew Breitbart Hacked the Media." *Wired*, March 11, 2010. Accessed September 1, 2021. https://www.wired.com/2010/03/ff-andrew-brietbart/.

Tomkins, Al. "Anatomy of a Pulitzer: Q&A with Hull and Priest." PoynterOnline uploaded by New York University, April 8, 2008. Accessed September 1, 2021. https://undercover.hosting.nyu.edu/s/undercover-reporting/item/11743.

Weinstein, Eric. "Eric Weinstein (Solo), Ep. #018 of The Portal – Slipping the DISC: State of the Portal/Chapter 2020." February 13, 2020. YouTube video, 1:03:35. Accessed September 1, 2021. https://www.youtube.com/watch?app=desktop&v=QxnkGymKuuI.

## CHAPTER 3

CNN. "Chris Cuomo Defends James O'Keefe on CNN." May 17, 2015. Project Veritas website, 0:13. Accessed September 1, 2021. https://www.projectveritas.com/news/chris-cuomo-defends-james-okeefe-on-cnn/.

Havens, John C. "The Price of Haggling for Your Personal Data: It's not just about money." *Slate*, March 14, 2017. Accessed September 1, 2021. https://slate.com/technology/2014/03/haggling-for-your-personal-data-isnt-just-about-money.html.

Jenkins, Jr., Holman W. "How to Have More Police Shootings." *Wall Street Journal*, April 23, 2021. Accessed August 31, 2021. https://www.wsj.com/articles/how-to-have-more-police-shootings-11619213893.

Markel, Dr. Howard. "How Nellie Bly went undercover to expose abuse of the mentally ill." PBS NewsHour, May 5, 2018. Accessed September 1, 2021. https://www.pbs.org/newshour/nation/how-nellie-bly-went-undercover-to-expose-abuse-of-the-mentally-ill.

Project Veritas. "PART 1: CNN Director ADMITS Network Engaged in 'Propaganda' to Remove Trump from Presidency." April 13, 2021. YouTube video, 8:58. Accessed September 1, 2021. https://www.youtube.com/watch?v=Dv8Zy-JwXr4&t=17s.

Project Veritas. "Project Veritas | FB exec says Zuckerberg is too powerful." March 16, 2021. YouTube video, 2:01. Accessed September 1, 2021. https://www.youtube.com/watch?v=DRXeSJmeigc.

Project Veritas. "VIDEO: Leaked ABC News Insider Recording EXPOSES #EpsteinCoverup 'We had Clinton, We had Everything.'" November 5, 2019. YouTube video, 7:36. Accessed September 1, 2021. https://www.youtube.com/watch?v=3lfwkTsJGYA.

Smith, Emily. "ABC Scrambles to Figure Out Identity of Amy Robach Leaker, Who Goes by 'Ignotus,'" *Page Six*, November 12, 2019. Accessed September 1, 2021. https://pagesix.com/2019/11/12/abc-scrambles-to-figure-out-identity-of-amy-robach-leaker-who-goes-by-ignotus/.

Wolff, Michael. "'Fire and Fury' author Michael Wolff: 'I absolutely' spoke to President Trump." Originally broadcast by NBC on *The Today Show*, January 5, 2018. Accessed September 1, 2021. https://www.today.com/video/-fire-and-fury-author-michael-wolff-i-absolutely-spoke-to-president-trump-1130041411871.

# CHAPTER 4

Ballasy, Nicholas. "Joy Villa and Sebastian Gorka Clash with Reporter in Rose Garden." July 11, 2019. YouTube video, 2:59. Accessed September 1, 2021. https://www.youtube.com/watch?v=WV1Y02KOTak.

Boburg, Shawn, Aaron C. Davis and Alice Crites. "A woman approached The Post with dramatic, and false, tale about Roy Moore. She appears to be part of undercover sting operation." *The Washington Post*, November 27, 2017. Accessed September 1, 2021. https://www.washingtonpost.com/investigations/a-woman-approached-the-post-with-dramatic--and-false--tale-about-roy-moore-sje-appears-to-be-part-of-undercover-sting-operation/2017/11/27/0c2e335a-cfb6-11e7-9d3a-bcbe2af-58c3a_story.html.

The Editorial Board. "Donor Disclosure at the Supreme Court." *The Wall Street Journal*, April 23, 2021. Accessed September 1, 2021. https://www.wsj.com/articles/donor-disclosure-arrives-at-the-supreme-court-11619217816.

Fears, Darryl and Carol D. Leonnig. "Duo in ACORN Videos Say Effort Was Independent." *The Washington Post*, September 18, 2009. Accessed September 1, 2021. https://www.washingtonpost.com/nation/2009/09/18/duo-acorn-videos-say-effort-was-independent/?sid=ST2011020203536.

Grove, Lloyd. "It's Impossible To Shame James O'Keefe's Project Veritas." *Daily Beast*, December 2, 2017. Accessed September 1, 2021. https://www.thedailybeast.com/its-impossible-to-shame-james-okeefes-project-veritas.

@JoeNBC,"The Education Secretary's brother has hired FOREIGN SPIES to target political rivals of Donald Trump. Disgusting." Twitter, March 7, 2020. Accessed September 1, 2021. https://twitter.com/joenbc/status/1236330166865014785?lang=en.

@LauraLoomer. "A reporter from @Buzzfeed just tried to get me to speak negatively about @JamesOKeefeIII. I would give James O'Keefe my kidney if he needed it, because that's how much I respect him. If you come for O'Keefe, I will come for you. @Project_Veritas." Twitter, unknown date. Accessed before account suspension. https://twitter.com/lauraloomer/status/935523259654856704.

Markay, Lachlan. "James O'Keefe Donor Flees Over Failure to Disclose Criminal Record." *Daily Beast*, December 11, 2017. Accessed September 1, 2021. https://www.thedailybeast.com/james-okeefe-donor-flees-over-failure-to-disclose-criminal-record.

Markay, Lachlan. "James O'Keefe's Big-Money Donors Revealed." *Daily Beast*, December 8, 2017. Accessed September 1, 2021. https://www.thedailybeast.com/james-okeefes-big-money-donors-revealed.

Mazzetti, Mark and Adam Goldman. "Erik Prince Recruits Ex-Spies to Help Infiltrate Liberal Groups." *The New York Times*, March 7, 2020. Accessed September 1, 2021. https://www.nytimes.com/2020/03/07/us/politics/erik-prince-project-veritas.html.

McGreal, Chris. "Congress cuts funding to embattled anti-poverty group Acorn." *The Guardian*, September 21, 2009. Accessed September 1, 2021. https://www.theguardian.com/world/2009/sep/21/acorn-prostitution-videos.

Molloy, Tom. "Brian J. Karem, Reporter Who Defied Team Trump, Went to Jail to Protect Sources." *The Wrap*, June 27, 2017. Accessed September 1, 2021. https://www.thewrap.com/brian-j-karem-who-defended-media-at-white-house-press-briefing-once-went-to-jail-to-protect-a-source/.

Olson, William J., Herbert W. Tutus and Robert J. Olson. "Journalist Shield Laws: A Constitutional Conundrum." *American Thinker*, June 1, 2015. Accessed September 1, 2021. https://www.americanthinker.com/articles/2015/06/journalist_shield_laws_a_constitutional_conundrum.html.

Project Veritas. "Project Veritas Legal Victories." ProjectVeritas.com, 2021. Accessed September 1, 2021. https://www.projectveritas.com/project-veritas-legal-victories/.

Smith, Greg B. "Schemer behind Roy Moore setup of Washington Post hid criminal conviction in his N.Y. tax filings." *New York Daily News*, November 30, 2017. Accessed September 1, 2021. https://www.nydailynews.com/new-york/schemer-behind-moore-setup-hid-criminal-conviction-tax-filing-article-1.3668635.

Reporters Committee for Freedom of the Press. "Those who paid the price." Rcfp.org, unknown date. Accessed September 1, 2021. https://www.rcfp.org/journals/news-media-and-law-spring-2015/those-who-paid-price/.

Slattery, Denis. "Billionaire Robert Mercer donated $25G to James O'Keefe's nonprofit Project Veritas." *New York Daily News*, December 2, 2017. Accessed September 1, 2021. https://www.nydailynews.com/news/politics/billionaire-robert-mercer-donated-25g-schemer-james-o-keefe-article-1.3670260.

Suro, Roberto. "Texas Reporter Jailed for Withholding Names." *The New York Times*, June 30, 1990. Accessed September 1, 2021. https://www.nytimes.com/1990/06/30/us/texas-reporter-is-jailed-for-withholding-names.html.

Washington Post. "Gorka to Karem: 'You're not a journalist, you're a punk.'" July 11, 2019. YouTube video, 2:34. Accessed September 1, 2021. https://www.youtube.com/watch?v=zRogWTuS5HI.

## CHAPTER 5

Dunlap, David W. "Looking Back: 1896 'Without Fear or Favor.'" *The New York Times*, August 14, 2015. Accessed August 31, 2021. https://www.nytimes.com/2015/09/12/insider/1896-without-fear-or-favor.html.

Lelyveld, Philip. "Vice's Shane Smith: 'Young people are angry and leaving TV in droves.'" Philip Lelyveld's blog, entry posted March 2, 2014. Accessed September 1, 2021. http://philiplelyveld.com/?p=8201.

Project Veritas. "Project Veritas Features – Pinterest Insider Speaks Out: The tech companies can't fight us all." June 13, 2019. YouTube video, 19:33. Accessed August 30, 2021. https://www.youtube.com/watch?v=yuX-87JFzLFc.

Project Veritas. "'Socialist' ABC Reporter Admits Bosses Spike News Important to Voters, 'Don't Give Trump Credit.'" February 26, 2020. YouTube video, 7:31. Accessed September 1, 2021. https://www.youtube.com/watch?v=SZG1v5EcwUI&t=365s.

## CHAPTER 6

"Assange's Call to the State Department." assangedefense.org. August 26, 2011. Accessed September 23, 2021. https://assangedefense.org/press-release/assanges-call-to-the-state-department/.

"Appendix H: Approaches." Intelligence, *GlobalSecurity.org*. Page last updated April 26, 2005. Accessed September 23, 2021. https://www.globalsecurity.org/intell/library/policy/army/fm/fm34-52/app-h.htm.

Boburg, Shawn and Jacob Bogage. "Postal worker recanted allegations of ballot tampering, officials say." *The Washington Post*, November 10, 2020. Accessed August 30, 2021. https://www.washingtonpost.com/investigations/postal-worker-fabricated-ballot-pennsylvania/2020/11/10/99269a7c-2364-11eb-8599-406466ad1b8e_story.html.

Boburg, Shawn, Jacob Bogage, and Dalton Bennett. "Audio recording shows Pa. postal worker recanting ballot-tampering claim." *The Washington Post*. November 11, 2020. Accessed September 23, 2021. https://www.washingtonpost.com/investigations/postal-worker-hopkins-ballot-pennsylvania/2020/11/11/c9b70eda-2470-11eb-8599-406466ad-1b8e_story.html.

Brandeisky, Kara and Stephen Suen, "Has the Gov't Lied on Snooping? Let's Go to the Videotape." ProPublica, July 20, 2013. Accessed September 23, 2021. https://projects.propublica.org/graphics/nsa-claims.

Cannon, Celeste. "Sen. Graham to follow-up on postal worker alleging some ballots were backdated." WACH FOX-57. November 7, 2020. Accessed September 23, 2021. https://wach.com/news/local/sen-lindsey-graham-to-follow-up-on-postal-worker-alleging-some-ballots-were-backdated.

@Cernovich, "Holy f*ck, this is an interrogation technique where the federal agent tries to use stress tactics to implant a false memory into the interview subject. You rarely get stuff like this on audio." Twitter, November 10, 2020. Accessed September 23, 2021. https://twitter.com/Cernovich/status/1326325556086910977.

*Chernobyl*. "Open Wide, O Earth." Episode 3, originally aired on HBO May 20, 2019.

Croft, Jane. "Jennifer Robinson: 'Assange had information. That made him dangerous." *Financial Times*, January 8, 2021. Accessed September 23, 2021. https://www.ft.com/content/16b8cfb2-4934-4e88-9686-ff09172e8258.

Darcy, Oliver. "CNN settles lawsuit with Nick Sandmann stemming from viral video controversy." CNN Business. January 7, 2020. Accessed September 23, 2021. https://www.cnn.com/2020/01/07/media/cnn-settles-lawsuit-viral-video/index.html.

Devine, Miranda. "FBI's failures to protect patriotic whistleblowers, then and now." *New York Post*. November 11, 2020. Accessed September 23, 2021. https://nypost.com/2020/11/11/fbis-failures-to-protect-whistleblowers-then-and-now-devine/.

@DingoPrincess1, "Project Veritas? Really? So disappointed in you …" Twitter, December 16, 2020. Accessed September 23, 2021. https://twitter.com/DingoPrincess1/status/1339251928048545792?s=20.

Earle, Geoff. "Mailman who Donald Trump called 'a patriot' for claiming he heard possible election fraud told Postal Inspectors 'I didn't hear the whole story – my mind probably added the rest.'" *Daily Mail.* November 11, 2020. Accessed September 23, 2021. https://www.dailymail.co.uk/news/article-8939791/Mailman-Trump-called-patriot-possible-fraud-claim-says-didnt-hear-story.html.

Fairbanks, Cassandra. "BREAKING: Project Veritas Releases Shocking Never-Before-Heard Phone Call Between Julian Assange and Hillary Clinton's State Department." The Gateway Pundit, December 16, 2020. Accessed September 23, 2021. https://www.thegateway-pundit.com/2020/12/breaking-project-veritas-releases-shocking-never-heard-phone-call-julian-assange-hillary-clintons-state-department/.

Farhi, Paul. "Washington Post settles lawsuit with family of Kentucky teenager." *The Washington Post.* July 24, 2020. Accessed September 23, 2021. https://www.washingtonpost.com/lifestyle/style/washington-post-settles-lawsuit-with-family-of-kentucky-teenager/2020/07/24/ae42144c-cdbd-11ea-b0e3-d55bda07d66a_story.html.

@jamesokeefeiii. "People come to @Project_Veritas with recordings because there's nowhere else to go. Journalists[TM] are afraid to break new ground, afraid to be in an exposed position, and afraid to challenge the state's narrative." Twitter, December 16, 2020. Accessed before permanent suspension.

Lee, Meredith. "The charges against Julian Assange, explained." PBS NewsHour, April 11, 2019. Accessed September 23, 2021. https://www.pbs.org/newshour/world/the-charges-against-julian-assange-explained.

Meredith Digital Staff. "Report: Postal worker recants claim of ballot-tampering." WFSB. November 11, 2020. Accessed September 23, 2021. https://www.wfsb.com/report-postal-worker-recants-claims-of-ballot-tampering/article_2e00bb48-18c4-566e-a4c6-3cc1df010d1a.html.

O'Keefe, James. "#MailFraud." November 11, 2020. Facebook video, 3:19. Accessed September 23, 2021. https://www.facebook.com/JamesOKeefeAuthor/videos/774628580067111/?vh=e&d=n.

@OversightDems. "BREAKING NEWS: Erie, Pa. #USPS whistleblower completely RECANTED his allegations of a supervisor tampering with mail-in ballots after being questioned by investigators, according to IG." Twitter, November 10, 2020. Accessed September 23, 2021. https://twitter.com/OversightDems/status/1326289047933816836.

Palmer, Ewan. "Sen. Graham Silent on Biden Win after Trump Campaign Sends Affidavit from USPS Worker Citing 'Backdated Ballots.'" *Newsweek*. November 8, 2020. Accessed September 23, 2021. https://www.newsweek.com/lindsey-graham-voter-fraud-affadvit-pennsylvania-joe-biden-1545820.

Picket, Kerry. "Lindsey Graham calls for DOJ investigation after USPS whistleblower affidavit alleges ballot fraud." *Washington Examiner*. November 7, 2020. Accessed September 23, 2021. https://www.washingtonexaminer.com/news/lindsey-graham-calls-for-doj-investigation-after-usps-whistleblower-affidavit-alleges-ballot-fraud.

Project Veritas. "Another Facebook Insider Details Political Censorship: Current HR Exec 'No One Has White Man's Back.'" June 25, 2020. YouTube video, 17:57. Accessed September 23, 2021. https://www.youtube.com/watch?v=9O8p4zK8ywY&t=133s.

Project Veritas. "BREAKING: PA USPS Whistleblower Richard Hopkins Goes Public; Confirms Federal Investigation." November 6, 2020. YouTube video, 2:19. Accessed September 23, 2021. https://www.youtube.com/watch?v=J-D-2GOswwA.

Project Veritas. "Current Sr. Google Engineer Goes Public on Camera: Tech is 'dangerous,' 'taking sides.'" July 24, 2019. YouTube video, 14:01. Accessed September 23, 2021. https://www.youtube.com/watch?v=ric-I5t66cj8.

Project Veritas. "Facebook Content Moderator: 'If Someone's Wearing MAGA Hat, I'm Going to Delete Them for Terrorism.'" June 23, 2020. YouTube video, 19:55. Accessed September 23, 2020. https://www.youtube.com/watch?v=l7o4A16QCxE&t=3s.

Project Veritas. "Google 'Machine Learning Fairness' Whistleblower Goes Public, says: 'burden lifted off of my soul.'" August 14, 2019. YouTube video, 19:34. Accessed September 23, 2021. https://www.youtube.com/watch?v=g1VeElBAeas&t=5s.

Project Veritas. "MAIL FRAUD UPDATE: Federal investigators in Michigan investigating USPS after Veritas Whistleblower." November 5, 2020. YouTube video, 0:44. Accessed September 23, 2021. https://www.youtube.com/watch?v=4rhrsvoRF8k.

Project Veritas. "Michigan USPS Whistleblower Details Directive From Superiors To Back-Date Late Mail-In-Ballots Nov 3." November 4, 2020. YouTube video, 2:19. Accessed September 23, 2021. https://www.youtube.com/watch?v=fS6xOuhsiJw.

Project Veritas. "PART 1: CNN Insider Blows Whistle on Network President Jeff Zucker's Personal Vendetta Against POTUS." October 14, 2019. YouTube video, 19:50. Accessed September 23, 2021. https://www.youtube.com/watch?v=m7XZmugtLv4.

Project Veritas. "Pennsylvania USPS Whistleblower Exposes Anti-Trump Postmaster's Illegal Order To Back-Date Ballots." November 5, 2020. YouTube video, 2:18. Accessed September 23, 2021. https://www.youtube.com/watch?v=AR_XpJ287Iw.

Project Veritas. "Project Veritas Features – Pinterest Insider Speaks Out: The tech companies can't fight us all." June 13, 2019. YouTube video, 19:33. Accessed August 30, 2021. https://www.youtube.com/watch?v=yuX-87JFzLFc.

Project Veritas. "Project Veritas Offers $25k Reward for Tips Related to Election, Voter & Ballot Fraud in PA." November 9, 2020. YouTube video, 1:40. Accessed September 23, 2021. https://www.youtube.com/watch?v=51OYPRGhv2A.

Project Veritas. "RAW AUDIO: USPS Whistleblower Richard Hopkins FULL COERCIVE INTERROGATION By Federal Agents." November 11, 2020. YouTube video, 2:02:49. Accessed September 23, 2021. https://www.youtube.com/watch?v=QkNkQ2nDQfc&t=275s.

Project Veritas. "USPS Whistleblower Richard Hopkins Gives New Interview Detailing Coercion Tactics Used By Fed Agents." November 11, 2020. YouTube video, 7:02. Accessed September 23, 2021. https://www.youtube.com/watch?v=gKhXBU_IgYo&t=262s.

Project Veritas. "USPS Whistleblower Richard Hopkins: I DID NOT RECANT.'" November 10, 2020. YouTube video, 0:46. Accessed September 23, 2021. https://www.youtube.com/watch?v=ibU5KVFCg4Y.

Richardson, Valerie. "Richard Hopkins, Pa. postal whistleblower placed on unpaid leave, raises $233,000 on crowdfunding." *The Washington Times*. November 17, 2020. Accessed September 23, 2021. https://www.washingtontimes.com/news/2020/nov/17/richard-hopkins-pa-postal-whistleblower-placed-unp/.

Sack, Kevin. "Richard Jewell, 44, Hero of Atlanta Attack, Dies." *The New York Times*. August 30, 2007. Accessed September 23, 2021. https://www.nytimes.com/2007/08/30/us/30jewell.html?n=Top/Reference/Times%20Topics%20/Subjects/O/Olympic%20Games.

@Snowden, "The extraordinary recording (which I had never heard before) confirms claims that @Wikileaks made for years, but its critics dismissed as lies. 1) Assange DID seek to minimize risks to individuals. 2) Bulk release of cables was forced, not intentional," Twitter, December 16, 2020. Accessed September 23, 2021. https://twitter.com/Snowden/status/1339250586651414537?s=20.

@Snowden, "The source of a given piece of information is a hell of a lot less important than if that information is true," Twitter, December 16, 2020. Accessed September 23, 2021. https://twitter.com/snowden/status/1339252843308605440?lang=en.

Timcast IRL. "WaPo Says Postal Worker RECANTED Statement About Voter Fraud, He Did NOT, IT's A CRAZY Story." November 11, 2020. YouTube video, 17:17. Accessed September 23, 2021. https://www.youtube.com/watch?v=NqvLaiOhw5s.

Turley, Jonathan. "Clappers' actions sure do look like political manipulations." *The Hill*, April 28, 2018. Accessed September 23, 2021. https://thehill.com/opinion/white-house/385351-clappers-actions-sure-look-like-political-manipulations.

Walsh, Joe. "Mailman Recants Bogus Voter Fraud Allegation That Launched a GOP Conspiracy." *Forbes*. November 10, 2020. Accessed September 23, 2021. https://www.forbes.com/sites/joewalsh/2020/11/10/mailman-recants-bogus-voter-fraud-allegation-that-launched-a-gop-conspiracy/?sh=3a59f39b7c05.

## CHAPTER 7

Braun, Bob. "Heroic N.J. teacher was sacrificed for political cause in hidden video." *NJ.com*, November 14, 2010. Accessed September 24, 2021. https://www.nj.com/njv_bob_braun/2010/11/braun_heroic_nj_teacher_was_sa.html.

Cooper, Anderson. "Landmark Terror Trial; Palin Considering White House Run; Great Apes Raised with Language." Anderson Cooper 360 Degrees Transcript. CNN, November 17, 2010. Accessed September 24, 2021. https://transcripts.cnn.com/show/acd/date/2010-11-17/segment/02.

Crook, Andrew. "Judge Allows AFT to Examine Project Veritas Documents." AFT Press Release, aft.org, July 20, 2018. Accessed September 25, 2021. https://www.aft.org/press-release/judge-allows-aft-examine-project-veritas-documents.

Fogarty, Ruth. "French journalist goes undercover with Islamic State terror cell." ABC News, July 11, 2016. Accessed September 25, 2021. https://www.abc.net.au/news/2016-07-11/undercover-with-an-islamic-state-terror-cell/7583246

*The Insider.* Directed by Michael Mann. Touchstone Pictures, 1999.

Harmata, Claudia. "Amy Robach Walks Back Leaked Video Claiming ABC 'Quashed' Jeffrey Epstein Story: 'I Was Upset.'" People.com, November 5, 2019. Accessed September 24, 2021. https://people.com/tv/amy-robach-walks-back-jeffrey-epstein-video/.

"Hunter S. Thompson: in his own words; a selection of the best-remembered quotes from the master of the one-liner." *The Guardian*, February 21, 2005. Accessed September 24, 2021. https://www.theguardian.com/books/2005/feb/21/huntersthompson.

Jackson, Aiden. "Asking the Question: What ARE ABC's Editorial Standards?" *Newsbusters.org*, November 11, 2019. Accessed September 25, 2021. https://www.newsbusters.org/blogs/nb/aiden-jackson/2019/11/11/asking-question-what-are-abcs-editorial-standards.

Jefferson, Thomas. "Letter to Edward Carrington." Edited by Stephen D. Solomon. *FirstAmendmentWatch.org*, November 27, 2017. Accessed September 24, 2021. https://firstamendmentwatch.org/history-speaks-letters-thomas-jefferson-edward-carrington.

Marcelo, Philip. "Court weighs ban on secret recordings of public officials." *AP News*, January 8, 2020. Accessed September 25, 2021. https://apnews.com/article/e878409031d8310f88bb95c097a953d8

Miner, Michael. "To Investigate and Advocate." *Chicago Reader*, July 15, 2010. Accessed September 25, 2021. https://chicagoreader.com/news-politics/to-investigate-and-advocate/.

Mmater2. "Dean Baquet On O'Keefe and Sin – 101217." October 12, 2017. YouTube video, 2:31. Accessed September 25, 2021. https://www.youtube.com/watch?v=vgCmtAW1UgU.

Project Veritas. "Dem Operative in Lawsuit Deposition Answer for "Gotcha B*tch" Attack & Their Selective Editing." April 15, 2020. YouTube video, 9:59. Accessed September 24, 2021. https://www.youtube.com/watch?v=bmLMswsSw08&t=78s.

Project Veritas. "PART 3: CNN Field Manager: Zucker's 9am Calls 'BS;'… Totally Left-Leaning…Don't Want to Admit it." October 17, 2019. YouTube video, 15:48. Accessed September 24, 2021. https://www.youtube.com/watch?v=qbQwAQ0tDTQ&t=171s.

Project Veritas. "Project Veritas Legal Victories: Dismissal Dianne Barrow v. Project Veritas." ProjectVeritas.com. Accessed September 25, 2021. https://www.projectveritas.com/project-veritas-legal-victories/.

Project Veritas. "PV Releases Deposition Tapes Showing American Federation of Teachers Wants to Bleed Us Dry." January 24, 2020. YouTube video, 5:27. Accessed September 25, 2021. https://www.youtube.com/watch?v=X0kjaDxSUUU&t=1s.

Project Veritas. "Teachers Union Gone Wild – Volume I." October 25, 2010. YouTube video, 4:59. Accessed September 24, 2021. https://www.youtube.com/watch?v=WdqQTIQhn5A.

Project Veritas. "Undercover Common Core Vid: Exec Says 'I hate kids…it's all about the money.'" January 12, 2016. YouTube video, 7:49. Accessed September 25, 2021. https://www.youtube.com/watch?v=c8tZGl1SVs0.

Project Veritas. "Undercover Common II: Another Top Publishing Exec: 'It's never about the kids.'" January 14, 2016. YouTube video, 4:46. Accessed September 25, 2021. https://www.youtube.com/watch?v=kAc-fuKbKqK8.

Renda, Matthew. "Publishing Exec Blames Firing on Right-Wing Sting." Courthouse News Service, June 23, 2017. Accessed September 25, 2021. https://www.courthousenews.com/fired-sales-exec-sues-employ-er-right-wing-sting/.

Rothschild, Daniel M. "Policy Is Also Downstream of Culture." *Discourse Magazine*, June 3, 2021. Accessed September 24, 2021. https://www.discoursemagazine.com/ideas/2021/06/03/policy-is-also-down-stream-of-culture/.

Sanburn, Josh. "'The Kennedy Machine Buries What Really Happened': Revisiting Chappaquiddick, 50 Years Later." *Vanity Fair Magazine*, July 17, 2019. Accessed September 25, 2021. https://www.vanityfair.com/style/2019/07/chappaquiddick-anniversary-kennedy-kopechne.

Shotter, James and Max Seddon. "How Belarus's protesters staged a digital revolution." *Financial Times*, February 27, 2021. Accessed September 25, 2021. https://www.ft.com/content/a68a1c28-fdd0-4800-9339-6ca1e81d456a.

Solzhenitsyn Center. "Harvard Address." April 12, 2013. YouTube video, 1:02:29. Accessed August 31, 2021. https://www.youtube.com/watch?v=WuVG8SnxxCM.

## CHAPTER 8

Borchers, Callum. "It's almost as though Michael Wolff is trying to make journalists looks bad." *The Washington Post*, January 10, 2018. Accessed September 25, 2021. https://www.washingtonpost.com/news/the-fix/wp/2018/01/10/its-almost-like-michael-wolff-is-trying-to-make-journalists-look-bad/?variant=45bcfc8a951d56c3.

@brianstelter. "Per @farhip, ABC News has suspended correspondent David Wright 'for unguarded remarks he made in a video by operatives of Project Veritas.' The video has not been released yet." Twitter, February 26, 2020. Accessed September 25, 2021. https://twitter.com/brianstelter/status/1232645704436387842.

@cwarzel. "i realize i look like a total boob here because i'm attempting to engage or even spend time responding to ppl who seem to operate exclusively in bad faith. i get that. i also see that this is a huge story on half the internet and i still struggle w/ how to address that if at all," Twitter, June 24, 2019. Accessed September 25, 2021. https://twitter.com/cwarzel/status/1143246752331358208?s=20.

"Ethical Journalism: A Handbook of Values and Practices for the News and Editorial Departments," Section 62. *The New York Times*, July 28, 2004. Accessed September 25, 2021. https://www.nytimes.com/editorial-standards/ethical-journalism.html.

@ezraklein. "If there is a problem with Wright's work – if it was false or wrong or misleading – he should be fired. The idea that he shouldn't have, or on his own time, express, personal views is absurd." Twitter, February 26, 2020.

Farhi, Paul. "ABC News suspends correspondent David Wright after comments about Trump coverage, socialism, in Project Veritas sting." *The Washington Post*, February 26, 2020. Accessed September 25, 2021. https://www.washingtonpost.com/lifestyle/media/abc-news-suspends-correspondent-david-wright-after-project-veritas-sting/2020/02/26/764efc06-5849-11ea-9b35-def5a027d470_story.html.

Kim, Eun Kyung. "Michael Wolff says he 'absolutely' spoke to President Trump for his tell-all book." Today.com, January 5, 2018. Accessed September 25, 2021. https://www.today.com/news/michael-wolff-says-he-absolutely-spoke-president-donald-trump-fire-t120837.

Kurtz, Howard. "Hidden Network Cameras: A Troubling Trend? Critics Complain of Deception as Dramatic Footage Yields High Ratings." *The Washington Post*, November 30, 1992. Accessed September 25, 2021. https://www.washingtonpost.com/archive/politics/1992/11/30/hidden-network-cameras-a-troubling-trend-critics-complain-of-deception-as-dramatic-footage-yields-high-ratings/56867af5-ccd6-4aa7-8ed1-46caa5a3186f/.

Payton, Bre. "Top NYT Editor Confesses: We Don't Understand Religion At All." *The Federalist*, December 12, 2016. Accessed September 25, 2021. https://thefederalist.com/2016/12/12/top-nyt-editor-confesses-dont-understand-religion/.

Peters, Jeremy W. and Lizette Alvarez. "After Orlando, a Political Divide on Gay Rights Still Stands." *The New York Times*, June 15, 2016. Accessed September 25, 2021. https://www.nytimes.com/2016/06/16/us/after-orlando-a-political-divide-on-gay-rights-still-stands.html.

Project Veritas. "America Pravda, NYT Part I – Slanting the News & A Bizarre Comey Connection." October 10, 2017. YouTube video, 14:38. Accessed September 25, 2021. https://www.youtube.com/watch?v=D5854-qAqkM&t=376s.

Project Veritas. "American Pravda, NYT Part II – Exploiting Social Media & Manipulating the News." October 11, 2017. YouTube video, 11:37. Accessed September 25, 2021. https://www.youtube.com/watch?v=r0c1B-ph1jrQ.

Project Veritas. "American Pravda, NYT Part III – Senior Homepage Editor Reveals Biased Political Agenda at NYT." October 17, 2017. YouTube video, 13:17. Accessed September 25, 2021. https://www.youtube.com/watch?v=uOBuGCd39Xw&t=43s.

Project Veritas. "O'Keefe Response: NYT Exec Editor Calls Him 'despicable,' Says Veritas Videos, 'damaging.'" October 12, 2017. YouTube video, 5:46. Accessed September 25, 2021. https://www.youtube.com/watch?v=9NykOtRVjkE.

Project Veritas. "Project Veritas Senior Journalist Christian Hartsock confronts NYT Executive Editor Dean Baquet." February 3, 2021. YouTube video, 1:33. Accessed September 25, 2021. https://www.youtube.com/watch?v=dH7W5Rs8C7w.

Project Veritas. "'Socialist' ABC Reporter Admits Bosses Spike News Important to Voters, 'Don't Give Trump credit.'" February 26, 2021. YouTube video, 7:31. Accessed September 25, 2021. https://www.youtube.com/watch?v=SZG1v5EcwUI&t=42s.

Sinclair, Upton. "What Life Means to Me." *The Cosmopolitan*, October 31, 1906: 591-595. Accessed September 25, 2021. https://undercover. hosting.nyu.edu/s/undercover-reporting/item/12158#:~:text=Description:Sinclair%20contributes%20to%20Cosmopolitan's,socialism%20 and%20the%20Socialist%20movement.

Smith, Ben. "The Times Took 19 Days to Report an Accusation Against Biden. Here's Why." *The New York Times*, April 13, 2020. Accessed September 25, 2021. https://www.nytimes.com/2020/04/13/business/media/joe-biden-tara-reade-new-york-times.html.

Smith, Emily. "ABC Scrambles to Figure Out Identity of Amy Robach Leaker, Who Goes by 'Ignotus,'" *Page Six*, November 12, 2019. Accessed September 1, 2021. https://pagesix.com/2019/11/12/abc-scrambles-to-figure-out-identity-of-amy-robach-leaker-who-goes-by-ignotus/.

"Social Media Guidelines for the Newsroom." *The New York Times*, updated November 3, 2020. Accessed September 25, 2021. https://www.nytimes.com/editorial-standards/social-media-guidelines.html.

The Right Scoop. "CNN's Brian Stelter writes about the REAL villains of ABC News spiking the Epstein story." Therightscoop.com, November 6, 2019. Accessed September 25, 2021. https://therightscoop.com/cnns-brian-stelter-writes-about-the-real-villains-of-abc-news-spiking-the-epstein-story/.

"The Times Responds to Project Veritas Video." *The New York Times*, October 10, 2017. Accessed September 25, 2021. https://www.nytimes.com/2017/10/10/reader-center/project-veritas-video.html.

Weinstein, Eric. "James O'Keefe on The Portal, Ep. #026 (w E Weinstein) – What is (and isn't) Journalism in the 21stC." April 20, 2020. YouTube video, 2:25:27. Accessed September 25, 2021. https://www.youtube.com/watch?v=31CvsBlKGYg.

## CHAPTER 9

Astor, Maggie. "Project Veritas Video Was a 'Coordinated Disinformation Campaign,' Researchers Say." *The New York Times*, September 29, 2020. Accessed September 26, 2021. https://www.nytimes.com/2020/09/29/us/politics/project-veritas-ilhan-omar.html.

@brianstelter. "awatching fox, seeing the talk shows promote project veritas, i googled for a reliable news account about what's going on…and…can't really find one." Twitter, June 25, 2019. Accessed September 26, 2021. https://twitter.com/brianstelter/status/1143685846425624578?s=20

Budryk, Zack. "50 former intelligence officials warn NY Post story sounds like Russian disinformation." *The Hill*, October 20, 2020. Accessed September 26, 2021. https://thehill.com/homenews/campaign/521823-50-former-intelligence-officials-warn-ny-post-story-sounds-like-russian.

Buettner, Russ, Susanne Craig, and Mike McIntire. "Long-concealed Records Shot Trump's Chronic Losses and Years of Tax Avoidance." *The New York Times*, September 27, 2020. Accessed September 26, 2021. https://www.nytimes.com/interactive/2020/09/27/us/donald-trump-taxes.html.

Caldera, Camille. "Fact check: No proof of alleged voter fraud scheme or connection to Rep. Ilhan Omar." *USA Today*, October 16, 2020. Accessed September 26, 2021. https://www.usatoday.com/story/news/factcheck/2020/10/16/fact-check-project-veritas-no-proof-voter-fraud-scheme-link-ilhan-omar/3584614001/.

@cwarzel. "so it seems to me that this 'investigation' about Google's bias is really just a bunch of non technical ppl mixing up algorithmic bias w/ political bias. am i wrong? could one of you smart technologists who follow me explain?" Twitter, June 24, 2019. Accessed September 26, 2021. https://twitter.com/cwarzel/status/1143243043782311936?s=20.

@cwarzel. "i mean obviously the video snippets from their 'whistleblower' are all completely contextless and thus not to be taken seriously. but the part about fairness and algos. that's just them seeing the word bias and not understanding what it means, right?" Twitter, June 24, 2019. Accessed September 26, 2021. https://twitter.com/cwarzel/status/1143243370489188352?s=20.

@cwarzel. "i realize i look like a total boob here because i'm attempting to engage or even spend time responding to ppl who seem to operate exclusively in bad faith. i get that. i also see that this is a huge story on half the internet and i still struggle w/ how to address that if at all," Twitter, June 24, 2019. Accessed September 25, 2021. https://twitter.com/cwarzel/status/1143246752331358208?s=20.

Davidson, Chelsea, Michael Jacobs, Carlos Martinez, Spencer McManus, and Yegina Whang. "The 2020 Minnesota Primary in the Wake of Coronavirus." The Lawfare blog, entry posted September 15, 2020. Accessed September 26, 2021. https://www.lawfareblog.com/2020-minnesota-primary-wake-coronavirus.

Devine, Miranda. "Project Veritas uncovers 'ballot harvesting fraud' in Minnesota." *New York Post*, September 27, 2020. Accessed September 26, 2021. https://nypost.com/2020/09/27/project-veritas-uncovers-ballot-harvesting-fraud-in-minnesota/.

Ganguly, Aditi. "Which 2 trillion Dollar Tech Giant Is a Better Buy: Apple or Microsoft?" *StockNews.com*, July 8, 2021. Accessed September 26, 2021. https://stocknews.com/news/aapl-msft-which-2-trillion-dollar-tech-giant-is-a-better-buy/.

Gennai, Jen. "This is not how I expected Monday to go!" *Medium* blog, entry posted June 24, 2019. Accessed September 26, 2021. https://medium.com/@gennai.jen/this-is-not-how-i-expected-monday-to-go-e92771c7aa82.

Howley, Patrick. "Obamacare Architect: Lack of Transparency Was Key Because 'Stupidity Of The American Voter' Would Have Killed Obamacare." *Daily Caller*, November 9, 2014. Accessed September 26, 2021. https://dailycaller.com/2014/11/09/obamacare-architect-lack-of-transparency-was-key-because-stupidity-of-the-american-voter-would-have-killed-obamacare/.

"Inside YouTube's 'numerous policy changes' during the pandemic." Reliable Sources video, CNN, April 19, 2019. Accessed September 26, 2021. https://www.cnn.com/videos/business/2020/04/19/inside-you-tubes-numerous-policy-changes-during-the-pandemic.cnn.

Klasfeld, Adam. "Project Veritas Sues *New York Times* for Calling Group 'Deceptive'," Law & Crime, October 30, 2020. Accessed September 26, 2021. https://lawandcrime.com/lawsuit/project-veritas-sues-new-york-times-for-calling-them-deceptive/.

Lee, Edmund. "Bari Weiss Resigns From New York Times Opinion Post: In a letter posted online Tuesday, she cites 'bullying by colleagues' and an 'illiberal environment." *The New York Times*, July 14, 2020. Accessed September 26, 2021. https://www.nytimes.com/2020/07/14/business/media/bari-weiss-resignation-new-york-times.html.

@leninsidious. "Check out the ratio on this clown." Twitter, June 26, 2019. Accessed September 26, 2021. https://twitter.com/LeninSidious/status/1143985166206959616?s=20.

Lyden, Tom. "Subject of Project Veritas voter fraud story says he was offered bribe." Fox 9 KMSP, October 6, 2020. Accessed September 26, 2021. https://www.fox9.com/news/subject-of-project-veritas-voter-fraud-story-says-he-was-offered-bribe.

McMillan, Robert. "Twitter Unlocks New York Post Account After Two-Week Standoff." *The Wall Street Journal*, October 30, 2020. Accessed September 26, 2021. https://www.wsj.com/articles/twitter-reinstates-new-york-post-account-11604096659.

Morris, Emma-Jo and Gabrielle Fonrouge. "Smoking-gun email reveals how Hunter Biden introduced Ukrainian businessman to VP dad." *New York Post*, October 14, 2020. Accessed September 26, 2021. https://nypost.com/2020/10/14/email-reveals-how-hunter-biden-introduced-ukrainian-biz-man-to-dad/.

Murphy, Heather. "Snopes Retracts 60 Articles Plagiarized by Co-Founder: Our Staff Are Gutted." *The New York Times*, August 13, 2021. Accessed September 26, 2021. https://www.nytimes.com/2021/08/13/business/media/snopes-plagiarism-David-Mikkelson.html.

PBS NewsHour. "What we know and don't know about these video alleging illicit strategies by Democrats." October 19, 2016. YouTube video, 3:35. Accessed September 26, 2021. https://www.youtube.com/watch?v=cZGY5ugMF4M.

Project Veritas. "Google 'Machine Learning Fairness' Whistleblower Goes Public, says: 'burden lifted off of my soul.'" August 14, 2019. YouTube video, 19:34. Accessed September 26, 2021. https://www.youtube.com/watch?v=g1VeElBAeas&t=5s.

Project Veritas. "Google Program Manager: Google 'Trying to Play God' via 'Drivers of Algorithms' in 2020 Election." October 19, 2020. YouTube video, 8:43. Accessed September 26, 2021. https://www.youtube.com/watch?v=w9uT8zve9wk&t=51s.

Project Veritas. "Ilhan Omar connected Ballot Harvester in cash-for-ballots scheme: 'Car is full' of absentee ballots." September 27, 2020. YouTube video, 16:42. Accessed September 26, 2021. https://www.youtube.com/watch?v=ZWK56l2VaLY&t=114s.

Project Veritas. "James O'Keefe goes NUCLEAR in debunking bogus Fox 9 report that defends illegal ballot harvesting." October 6, 2020. YouTube video, 9:07. Accessed September 26, 2021. https://www.youtube.com/watch?v=tAZfQ7CpdKk.

Project Veritas. "LEGAL UPDATE: NYT FORCED by court to ANSWER Veritas's defamation allegations, STUNNING Admissions." April 18, 2021. YouTube video, 9:44. Accessed September 26, 2021. https://www.youtube.com/watch?v=3mbkd2yll14.

Project Veritas. "Omar Connected Harvester SEEN Exchanging $200 for General Election Ballot, 'We don't care illegal.'" September 28, 2020. YouTube video, 13:49. Accessed September 26, 2021. https://www.youtube.com/watch?v=MV7oDl8yDZk&t=426s.

Project Veritas. "Veritas Re-Uploads Google Expose Taken Down By You-Tube Ahead of White House Social Media Summit." July 11, 2019. YouTube video, 25:10. Accessed September 26, 2021. https://www.youtube.com/watch?v=csP4z8dR6X0.

Roose, Kevin. "Facebook and Twitter Dodge a 2016 Repeat, and Ignite a 2020 Firestorm." *The New York Times*, October 15, 2020. Accessed September 26, 2021. https://www.nytimes.com/2020/10/15/technology/facebook-twitter-nypost-hunter-biden.html.

Shabad, Rebecca. "Trump chief of staff Mark Meadows refuses to speak to reporters with mask on." ABC News, October 12, 2020. Accessed September 26, 2021. https://www.nbcnews.com/politics/white-house/trump-chief-staff-mark-meadows-refuses-speak-reporters-mask-n1242990.

@navymig. "You Googled Google for reliable news about Google suppressing Google results Google doesn't like? This is Inception level stupid." Twitter, June 26, 2019. Accessed September 26, 2021. https://twitter.com/navymig/status/1143770377861992449?s=20.

@snowden. "The source of a given piece of information is a hell of a lot less important than if that information is true." Twitter, December 16, 2020.

"Social Media and Content Monitoring: Executives from Facebook, Twitter and Google testified on Capitol Hill about efforts to counter online terror content, hate speech, and misinformation on their platforms." C-SPAN, June 26, 2019. Accessed September 26, 2021. https://www.c-span.org/video/?462052-1/social-media-content-monitoring.

Stelter, Brian. "YouTube CEO says people are discovering different kinds of videos as the pandemic rages." CNN Business, April 24, 2020. Accessed September 26, 2021. https://www.cnn.com/2020/04/23/media/youtube-videos-pandemic/index.html.

The Rubin Report. "Leaked CNN Tapes Revealed: Project Veritas Exposes Media's Agenda." December 2, 2020. YouTube video, 37:00.

*The Usual Suspects*. Directed by Bryan Singer. Bad Hat Harry Productions, 1985.

Weiss, Bari. "Resignation Letter." Bariweiss.com, July 14, 2020. Accessed September 26, 2021. https://www.bariweiss.com/resignation-letter.

Zilber, Ariel. "Donald Trump demands US attorneys launch an investigation into Ilhan Omar following report her supporters 'illegally harvested ballots in Minnesota.'" *DailyMail*, September 28, 2020. Accessed September 26, 2021. https://www.dailymail.co.uk/news/article-8779895/Donald-Trump-demands-attorneys-launch-investigation-Ilhan-Omar-harvested-ballots.html.

## CHAPTER 10

Brenan, Megan. "Americans Remain Distrustful of Mass Media." Gallup, September 30, 2020. Accessed September 26, 2021. https://news.gallup.com/poll/321116/americans-remain-distrustful-mass-media.aspx.

Burns, Alexander. "Shooting Is Latest Eruption in a Grim Ritual of Rage and Blame." *The New York Times*, June 14, 2017. Accessed September 27, 2021. https://www.nytimes.com/2017/06/14/us/baseball-shooting-is-latest-eruption-in-a-grim-ritual-of-rage-and-blame.html.

CUNY TV. "Television in America: An Autobiography – Daniel Schorr." Taped January 1, 2003. YouTube video, 55:53. Accessed September 27, 2021. https://www.youtube.com/watch?v=ysLmQj--DZA.

Dean Baquet interview with Christiane Amanpour, "NY Times editor: Trump has damaged the press," Amanpour on CNN, January 12, 2018. Accessed September 26, 2021. https://www.cnn.com/videos/politics/2018/01/12/intv-amanpour-dean-baquet.cnn.

Delkic, Melina. "Ready, Set, Embargo." *The New York Times*, August 11, 2018. Accessed September 26, 2021. https://www.nytimes.com/2018/08/11/insider/embargoes-reporting.html.

Dugyala, Rashika. "NYT opinion editor resigns after outrage over Tom Cotton op-ed," Politico, June 7, 2020. Accessed September 27, 2021. https://www.politico.com/news/2020/06/07/nyt-opinion-bennet-resigns-cotton-op-ed-306317.

Gerstein, Josh. "Appeals court revives Palin libel suit against *New York Times*." Politico, August 6, 2019. Accessed September 27, 2021. https://www.politico.com/story/2019/08/06/palin-libel-suit-new-york-times-1449103.

"Journalism." The New York Times Company. Accessed September 26, 2021. https://www.nytco.com/journalism/.

Kennedy, John F. "Address on the 20th Anniversary of the Voice of America." American Rhetoric Online Speech Bank, February 28, 1962. Accessed September 26, 2021. https://www.americanrhetoric.com/speeches/jfkvoiceofamerica.htm.

Kruzel, John. "No evidence Sarah Palin's PAC incited shooting of Rep. Gabby Giffords." PolitiFact.com, June 15, 2017. Accessed September 27, 2021. https://www.politifact.com/factchecks/2017/jun/15/new-york-times-editorial-board/no-evidence-sarah-palins-pac-incited-shooting-rep-/.

Gorton, Stephanie. "Ida Tarbell: Reporting the Oil Region," *Belt Magazine*, March 3, 2020. Accessed September 27, 2021. https://beltmag.com/ida-tarbell-oil-region.

"Judicial Watch: Documents Show CA State Officials Coordinated with Big Tech to Censor Americans' Election Posts." Judicial Watch, April 27, 2021. https://www.judicialwatch.org/press-releases/ca-state-officials-big-tech/.

McCaughey, Betsy. "Justice Thomas shows how we can end Big Tech censorship for good." *New York Post*, April 6, 2021. Accessed September 27, 2021. https://nypost.com/2021/04/06/justice-thomas-shows-how-we-can-end-big-tech-censorship-for-good/.

Project Veritas. "LEGAL UPDATE: NYT FORCED by court to ANSWER Veritas's defamation allegations, STUNNING Admissions." April 18, 2021. YouTube video, 9:44. Accessed September 26, 2021. https://www.youtube.com/watch?v=3mbkd2yll14.

Project Veritas. "PART 1: CNN Director ADMITS Network Engaged in 'Propaganda' to Remove Trump from Presidency," April 13, 2021. YouTube video, 8:58. Accessed September 26, 2021. https://www.youtube.com/watch?v=Dv8Zy-JwXr4&t=18s.

"Schiff Sends Letter to Google, Facebook Regarding Anti-Vaccine Misinformation." Adam Chiff. chiff.house.gov, February 14, 2019. Accessed September 27, 2021. https://schiff.house.gov/news/press-releases/schiff-sends-letter-to-google-facebook-regarding-anti-vaccine-misinformation.

Timcast IRL. "Project Veritas Scores EPIC Win Against New York Times, Making The NYT Look Like LOSERS." April 29, 2021. YouTube video, 15:21. Accessed September 27, 2021. https://www.youtube.com/watch?v=7UG5g673NEY.

Turley, Jonathan. "Project Veritas Wins Victory Against New York Times in Defamation Action." The Jonathan Turley blog, entry posted March 21, 2021. Accessed August 30, 2021. https://jonathanturley.org/2021/03/21/project-veritas-wins-victory-against-new-york-times-in-defamation-action/.

York, Byron. "The New York Times's embarrassing defense in the Project Veritas case." *Washington Examiner*, March 24, 2021. Accessed September 27, 2021. https://www.washingtonexaminer.com/opinion/columnists/the-new-york-times-embarrassing-defense-in-the-project-veritas-case.

## CHAPTER 11

Babington, Thomas. "Macaulay." Representative Poetry Online, University of Toronto, 217-224. Accessed September 27, 2021. https://rpo.library.utoronto.ca/content/horatius

Britannica, T. Editors of Encyclopaedia. "Muckraker." *Encyclopedia Britannica*, April 14, 2020. Accessed September 27, 2021. https://www.britannica.com/topic/muckraker.

History.com Editors. "Alien and Sedition Acts." History.com, updated March 5, 2020. Accessed September 27, 2021. https://www.history.com/topics/early-us/alien-and-sedition-acts.

Lincoln, Abraham. "First Debate: Ottawa, Illinois, Mr. Lincoln's Speech." Lincoln Home. nps.gov, August 21, 1858. Accessed September 27, 2021. https://www.nps.gov/liho/learn/historyculture/debate1.htm.

Lincoln, Abraham. "House Divided Speech, June 16, 1858." Abraham Lincoln Online, 2018. Accessed September 27, 2021. http://www.abrahamlincolnonline.org/lincoln/speeches/house.htm.

*Network*. Directed by Sidney Lumet. Metro-Goldwyn-Mayer, 1976.

Richman, Barak and Francis Fukuyama. "How to Quiet the Megaphones of Facebook, Google and Twitter." *The Wall Street Journal*, updated February 12, 2021. Accessed September 27, 2021. https://www.wsj.com/articles/how-to-quiet-the-megaphones-of-facebook-google-and-twitter-11613068856.

Roosevelt, Theodore. "The Man with the Muck Rake." American Rhetoric Online Speech Bank, April 14, 1906. Accessed September 27, 2021. https://www.americanrhetoric.com/speeches/teddyrooseveltmuckrake.htm.

Solzhenitsyn, Aleksandr. "'Men Have Forgotten God': Aleksandr Solzhenitsyn's 1983 Templeton Address." *National Review*, December 11, 2018. Accessed September 27, 2021. https://www.nationalreview.com/2018/12/aleksandr-solzhenitsyn-men-have-forgotten-god-speech/.